THE
AMERICAN REVOLUTION
THROUGH BRITISH EYES

From the year 1778

The Gentleman who had dined with us at Dr. Percy's came in. Dr. Johnson attacked the Americans with intemperate vehemence of abuse. I said something in their favour; and added, that I was always sorry when he talked on that subject. This, it seems, exasperated him; though he said nothing at the time. The cloud was charged with sulphureous vapour, which was afterwards to burst in thunder . . . for he said, "I am willing to love all mankind *except an American:*" and his inflammable corruption bursting into horrid fire, he breathed out threatenings and slaughter, calling them "Rascalls—Robbers; Pirates;" and exclaiming, he'd "burn and destroy them." Miss Seward, looking to him with mild but steady astonishment, said, "Sir, this is an instance that we are always most violent against those whom we have injured." He was irritated still more by this delicate and keen reproach; and he roared out another tremendous volley, which one might fancy could be heard across the Atlantick. During this tempest I sat in great uneasiness, lamenting his heat of temper; till, by degrees, I diverted his attention to other topicks. . . .

From James Boswell, *Life of Samuel Johnson*

THE
AMERICAN REVOLUTION
THROUGH BRITISH EYES

edited by

Martin Kallich
Andrew MacLeish

Northern Illinois University

HARPER & ROW, PUBLISHERS
New York, Evanston, and London

The editors wish to thank the following publishers for permission
to reproduce materials included in this book: The Clarendon
Press for selections from *The Letters of James Boswell,* ed.
Chauncey Brewster Tinker, and from *The Letters of Robert
Burns,* ed. J. DeLancey Ferguson; Columbia University Press
for selections from Stella H. Sutherland, *Population Distribution
in Colonial America;* Harvard University Press for selections from
A British Fusilier in Revolutionary Boston, ed. Allen French;
Longmans, Green & Co. for selections from G. O. Trevelyan,
The American Revolution; Manchester University Press for selec-
tions from *Letters from America, 1773-1780,* ed. Eric Robson.

LIBRARY OF CONGRESS CATALOG CARD NUMBER: 62-4361

Preface

On August 11, 1776, news reached London that the Second Continental Congress, under its presiding officer, John Hancock, had formally proclaimed its Declaration of Independence. Six and one-half years later the revolt of Britain's American colonies had ended, the ties with the mother country were broken, and the foundations of the future greatness of the United States were laid. Certainly, it was no small accomplishment for a young nation of brash upstarts to free itself from a power whose imperial might was feared all over the world.

Brash upstarts the colonists must have been in the eyes of all Englishmen during the critical years of the Revolutionary War. Or were they? We may sometimes wonder how England really felt about America; why she behaved the way she did toward us. With these questions in mind, the present collection of documents has been assembled to help us get a different view of ourselves from the one we already have. This is the first published collection of documents giving the British point of view in significant depth. As such, it should remind us that our liberty, so painfully won, must be the subject of frequent reflection and re-examination. If we are able to see what the British thought of our stand on liberty during these critical years, we gain a perspective which makes reflection more fruitful.

The fact is that the British were by no means unanimous in their opinions concerning the future of the American colonies in the Empire. Many influential and intelligent British citizens considered the struggle with their fellow subjects deplorable and attempted to avert, or at least to lessen, the damage of a civil war with their brothers overseas.

This collection of documents illustrates the variety of British opinion on America from the time of the Stamp Act crisis of 1765, which precipitated the Revolution, to the Treaty of Paris in 1783, when the United States was recognized as an independent nation under international law. As epilogue, a few documents relating to the future republic have been included. All these papers reveal contemporary attitudes towards the major causes of the Revolution, the military struggle for independence, the final victory of the Americans, and their future as an independent people. Sensitive poets, patriotic and sincere politicians and lawyers, frivolous young and serious middle-aged military officers, partisan journalists and merchants, and impartial observers with no apparent stake in the outcome of the contest, but all devoted to their country with varying degrees of intensity, are represented in this cross-section of opinion on an issue that moved the heart as well as the mind.

Letters, poems, essays, debates in Parliament, and magazine commentaries are the sources of these expressions of opinion. In the Bibliography, additional works of authoritative historians are listed so that interested students can deepen their understanding of this important historical event or trace British opinion on this subject up to the present.

At the back of the book, topics for long and short papers and class discussion are included. Of varying degrees of difficulty, they are designed to appeal to students of differing interests and levels of ability. A few suggestions will involve the students in library research, for which the documents in this collection can be used as supplementary materials.

Because of the quantity and diverse quality of the documents, they have, for the most part, been arranged in chronological order over the years which the book covers. Most of the correspondence and memoirs have been placed in a separate section (Section VII) at the cost of interrupting chronological consistency. This arrangement teaches the student to handle the material as it is found in the original source. Further, the student is better able to get a comprehensive picture of one point of view should he refer to the correspondence for ideas. The Suggested Topics and the Index of Topics which appear at the end of the book will suggest to the student still other ways in which the material can be organized.

The statistics in Appendix B are the best figures available for the period and represent original and, in the case of population, later scholarly estimates.

The objective of the editors has been to present carefully edited texts as they would appear to the student if he himself were to go to the original sources. The user of this book may exploit its materials in any way he chooses. Page references to the original documents appear in brackets throughout the text. The opening page number of each selection is given as part of the introductory bibliographical note.

Most inconsistencies in spelling, particularly those within George III's correspondence, remain as they appear in the original documents.

Two Major Historical Sources: *The Gentleman's Magazine* and *The Annual Register*

Students of history wishing to view contemporary British historical documents of the eighteenth and nineteenth centuries have access to two magnificent sources, *The Annual Register* and *The Gentleman's Magazine*.

The latter, founded in 1731 by Edward Cave, who assumed the pseudonym of Sylvanus Urban, originally had as its purpose the presentation of news as well as the usual entertaining features to be found in the large number of daily and weekly magazines of the eighteenth century. Its appeal was to all classes of readers.

Among its many contributors during its 166 years of publication were men such as Samuel Johnson, James Boswell, Benjamin Franklin and the poets Mark Akenside and Christopher Smart. And it was Johnson who was in large part responsible for the truly original feature in *The Gentleman's Magazine*, the publication of parliamentary debates, one of which is included in this source book.

By 1754 the *Magazine* included much original material, and during the revolutionary period it became more valuable than ever as a great storehouse for the debates as well as antiquarian, biographical, historical, and scientific features.

The parliamentarian Edmund Burke was the first editor of *The Annual Register*, which began publication in 1758. Issued annually, it was a four-hundred page volume of general fact with literature and poetry composing the last one hundred pages or so. Some of the current news notes, poetry, and proclamations found in this source book are taken from *The Annual Register*.

Contents

I. The Origin of the American Crisis: Taxation

II. British Errors and American Resistance

III. The Year of Decision

IV. The War Against American Independence: "A Great National Cause"

V. British Confusion and American Victory

VI. Epilogue

VII. Memoirs and Correspondence

I

THE ORIGIN OF THE AMERICAN CRISIS: TAXATION

1. Basic Principles of Society

From William Blackstone, *Commentaries on the Laws of England*
(Oxford: Clarendon Press, 1765–69). Four volumes. Vol. I, p.
40.
Blackstone (1723–80) was professor of English law at Oxford
from 1758 to 1766 as well as Solicitor-General. His lectures, published under the above title, had a wide circulation in Great
Britain and were carefully studied in America.

As therefore the creator is a being, not only of infinite *power*, and
wisdom, but also of infinite *goodness*, he has been pleased so to con-
trive the constitution and frame of humanity, that we should want no
other prompter to enquire after and pursue the rule of right, but only
our own self-love, that universal principle of action. For he has so in-
timately connected, so inseparably interwoven the laws of eternal justice with the happiness of each individual, that the latter cannot be
attained but by observing the former; and, if the former be punctually
obeyed, it cannot but induce the latter. In consequence of which mutual connection of justice and human felicity, he has not per- [41]
plexed the law of nature with a multitude of abstracted rules and pre-
cepts, referring merely to the fitness or unfitness of things, as some
have vainly surmised; but has graciously reduced the rule of obedience
to this one paternal precept, "that man should pursue his own happiness." This is the foundation of what we call ethics, or natural law.
For the several articles into which it is branched in our systems, amount
to no more than demonstrating, that this or that action tends to man's
real happiness, and therefore very justly concluding that the performance of it is a part of the law of nature; or, on the other hand, that this
or that action is destructive of man's real happiness, and therefore that
the law of nature forbids it.

1

This law of nature, being co-eval with mankind and dictated by God himself, is of course superior in obligation to any other. It is binding over all the globe, in all countries, and at all times: no human laws are of any validity, if contrary to this; and such of them as are valid derive all their force, and all their authority, mediately or immediately from this original. . . .

[43] If man were to live in a state of nature, unconnected with other individuals, there would be no occasion for any other laws, than the law of nature, and the law of God. Neither could any other law possibly exist; for a law always supposes some superior who is to make it; and in a state of nature we are all equal, without any other superior but him who is the author of our being. But man was formed for society; and . . . is neither capable of living alone, nor indeed has the courage to do it. . . .

[91] I know it is generally laid down more largely, that acts of parliament contrary to reason are void. But if the parliament will positively enact a thing to be done which is unreasonable, I know of no power that can control it: and the examples usually alleged in support of this sense of the rule do none of them prove, that where the main object of a statute is unreasonable the judges are at liberty to reject it; for that were to set the judicial power above that of the legislature, which would be subversive of all government. . . .

[156] The power and jurisdiction of parliament, says Sir Edward Coke, is so transcendent and absolute, that it cannot be confined, either for causes or persons, within any bounds. . . . It hath sovereign and uncontrolable authority in making, confirming, enlarging, restraining, abrogating, repealing, reviving, and expounding of laws, concerning matters of all possible denominations, ecclesiastical, or temporal, civil, military, maritime, or criminal: this being the place where that absolute despotic power, which must in all governments reside somewhere, is entrusted by the constitution of these kingdoms. All mischiefs and grievances, operations and remedies, that transcend the ordinary course of the laws, are within the reach of this extraordinary tribunal. It can regulate or new model the succession to the crown; as was done in the reign of Henry VIII and William III. It can alter the established religion of the land; as was done in a variety of instances, in the reigns of King Henry VIII and his three children. It can change and create afresh even the constitution of the kingdom and of parliaments themselves; as was done by the act of union, and the several statutes for triennial and septennial elections. It can, in short, do everything that is not naturally impossible; and therefore some have not scrupled to call its power, by a figure rather too bold, the omnipotence of parliament. True, it is, that what they [the parliament] do, no authority upon earth can undo. [157] . . . and, as Sir Matthew Hale observes, this being the highest and greatest court, over which none other can have jurisdiction in the kingdom, if by any means a misgovernment should fall upon it, the subjects of this kingdom are left without all manner of remedy. . . . It must be owned that Mr. Locke, and other theoretical writers, have held that "there remains still inherent in the people a supreme power to remove or alter the legislative, when they

find the legislative act contrary to the trust reposed in them: for when such trust is abused, it is thereby forfeited, and devolves to those who have it." But however just this conclusion may be in theory, we cannot adopt it, nor argue from it, under any dispensation of government at present actually existing. For this devolution of power, to the people at large, includes in it a dissolution of the whole form of government established by that people, reduces all the members to their original state of equality and by annihilating the sovereign power repeals all positive laws whatsoever before enacted. No human laws will therefore suppose a case, which at once must destroy all law, and compel men to build afresh upon a new foundation; nor will they make provision for so desperate an event, as must render all legal provisions ineffectual. So long therefore as the English constitution lasts, we may venture to affirm, that the power of parliament is absolute and without control.

2. The Stamp Act

From Danby Pickering, ed., *The Statutes at Large* (Cambridge, 1762–1807). Forty-six volumes. Vol. XXVI, p. 179.

This act, an attempt to raise revenue in the American provinces in order to defray the expenses of the British government and army stationed there, passed through Parliament with little opposition and was signed March 22, 1765. The British ministry, believing it to be innocuous and just, hoped that the Americans would not object to this attempt to raise £60,000 with this revenue tax. Even before it became effective on November 1, 1765, it aroused bitter indignation in the American colonies. Meetings were held to denounce the policy, dangerous rioting took place, and the stamped papers, on their arrival from England, were in some provinces seized and destroyed by the populace.

An act for granting and applying certain stamp duties, and other duties, in the British colonies and plantations in America, towards further defraying the expences of defending, protecting, and securing the same. . . .

WHEREAS, by an act made in the last session of parliament, several duties were granted, continued, and appropriated, towards defraying the expences of defending, protecting, and securing, the British colonies and plantations in America: and whereas it is just and necessary, that provision be made for raising a further revenue within your Majesty's dominions in America, towards defraying the said expences . . . be it enacted . . . , That from and after the first day of November, one thousand seven hundred and sixty five, there shall be raised, levied, collected, and paid unto his Majesty, his heirs, and successors, throughout the colonies and plantations in America which now are, or here-after may be, under the dominion of his Majesty, his heirs and successors . . . [The statute then lists the various stamp taxes, ranging from three pence to four pounds on the following items: legal documents, registration and other official certificates, commercial bills of lading and sale, pamphlets and newspapers, cards, dice, legal papers, wills, certificates of academic degrees, licenses, contracts, deeds, and the like.]

[201] And it be further enacted . . . , That all monies which should arise by the several rates and duties hereby granted (except the necessary charges of raising, collecting, recovering, answering, paying, and accounting for the same, and the necessary charges from time to time incurred in relation to this act, and the execution thereof) shall be paid into the receipt of his Majesty's exchequer, and shall be entered separate and apart from all other monies, and shall be there reserved to be from time to time disposed of by parliament, towards further defraying the necessary expences of defending, protecting, and securing, the said colonies and plantations.

3. The Quartering Act

From Danby Pickering, ed., *The Statutes at Large* (Cambridge, 1762–1807). Forty-six volumes. Vol. XXVI, p. 305.

The Quartering Act was passed at the request of General Gage in order that he might enforce the Stamp Act and the Revenue Act of 1764. New York failed to comply in full with the terms of the Quartering Act; as a result, its assembly was suspended in 1767 by an act of Parliament.

An act to amend and render more effectual, in his Majesty's dominions in America, an act passed in this present session of parliament, intituled, An act for punishing mutiny and desertion, and for the better payment of the army and their quarters.

WHEREAS . . . [by the Mutiny Act of 1765] several regulations are made and enacted for the better government of the army, and their observing strict discipline, and for providing quarters for the army, and carriages on marches and [306] other necessary occasions, and inflicting penalties on offenders against the same act, and for many other good purposes therein mentioned; but the same may not be sufficient for the forces that may be employed in his Majesty's dominions in America: and whereas, during the continuance of the said act, there may be occasion for marching and quartering of regiments and companies of his Majesty's forces in several parts of his Majesty's dominions in America: and whereas the publick houses and barracks, in his

Majesty's dominions in America, may not be sufficient to supply quarters for such forces: and whereas it is expedient and necessary that carriages and other conveniences, upon the march of troops in his Majesty's dominions in America, should be supplied for that purpose: be it enacted . . . , That for and during the continuance of this act, and no longer, it shall and may be lawful to and for the constables, tithingmen, magistrates, and other civil officers of villages, towns, townships, cities, districts, and other places, within his Majesty's dominions in America, and in their default or absence, for any one justice of the peace inhabiting in or near any such village, township, city, district or place, and for no others; and such constables . . . and other civil officers as aforesaid, are hereby required to billet and quarter the officers and soldiers, in his Majesty's service, in the barracks provided by the colonies; and if there shall not be sufficient room in the said barracks for the officers and soldiers, then and in such case only, to quarter and billet the residue of such officers and soldiers for whom there shall not be room in such barracks in inns, livery stables, ale-houses, victualling-houses, and the houses of sellers of wine by retail . . . and in case there shall not be sufficient room for the officers and soldiers in such barracks, inns, victualling and other publick ale-houses, that in such and no other case, and upon no other account, it shall and may be lawful for the governor and council of each respective province in his Majesty's dominions in America, to authorize and appoint, and they are hereby directed and impowered to authorize and appoint, such proper person or persons as they shall think fit, to take, hire and make fit, and, in default of the said governor and council appointing and authorizing such person or persons, or in default of such person or persons so appointed neglecting or refusing to do their duty, in that case it shall and may be lawful for any two or more of his Majesty's justices of the peace in or near the said villages, towns, townships, cities, districts, and other places, and they are hereby required to take, hire, and make fit for the reception of his Majesty's forces, such and so many uninhabited houses, outhouses, barns, or other buildings, as shall be necessary to quarter therein the residue of such of- [307] ficers and soldiers for whom there should not be room in such barracks and publick houses as aforesaid. . . .

III. [Military officers taking upon themselves to quarter soldiers contrary to this act, or using any menace to civil officers to deter them from their duty, are to be cashiered. Persons aggrieved by being quartered on may complain to the justices, and be relieved.] . . .

[318] XXX. And be it further enacted . . . , That this act . . . shall continue and be in force in all his Majesty's dominions in America from the twenty fourth day of March, in the year one thousand seven hundred and sixty five, until the twenty fourth day of March in the year of our Lord one thousand seven hundred and sixty seven.

4. A Defense of Parliamentary Taxation of the American Colonies

From Soame Jenyns, *The Objections to the Taxation of our American Colonies, briefly considered* (1765), in *Miscellaneous Pieces* (London: T. Cadell, 1790). P. 421.

Soame Jenyns (1704–87) was a member of Parliament for Cambridge and Dunwich from 1754 to 1780, and in 1765 had been for many years a commissioner of the Board of Trade and Plantations. His essay on American taxation, published as a pamphlet in 1765, was very successful in England and provoked many replies in the colonies.

The right of the legislature of Great Britain to impose taxes on her American colonies, and the expediency of exerting that right in the present conjuncture, are propositions so indisputably clear that I should never have thought it necessary to have undertaken their defence, had not many arguments been lately flung out both in papers and conversation, which with insolence equal to their absurdity deny them both. As these are usually mixt up with several patriotic and favorite words such as Liberty, Property, Englishmen, etc., which are apt to make strong impressions on that more numerous part of mankind [422] who have ears but no understanding, it will not, I think, be improper to give them some answers: to this, therefore, I shall singly confine myself, and do it in as few words as possible, being sensible that the fewest will give least trouble to myself, and probably most information to my reader.

The great capital argument which I find on this subject, and which, like an Elephant at the head of a Nabob's army, being once overthrown, must put the whole into confusion, is this: that no Englishman is, or can be taxed, but by his own consent: by which must be meant one of these three propositions; either that no Englishman can be taxed without his own consent as an individual; or that no Englishman can be taxed without the consent of the persons he chuses to represent him; or that no Englishman can be taxed without the consent of the majority of all those, who are elected by himself and others of his fellow-subjects to represent them. Now let us impartially consider, whether any one of these propositions are in fact true: if not, then this wonderful structure which has been erected upon them falls at once to the ground, and like another Babel, perishes by a confusion of words, which the builders themselves are unable to understand.

First then, that no Englishman is or can be taxed but by his own consent as an individual: [423] this is so far from being true, that it is the very reverse of truth; for no man that I know of is taxed by his own consent, and an Englishman, I believe, is as little likely to be so taxed, as any man in the world.

6

Secondly, that no Englishman is, or can be taxed, but by the consent of those persons whom he has chose to represent him; for the truth of this I shall appeal only to the candid representatives of those unfortunate counties which produce cyder, and shall willingly acquiesce under their determination. [They were taxed without their consent.]

Lastly, that no Englishman is, or can be taxed, without the consent of the majority of those who are elected by himself, and others of his fellow-subjects, to represent them. This is certainly as false as the other two; for every Englishman is taxed, and not one in twenty represented: copyholders, leaseholders, and all men possessed of personal property only, chuse no representatives; Manchester, Birmingham, and many more of our richest and most flourishing trading towns send no members to Parliament, consequently cannot consent by their representatives, because they chuse none to represent them; yet are they not Englishmen? or are they not taxed?

I am well aware that I shall hear Locke, Sidney, Selden, and many other great names quoted [424] to prove that every Englishman, whether he has a right to vote for a representative, or not, is still represented in the British Parliament; in which opinion they all agree. On what principle of common-sense this opinion is founded I comprehend not, but on the authority of such respectable names I shall acknowledge its truth; but then I will ask one question, and on that I will rest the whole merits of the cause: Why does not this imaginary representation extend to America, as well as over the whole island of Great Britain? If it can travel three hundred miles, why not three thousand? If it can jump over rivers and mountains, why cannot it sail over the ocean? If the towns of Manchester and Birmingham, sending no representatives to Parliament, are notwithstanding there represented, why are not the cities of Albany and Boston equally represented in that assembly? Are they not alike British subjects? are they not Englishmen? or are they only Englishmen when they sollicit for protection, but not Englishmen, when taxes are required to enable this country to protect them?

But it is urged that the Colonies are by their charters placed under distinct Governments, each of which has a legislative power within itself, by which alone it ought to be taxed; that if this privilege is once given up, that liberty which every Englishman has a right to, is torn from them, they are all slaves, and all is lost.

[425] The liberty of an Englishman is a phrase of so various a signification, having within these few years been used as a synonymous term for blasphemy, bawdy, treason, libels, strong beer, and cyder, that I shall not here presume to define its meaning; but I shall venture to assert what it cannot mean; that is, an exemption from taxes imposed by the authority of the Parliament of Great Britain; nor is there any charter that ever pretended to grant such a privilege to any colony in America; and had they granted it, it could have had no force; their charters being derived from the crown, and no charter from the crown can possibly supersede the right of the whole Legislature: their charters are undoubtedly no more than those of all corporations, which

7

impower them to make byelaws, and raise duties for the purposes of their own police, for ever subject to the superior authority of Parliament; and in some of their charters the manner of exercising these powers is specified in these express words, "according to the course of other corporations in Great Britain:" and therefore they can have no more pretence to plead an exemption from this parliamentary authority, than any other corporation in England.

It has been moreover alledged, that, though Parliament may have power to impose taxes on the Colonies, they have no right to use it, [426] because it would be an unjust tax; and no supreme or legislative power can have a right to enact any law in its nature unjust: to this, I shall only make this short reply, that if Parliament can impose no taxes but what are equitable, and [if] the persons taxed are to be the judges of that equity, they will in effect have no power to lay any tax at all. No tax can be imposed exactly equal on all, and if it is not equal, it cannot be just, and if it is not just, no power whatever can impose it; by which short syllogism, all taxation is at an end; but why it should not be used by Englishmen on this side the Atlantic as well as by those on the other, I do not comprehend.

Thus much for the right. Let us now a little inquire into the expediency of this measure, to which two objections have been made; that the time is improper, and the manner wrong.

As to the first, can any time be more proper to require some assistance from our Colonies, to preserve to themselves their present safety, than when this Country is almost undone by procuring it? Can any time be more proper to impose some tax upon their trade, than when they are enabled to rival us in our manufactures, by the encouragement and protection which we have given them? Can any time be more proper to oblige them to settle handsome incomes on their governors, than [427] when we find them unable to procure a subsistence on any other terms than those of breaking all their instructions, and betraying the rights of their sovereign? Can there be a more proper time to compel them to fix certain salaries on their judges, than when we see them so dependent on the humours of their assemblies, that they can obtain a livelihood no longer than *quam diu se male gesserint* [that day upon which the evil befell them]? Can there be a more proper time to force them to maintain an army at their expence, than when that army is necessary for their own protection, and we are utterly unable to support it? Lastly; can there be a more proper time for this mother country to leave off feeding out of her own vitals, these children whom she has nursed up, than when they are arrived at such strength and maturity as to be well able to provide for themselves and ought rather with filial duty to give some assistance to her distresses?

As to the manner; that is, the imposing taxes on the Colonies by the authority of Parliament, it is said to be harsh and arbitrary; and that it would have been more consistent with justice, at least with maternal tenderness, for Administration here to have settled quotas on each of the colonies, and have then transmitted them with injunctions, that the sums allotted should be immediately raised by their respective legislatures, on the penalty of their being imposed by Parliament in

8

case of their [428] non-compliance. But was this to be done, what would be the consequence? Have their assemblies shewn so much obedience to the orders of the Crown, that we could reasonably expect, that they would immediately tax themselves on the arbitrary command of a minister? Would it be possible here to settle those quotas with justice, or would any one of the colonies submit to them, were they ever so just? Should we not be compared to those Roman tyrants, who used to send orders to their subjects to murder themselves within so many hours, most obligingly leaving the method to their own choice, but on their disobedience threatening a more severe fate from the hands of an executioner? And should we not receive votes, speeches, resolutions, petitions, and remonstrances in abundance, instead of taxes? In short, we either have a right to tax the Colonies or we have not: if Parliament is possessed of this right, why should it be exercised with more delicacy in America, than it has ever been even in Great Britain itself? If on the other hand, they have no such right, sure it is below the dignity as well as the justice of the Legislature, to intimidate the Colonies with vain threats, which they have really no right to put in execution.

One method indeed has been hinted at, and but one, that might render the exercise of this power in a British Parliament just and legal, which is the introduction of representatives from the [429] several colonies into that body; but as this has never seriously been proposed, I shall not here consider the impracticability of this method, nor the effects of it, if it could be practised; but only say that I have lately seen so many specimens of the great powers of speech, of which these American gentlemen are possessed, that I should be much afraid, that the sudden importation of so much eloquence at once, would greatly endanger the safety and government of this country; or in terms more fashionable, though less understood, this our most excellent constitution. If we can avail ourselves of these taxes on no other condition, I shall never look upon it as a measure of frugality; being perfectly satisfied that in the end it will be much cheaper for us to pay their army, than their orators. . . .

5. Pitt's Influence

From Frederic Harrison, *Chatham* (New York: Macmillan, 1905). P. 158.

Called the "Great Commoner," William Pitt, later the Earl of Chatham, was the principal leader of the Whigs. He enjoyed a tremendous popularity in England and America for his successful prosecution of the recent war against France. But he had been out of office since his resignation in October, 1761, and was incapacitated by ill health from participating in parliamentary affairs. He declined to join the Rockingham ministry, formed

9

in 1765, but supported that ministry's decision to repeal the Stamp Act (see document 6).

It may be taken as almost certain that, if Pitt had been in his place and in full possession of his powers, the disastrous policy of taxing the American colonies could not have been carried. But during the whole of the debates on Grenville's Stamp Act of 1765, Pitt was away at Bath, and disabled by gout. When [159] Lord Rockingham succeeded Grenville, one of his first and most beneficial measures was the Repeal of the Stamp Act, in 1766, and this was very largely due to the influence and eloquence of Pitt. Up to the beginning of the year 1766 Pitt remained in retirement at Bath. From there he wrote to Lord Shelburne protesting against "the making good by force there, preposterous and infatuated errors in policy here." In January 1766 he returned to the House of Commons after a long absence, with powers materially restored. The King's Speech turned on the disturbed state of the American colonies, where riots and violent opposition made the Stamp Act wholly unworkable. In fact, the American revolution was on the point of breaking out eight years earlier than it did. In the debates which brought about the Repeal of the Stamp Act, Pitt had a leading part. As these speeches are amongst the most authentic reports we possess, and as they contain many of his noblest utterances, it may be well to quote them at large:—

6. Pitt's Speech on the Stamp Act

From *Correspondence of William Pitt, Earl of Chatham*, ed. William S. Taylor and John Henry Pringle (London: John Murray, 1838–40). Four volumes. Vol. II, p. 365.
The following extract is from a speech by Pitt in the debate on the Address to the Throne, House of Commons (on the assembling of Parliament), January 14, 1766.

It is a long time, Mr. Speaker, since I have attended in parliament. When the resolution was taken in this House to tax America, I was ill in bed. If I could have endured to have been carried in my bed, so great was the agitation of my mind for the consequences, I would have solicited some kind hand to have laid me down on this floor, to have borne my testimony against it. It is now an act that has passed. I would speak with decency of every act of this House, but I must beg the indulgence of the House to speak of it with freedom.

I hope a day may soon be appointed to consider the state of the nation with respect to America. I hope gentlemen will come to this debate with all the temper and impartiality that his Majesty recom-

mends, and the importance of the subject requires—*a subject of greater*
[366] *importance than ever engaged the attention of this House;* that
subject only excepted, when, nearly a century ago, it was the question,
whether you yourselves were to be bound or free.

In the meantime, as I cannot depend upon health for any future
day, such is the nature of my infirmities, I will beg to say a few words
at present, leaving the justice, the equity, the policy, the expediency of
the act, to another time. I will only speak to one point, a point which
seems not to have been generally understood—I mean [as] *to the right*
[to tax]. Some gentlemen . . . seem to have considered it as a point
of honour. If gentlemen consider it in that light, they leave all measures of right and wrong, to follow a delusion that may lead to destruction. It is my opinion that this kingdom has no right to lay a tax upon
the colonies. At the same time, I assert the authority of this kingdom
over the colonies to be sovereign and supreme in every circumstance of
government and legislation whatsoever. They [the colonists] are the
subjects of this kingdom, equally entitled with yourselves to all the
natural rights of mankind and the peculiar privileges of Englishmen:
equally bound by its laws, and equally participating of the constitution
of this free country. The Americans are the sons, not the bastards of
England. Taxation is no part of the governing or legislative power. The
taxes are a voluntary gift and grant of the Commons alone. In legislation, the three estates of the realm are alike concerned; but the con-
currency of the Peers and the Crown to a tax is only necessary to close
[clothe] it with the form of a law. . . .

[367] There is an idea in some, that the colonies are virtually represented in this House. I would fain know by whom an American is
represented here? Is he represented by any knight of the shire in any
county in this kingdom? Would to God that respectable representation was augmented to a greater number! Or will you tell him that he
is represented by any representative of a borough,—a borough which
perhaps its own representatives never saw? That is what is called the
"rotten part of the constitution." It cannot continue a century: if it
does not drop, it must be amputated. The idea of a virtual representation of America in this House, is the most contemptible that ever
entered into the head of man.—It does not deserve a serious refutation.

The Commons of America, represented in their several assemblies,
have ever been in possession of the exercise of this, their constitutional
right, of giving and granting their own money. They would have been
slaves if they had not enjoyed it. At the same time, this kingdom, as
the supreme governing and legislative power, has always bound the
colonies by her laws, by her regulations, and restrictions in trade, in
navigation, in manufacturing—in every thing, except that of taking
their money out of their pockets without their consent. Here I would
draw the line,

> "[Est modus in rebus,] sunt certi denique fines,
> Quos ultra citraque nequit consistere rectum."

["There are fixed limits beyond which, and short of which, right cannot find a resting place." Horace, *Satires,* I, i, 106–7.]

11

7. Grenville Answers Pitt

From William Cobbett, *The Parliamentary History of Englana* (London: T. C. Hansard, 1806–20). Thirty-six volumes. Vol. XVI, p. 101.

George Grenville (1712–70), Prime Minister from April, 1763, to July, 1765, was primarily responsible for the series of parliamentary acts that provoked the crisis in Anglo-American relations. The chief of those who opposed the Rockingham ministry's more conciliatory policy, he answered Pitt's speech. An excerpt from his reply to Pitt is given here. The source is the debate on the Address to the Throne, House of Commons, January 14, 1766. Cobbett's work is the published source of information on the proceedings in Parliament during this period.

He began with censuring the ministry very severely, for delaying to give earlier notice to parliament of the disturbances in America. He said they began in July, and now we are in the middle of January; lately they were only occurrences; they are now grown to disturbances, to tumults, and riots. I doubt they border on open rebellion; and if the doctrine I have heard this day be confirmed, I fear they will lose that name, to take that of a revolution. The government over them being dissolved, a revolution will take place in America. I cannot understand the difference between external and internal taxes. They are the same in effect, and differ only in name. That this kingdom has the sovereign, the supreme legislative power over America, is granted. It cannot be denied; and taxation is a part of that sovereign power. It is one branch of the legislation. It is, it has been exercised, over those who are not, who were never represented. It is exercised over the India Company, the merchants of London, and the proprietors of the stocks, and over great manufacturing towns. It was exercised over the county palatine of Chester, and the bishoprick of Durham, before they sent any representatives to parliament. . . . Which [102] being done, he said: When I proposed to tax America, I asked the house, if any gentleman would object to the right; I repeatedly asked it, and no man would attempt to deny it. Protection and obedience are reciprocal. Great Britain protects America, America is bound to yield obedience. If not, tell me when the Americans were emancipated? When they want the protection of this kingdom, they are always very ready to ask it. That protection has always been afforded them in the most full and ample manner. The nation has run itself into an immense debt to give them this protection; and now they are called upon to contribute a small share towards the public expence, an expence arising from themselves, they renounce your authority, insult your officers, and break out, I might almost say, in open rebellion. The seditious spirit of the colonies owes its birth to factions in this

House. Gentlemen are careless of the consequences of what they say, provided it answers the purposes of opposition.

We were told to trod on tender ground; we were bid to expect disobedience. What was this, but telling the Americans to stand out against the law, to encourage their obstinacy with expectation of support from hence? Let us only hold out a little, they would say, our friends will soon be in power. Ungrateful people of America! Bounties have been extended to them. When I had the honour of serving the crown, while you yourselves were loaded with an enormous debt, you have given bounties on their lumber, on their iron, their hemp, and many other articles. You have relaxed, in their favour, the Act of Navigation, that palladium of British commerce; and yet I have been abused in all the public papers as an enemy to the trade of America. I have been particularly charged with giving orders and instructions to prevent the Spanish trade, and thereby stopping the channel by which alone North America used to be supplied with cash for remittances for this country. I defy any man to produce any such orders or instructions. I discouraged no trade but what was illicit, what was prohibited by act of parliament. . . . I offered to do every thing in my power to advance the trade of America. I was above giving an answer to anonymous calumnies; [103] but in this place, it becomes me to wipe off the aspersion.

8. Pitt Answers Grenville

From *Correspondence of William Pitt, Earl of Chatham*, ed. William S. Taylor and John Henry Pringle (London: John Murray, 1838–40). Four volumes. Vol. II, p. 369.

Pitt's speech in reply to Grenville was delivered in the House of Commons on January 14, 1766.

Gentlemen,—Sir, (to the speaker) I have been charged with giving birth to sedition in America. [Several] have spoken their sentiments with freedom against this unhappy Act, and that freedom has become their crime. Sorry I am to hear the liberty of speech in this House imputed as a crime. But the imputation shall not discourage me. It is a liberty I mean to exercise.

No gentleman ought to be afraid to exercise it. It is a liberty by which the gentleman who calumniates it might have profited, by which he ought to have profited. He ought to have desisted from his project. The gentleman tells us America is obstinate; America is almost in open rebellion. I rejoice that America has resisted. Three millions of people so dead to all the feelings of liberty as voluntarily to submit to be slaves, would have been fit instruments to make slaves of all the rest. I come

13

not here armed at all points with law cases and Acts of Parliament, with the statute book doubled down in dog's-ears, to defend the cause of liberty: if I had, I myself would have cited the two cases of Chester and Durham: I would have cited them, to have shewn that even under the most arbitrary reigns, Parliaments were ashamed of taxing people without their consent, and allowed them representatives. Why did the gentleman confine himself to Chester and Durham? He might have taken a higher example in Wales; Wales, that never was taxed by Parliament till it was incorporated. I would not debate a particular point of law with the gentleman. I know his abilities: I have been obliged by his diligent researches: but, for the defence of liberty upon a general principle, upon a constitutional principle, it is a ground upon which I stand firm; on which I dare meet any man. The gentleman tells us of many who are taxed, and are not represented—the India Company, merchants, stock-holders, manufacturers. Surely many of these are represented in other capacities, as owners of land, or as free-men of boroughs. It is a misfortune that more are not equally [actually?] represented: but they are all inhabitants, and, as such, are they not virtually represented? Many have it in their option to be actually represented: they have connections with those that elect, and they have influence over them. . . . Since the accession of King William, many ministers, some of great, others of more moderate abilities, have taken the lead of government. (He then went through the list of them bringing it down till he came to himself, giving a short sketch of the characters of each of them.) None of these, he said, thought or ever dreamed of robbing the colonies of their constitutional rights. That was reserved to mark [370] the era of the late administration: not that there were wanting some, when I had the honour to serve his Majesty, to propose to me to burn my fingers with an American stamp act. With the enemy at their back, with our bayonets at their breasts in the day of their distress, perhaps the Americans would have submitted to the imposition; but it would have been taking an ungenerous, an unjust advantage. The gentleman boasts of his bounties to America. Are not these bounties intended finally for the benefit of this kingdom? If they are not, he has misapplied the national treasures. I am no courtier of America; I stand up for this kingdom. I maintain that the Parliament has a right to bind, to restrain America.

Our legislative power over the colonies is sovereign and supreme. When it ceases to be sovereign and supreme, I would advise every gentleman to sell his lands, if he can, and embark for that country. Where two countries are connected together like England and her colonies, without being incorporated, the one must necessarily govern; the greater must rule the less; but so rule it, as not to contradict the fundamental principles that are common to both.

If the gentleman does not understand the difference between ex-ternal and internal taxes, I cannot help it; but there is a plain distinc-tion between taxes levied for the purposes of raising a revenue, and duties imposed for the regulation of trade, for the accommodation of the subject; although, in the consequences, some revenue might inci-dentally arise from the latter.

14

The gentleman asks, when were the colonies emancipated? But I desire to know, when were they made slaves? But I dwell not upon words. When I had the honour of serving his Majesty, I availed myself of the means of information which I derived from my office. I speak, therefore, from knowledge. My materials were good. I was at pains to collect, to digest, to consider them; and I will be bold to affirm, that the profits to Great Britain from the trade of the colonies, through all its branches, are two millions a year. This is the fund that carried you triumphantly through the last war. The estates that were rented at two thousand pounds a year, threescore years ago, are at three thousand pounds at present. Those estates sold then from fifteen to eighteen years' purchase; the same may be now sold for thirty.

You owe this to America. This is the price that America pays you for her protection. . . . I dare [371] not say, how much higher these profits may be augmented. Omitting the immense increase of people, by natural population, in the northern colonies, and the emigration from every part of Europe, I am convinced the whole commercial system of America may be altered to advantage. You have prohibited where you ought to have encouraged; you have encouraged where you ought to have prohibited. Improper restraints have been laid on the continent in favour of the islands [the West Indies]. . . .

The gentleman must not wonder he was not contradicted, when, as the minister, he asserted the right of parliament to tax America. I know not how it is, but there is a modesty in this house which does not choose to contradict a minister. I wish gentlemen would get the better of this modesty: Even that chair, Sir, sometimes looks towards St. James's [the King's palace]; if they do not, perhaps the collective body may begin to abate of its respect for the representative. . . .

[372] A great deal has been said without doors of the power, of the strength of America. It is a topic that ought to be cautiously meddled with. In a good cause, on a sound bottom, the force of this country can crush America to atoms. I know the valour of your troops. I know the skill of your officers. There is not a company of foot that has served in America out of which you may not pick a man of sufficient knowledge and experience to make a governor of a colony there. But on this ground, on the Stamp Act, which so many here will think a crying injustice, I am one who will lift up my hands against it.

In such a cause, your success would be hazardous. America, if she fell, would fall like the strong man Samson; she would embrace the pillars of the state, and pull down the constitution along with her. Is this your boasted peace? Not to sheathe the sword in its scabbard, but to sheathe it in the bowels of your countrymen? Will you quarrel with yourselves, now that the whole House of Bourbon is united against you? While France disturbs your fisheries in Newfoundland, embarrasses your slave trade to Africa, and withholds from your subjects in Canada their property stipulated by treaty. . . .

The Americans have not acted in all things with prudence and temper; they have been wronged; they have been driven to madness by injustice. Will you punish them for the madness you have occasioned? Rather let prudence and temper come first from this side. I will undertake for America that she will follow the example. There are two lines in a ballad of Prior's, of a man's behaviour to his wife, so applicable to you and your colonies, that I cannot help repeating them:

> "Be to her faults a little blind;
> Be to her virtues very kind."

Upon the whole, I will beg leave to tell the House what is really my opinion. It is, that the Stamp Act be repealed absolutely, totally, and immediately; that the reason for the repeal be assigned because it was founded on an erroneous principle. At the [373] same time, let the sovereign authority of this country over the colonies be asserted in as strong terms as can be devised, and be made to extend to every point of legislation whatsoever; that we may bind their trade, confine their manufactures, and exercise every power whatsoever—except that of taking money out of their pockets without their consent.

["The Commons House of South Carolina unanimously voted to Pitt a colossal statue in Charleston 'in grateful memory of his services to America'—'for defending the freedom of Americans, the true sons of England, by promoting a Repeal of the Stamp Act in 1766.' The inscription was as follows: 'Time shall sooner destroy this mark of their esteem than erase from their minds the just sense of his patriotic virtue.' The statue still remains, but the right arm was broken off by a British cannon shot in 1780." Frederic Harrison, *Chatham* (New York: Macmillan, 1905), p. 168.]

9. Petition of the London Merchants Against the Stamp Act

From William Cobbett, *The Parliamentary History of England* (London: T. C. Hansard, 1806–20). Thirty-six volumes. Vol. XVI, p. 133.
The Americans reacted to British taxation with a boycott of goods manufactured in Great Britain. The following petition, presented to the House of Commons on January 17, 1766, represents a typical reaction of the English merchants and manufacturers to the effect of the American non-importation policy.

A petition of the merchants of London, trading to North America, was presented to the House, and read; setting forth;
"That the petitioners have been long concerned in carrying on the trade between this country and the British colonies on the continent of North America and that they have annually exported very large quantities of British manufactures, consisting of woolen goods of all

kinds, cottons, linens, hardware, shoes, household furniture, and almost
without exception of every other species of goods manufactured in
these kingdoms, besides other articles imported from abroad, chiefly
purchased with our manufactures and with the produce of our colonies;
by all which, many thousand manufacturers, seamen and labourers,
have been employed, to the very great and increasing benefit of this
nation; and that, in return for these exports, the petitioners have received from the colonies, rice, indigo, tobacco, naval stores, oil, whale
fins, furs, and lately potash, with other commodities, besides remittances by bills of exchange and bullion, obtained by the colonists in
payment for articles of their produce, not required for the British
market, and therefore exported to other places; and that, from the
nature of this trade, consisting of British manufactures exported, and
of the import of raw materials from America, many of them used in
our manufactures, and all of them tending to lessen our dependence
on neighboring states, it must be deemed of the highest importance in
the commercial system of this nation; and that this commerce, so beneficial to the [134] state, and so necessary for the support of multitudes,
now lies under such difficulties and discouragement, that nothing less
than its utter ruin is apprehended, without the immediate interposition of parliament; and that, in consequence of the trade between the
colonies and the mother country, as established and as permitted for
many years, and of the experience which the petitioners have had of
the readiness of the Americans to make their just remittances to the
utmost of their real ability, they have been induced to make and venture such large exportations of British manufactures, as to leave the
colonies indebted to the merchants of Great Britain in the sum of
several millions sterling; and that at this time the colonists, when
pressed for payment, appeal to past experience, in proof of their willingness; but declare it is not in their power, at present, to make good their
engagements, alleging, that the taxes and restrictions laid upon them,
and the extension of the jurisdiction of vice admiralty courts established by some late acts of parliament, particularly by an act passed
in the fourth year of his present Majesty, for granting certain duties in
the British colonies and plantations in America, and by an act passed
in the fifth year of his present Majesty, for granting and applying
certain stamp duties, and other duties, in the British colonies and
plantations in America, with several regulations and restraints, which,
if founded in acts of parliament for defined purposes, are represented
to have been extended in such a manner as to disturb legal commerce
and harass the fair trader, have so far interrupted the usual and former
most fruitful branches of their commerce, restrained the sale of their
produce, thrown the state of the several provinces into confusion, and
brought on so great a number of actual bankruptcies, that the former
opportunities and means of remittances and payments are utterly lost
and taken from them; and that the petitioners are, by these unhappy
events, reduced to the necessity of applying to the House, in order to
secure themselves and their families from impending ruin; to prevent
a multitude of manufacturers from becoming a burthen to the community, or else seeking their bread in other countries, to the irretriev-

able loss of this kingdom; and to preserve the strength of this nation entire, its commerce flourishing, the revenues increasing, our navigation, the bul- [135] wark of the kingdom, in a state of growth and extension, and the colonies from inclination, duty, and interest, firmly attached to the mother country; and therefore praying the consideration of the premises, and entreating such relief, as to the House shall seem expedient."

This Petition was referred to a Committee of the whole House, as were also the following petitions, viz. [of the merchants, etc., of Bristol, Liverpool, Halifax, Leeds, Lancaster, Manchester, Leicester, Bradford, etc.] . . . all complaining of a great decay in the trade to the North American colonies, owing to the late obstructions and embarrassments laid thereon, and praying relief. . . .

10. Benjamin Franklin Discusses
Repeal of the Stamp Act

From *The Gentleman's Magazine*. Vol. XXXVII (July, 1767), p. 368.
Franklin, Deputy Postmaster-General of North America and agent for Pennsylvania, was asked 174 questions, some by opponents and some by friends of the Stamp Act. Franklin's replies were published immediately; widely read, they greatly increased his influence in America and his reputation in England.

THE EXAMINATION OF DOCTOR BENJAMIN FRANKLIN, RELATIVE TO THE REPEAL OF THE AMERICAN STAMP ACT IN 1766.

From this examination of Dr. Franklin, the reader may form a clearer and more comprehensive idea of the state and disposition of America, of the expediency or inexpediency of the measure in question, and of the character and conduct of the minister who proposed it, than from all that has been written upon the subject in newspapers and pamphlets, under the titles of essays, letters, speeches, and considerations, from the first moment of its becoming the object of public attention till now.

The questions are put with great subtilty and judgment, and they are answered with such deep and familiar knowledge of the subject, such precision and perspicuity, such temper and yet such spirit, as do the greatest honour to Dr. Franklin, and justify the general opinion of his character and abilities. . . .

11. The Examination of Benjamin Franklin in Parliament

From Willam Cobbett, *The Parliamentary History of England* (London: T. C. Hansard, 1806–20). Thirty-six volumes. Vol. XVI, p. 137.

Q. What is your name, and place of abode?—A. Franklin, of Philadelphia.

Do the Americans pay any considerable taxes among themselves?—Certainly many, and very heavy taxes.

What are the present taxes in Pennsylvania, laid by the laws of the colony?—There are taxes on all estates real and personal, a poll-tax, a tax on all offices, professions, trades, and businesses, according to their profits; an excise on all wine, rum, and other spirit; and a duty of ten pounds per head on all negroes imported, with some other duties.

For what purposes are those taxes laid?—For the support of the civil and military establishments of the country, and to discharge the heavy debt contracted in the last war.

How long are those taxes to continue?—Those for discharging the debt are to continue till 1772, and longer, if the debt should not be then all discharged. The others must always continue.

Was it not expected that the debt would have been sooner discharged?—It was, when the peace was made with France and Spain; but a fresh war breaking out with the Indians, a fresh load of debt was incurred, and the taxes, of course, continued longer by a new law. . . .

[138] Are not the colonies, from their circumstances, very able to pay the stamp duty?—In my opinion, there is not gold and silver enough in the colonies to pay the stamp duty for one year.

Don't you know that the money arising from the stamps was all to be laid out in America?—I know it is appropriated by the act to the American service; but it will be spent in the conquered colonies, where the soldiers are, not in the colonies that pay it. . . .

[139] Do you think it right, that America should be protected by this country, and pay no part of the expence?—That is not the case. The colonies raised, clothed and paid, during the last war, near 25,000 men, and spent many millions.

[140] Were you not reimbursed by parliament?—We were only reimbursed what, in your opinion, we had advanced beyond our proportion, or beyond what might reasonably be expected from us; and it was a very small part of what we spent. Pennsylvania, in particular, disbursed about 500,000, and the reimbursements, in the whole, did not exceed 60,000. . . .

Do not you think the people of America would submit to pay the stamp duty, if it was moderated?—No, never, unless compelled by force of arms. . . .

What was the temper of America towards Great Britain before the year 1763?—The best in the world. They submitted willingly to the government of the crown, and paid, in [141] all their courts, obedience to acts of parliament. Numerous as the people are in the several old provinces, they cost you nothing in forts, citadels, garrisons or armies, to keep them in subjection. They were governed by this country at the expence only of a little pen, ink, and paper. They were led by a thread. They had not only a respect, but an affection for Great Britain, for its laws, its customs and manners, and even a fondness for its fashions, that greatly increased the commerce. Natives of Britain were always treated with particular regard; to be an Old-English man was, of itself, a character of some respect, and gave a kind of rank among us.

And what is their temper now?—O, very much altered.

Did you ever hear the authority of parliament to make laws for America questioned till lately?—The authority of parliament was allowed to be valid in all laws, except such as should lay internal taxes. It was never disputed in laying duties to regulate commerce. . . .

In what light did the people of America use to consider the parliament of Great Britain?—They considered the parliament as the great bulwark and security of their liberties and privileges, and always spoke of it with the utmost respect and veneration. Arbitrary ministers, they thought, might possibly, at times, attempt to oppress them; but they relied on it, that the parliament, on application, would always give redress. They remembered, with gratitude, a strong instance of this, when a bill was brought into parliament, with a clause to make royal instructions laws in the colonies, which the House of Commons would not pass, and it was thrown out.

And have they not still the same respect for parliament?—No; it is greatly lessened.

To what causes is that owing?—To a concurrence of causes; the restraints lately laid on their trade, by which the [142] bringing of foreign gold and silver into the colonies was prevented; the prohibition of making paper money among themselves; and then demand a new and heavy tax by stamps; taking away at the same time, trials by juries, and refusing to receive and hear their humble petitions.

Don't you think they would submit to the Stamp Act, if it was modified, the obnoxious parts taken out, and the duty reduced to some particulars of small moment?—No; they will never submit to it. . . .

Have not you heard of the resolution of this House, and of the House of Lords, asserting the right of parliament relating to America, including a power to tax the people there?—Yes, I have heard of such resolutions.

What will be the opinion of the Americans on those resolutions?—They will think them unconstitutional and unjust.

Was it an opinion in America before 1763, that the parliament had no right to lay taxes and duties there?—I never heard any objection to the right of laying duties to regulate commerce; but a right to lay internal taxes was never supposed to be in parliament, as we are not represented there.

On what do you found your opinion, that the people in America

20

made any such distinction?—I know that whenever the subject has occurred in conversation where I have been present, it has appeared to be the opinion of every one, that we could not be taxed in a parliament where we were not represented. But the payment of duties laid by act of parliament, as regulations of commerce, was never disputed. . . .

[144] You say the colonies have always submitted to external taxes, and object to the right of parliament only in laying internal taxes; now can you show that there is any kind of difference between the two taxes to the colony on which they may be laid?—I think the difference is very great. An external tax is a duty laid on commodities imported; that duty is added to the first cost, and other charges on the commodity, and when it is offered to sale, makes a part of the price. If the people do not like it at that price, they refuse it; they are not obliged to pay it. But an internal tax is forced from the people without their consent, if not laid by their own representatives. The Stamp Act says, we shall have no commerce, make no exchange of property with each other, neither purchase nor grant, nor recover debts; we shall neither marry nor make our wills, unless we pay such sums, and thus it is intended to extort our money from us, or ruin us by the consequences of refusing to pay it. . . .

[145] Considering the resolutions of parliament as to the right, do you think, if the Stamp Act is repealed, that the North Americans will be satisfied?—I believe they will.

Why do you think so?—I think the resolutions of right [the Declaration of Right] will give them very little concern, if they are never attempted to be carried into practice. The colonies [146] will probably consider themselves in the same situation, in that respect, with Ireland: they know you claim the same right with regard to Ireland, but you never exercise it. And they may believe you never will exercise it in the colonies, any more than in Ireland, unless on some very extraordinary occasion.

But who are to be the judges of that extraordinary occasion? Is not the parliament?—Though the parliament may judge of the occasion, the people will think it can never exercise such right, till representatives from the colonies are admitted into parliament, and that whenever the occasion arises, representatives will be ordered. . . .

[147] Did the Americans ever dispute the controuling power of parliament to regulate the commerce?—No.

Can any thing less than a military force carry the Stamp Act into execution?—I do not see how a military force can be applied to that purpose.

Why may it not?—Suppose a military force sent into America, they will find nobody in arms; what are they then to do? They cannot force a man to take stamps who chuses to do without them. They will not find a rebellion; they may indeed make one.

If the act is not repealed, what do you think will be the consequences?—A total loss of the respect and affection the people of America bear to this country, and of all the commerce that depends on that respect and affection.

How can the commerce be affected?—You will find, that if the act

21

is not repealed, they will take very little of your manufactures in a short time. . . .

[148] Suppose an act of internal regulations connected with a tax, how would they receive it?—I think it would be objected to.

Then no regulation with a tax would be submitted to?—Their opinion is, that when aids to the crown are wanted, they are to be asked of the several assemblies according to the old established usage, who will, as they have always done, grant them freely. And that their money ought not to be given away, without their consent, by persons at a distance, unacquainted with their circumstances and abilities. The granting aids to the crown, is the only means they have of recommending themselves to their sovereign, and they think it extremely hard and unjust, that a body of men, in which they have no representatives, should make a merit to itself of giving and granting what is not its own, but theirs, and deprives them of a right they esteem of the utmost value and importance, as it is the security of all their other rights. . . . [152] America has been greatly misrepresented and abused here, in papers, and pamphlets, [153] and speeches, as ungrateful, and unreasonable, and unjust, in having put this nation to immense expence for their defence, and refusing to bear any part of that expence. The colonies raised, paid, and clothed, near 25,000 men during the last war, a number equal to those sent from Britain, and far beyond their proportion; they went deeply into debt in doing this, and all their taxes and estates are mortgaged, for many years to come, for discharging that debt. Government, here, was at that time very sensible of this. The colonies were recommended to parliament. Every year the King sent down to the House a written message to this purpose, that his Majesty, being highly sensible of the zeal and vigour with which his faithful subjects in North America had exerted themselves, in defence of his Majesty's just rights and possessions, recommended it to the House to take the same into consideration and enable him to give them a proper compensation. You will find those messages on your own journals every year of the war to the very last, and you did accordingly give £200,000 annually to the crown, to be distributed in such compensation to the colonies. This is the strongest of all proofs that the colonies, far from being unwilling to bear a share of the burden, did exceed their proportion; for if they had done less, or had only equalled their proportion, there would have been no room or reason for compensation. Indeed the sums reimbursed them, were by no means adequate to the expence they incurred beyond their proportion; but they never murmured at that; they esteemed their sovereign's approbation of their zeal and fidelity, and the approbation of this House, far beyond any other kind of compensation; therefore there was no occasion for this act, to force money from a willing people; they had not refused giving money for the purposes of the act; no requisition had been made: they were always willing and ready to do what could reasonably be expected from them, and in this light they wish to be considered.

But suppose Great Britain should be engaged in a war in Europe, would North America contribute to the support of it?—I do think they would, as far as their circumstances would permit. They consider themselves as a part of the British empire, and as having one common interest with it; they may be looked on here as foreigners, but they do not consider themselves as such. They are zealous for the [154] honour and prosperity of this nation, and while they are well used, will always be ready to support it, as far as their little power goes. In 1739 they were called upon to assist in the expedition against Carthagena, and they sent 3,000 men to join your army. It is true Carthagena is in America, but as remote from the northern colonies as if it had been in Europe. . . .

[155] Was not the late war with the Indians [Pontiac], since the peace with France, a war for America only?—Yes; it was more particularly for America than the former, but it was rather a consequence or remains of the former war, the Indians not having been thoroughly pacified, and the Americans bore by much the greatest share of the expence. It was put an end to by the army under general Bouquet; there were not above 300 regulars in that army, and above 1000 Pennsylvanians.

Is it not necessary to send troops to America, to defend the Americans against the Indians?—No, by no means; it never was necessary. They defended themselves when they were but a handful, and the Indians much more numerous. They continually gained ground, and have driven the Indians over the mountains, without any troops sent to their assistance from this country. And can it be thought necessary now to send troops for their defence from those diminished Indian tribes, when the colonies are become so populous, and so strong? There is not the least occasion for it; they are very able to defend themselves.

Do you say there were no more than 300 regular troops employed in the late Indian war?—Not on the Ohio, or the frontiers of Pennsylvania, which was the chief part of the war that affected the colonies. There were garrisons at Niagara, Fort Detroit, and those remote posts kept for the sake of your trade; I did not reckon them, but I believe that on the whole the number of Americans, or provincial troops, employed in the late [French and Indian] war, was greater than that of the regulars. I am not certain, but I think so. . . .

[158] How . . . could the assembly of Pennsylvania assert, that laying a tax on them by the Stamp Act was an infringement of their rights?—They understand it thus: by the same charter, and otherwise, they are entitled to all the privileges and liberties of Englishmen; they find in the Great Charters, and the Petition and Declaration of Rights, that one of the privileges of English subjects is, that they are not to be taxed but by their common consent; they have therefore relied upon it, from the first settlement of the province, that the parliament never would, nor could, by colour of that clause in the charter, assume a right of taxing them, till it had qualified itself to exercise such right, by admitting representatives from the people to be taxed, who ought to make a part of that common consent.

Are there any words in the charter that justify that construction?—The common rights of Englishmen, as declared by Magna Charta, and the Petition of Right, all justify it. . . .

[160] If the Stamp Act should be repealed, would it induce the

assemblies of America to acknowledge the right of parliament to tax them, and would they erase their resolutions?—No, never.

Is there no means of obliging them to erase those resolutions?—None, that I know of; they will never do it, unless compelled by force of arms.

Is there a power on earth that can force them to erase them?—No power, how great soever, can force men to change their opinions. . . .

What used to be the pride of the Americans?—To indulge in the fashions and manufactures of Great Britain.

What is now their pride?—To wear their old clothes over again, till they can make new ones.——Withdrew.

The Committee of the whole House, having, in a great measure, finished their examination of persons and papers, it was at length moved, on the 21st of January, 1766,

That it is the opinion of this Committee, that the House be moved, that leave be given to bring in a Bill to repeal an Act passed in the last session of parliament intitled, 'An Act for granting and applying certain stamp duties, and other duties in the British colonies and plantations in [161] America, towards farther defraying the expences of defending, protecting, and securing the same, and for amending such parts of the several acts of parliament relating to the trade and revenues of the said colonies and plantations, as direct the manner of determining and recovering the penalties and forfeitures therein mentioned.'

It was afterwards proposed to leave out the word 'repeal,' and insert 'explain and amend.' Upon which there ensued a debate. The question was put, whether the word 'repeal' should stand. Ayes 275; Noes 167. Then the question was put and agreed to.

12. The Debate on the Declaratory Act and the Repeal of the Stamp Act

From William Cobbett, *The Parliamentary History of England* (London: T. C. Hansard, 1806–20). Thirty-six volumes. Vol. XVI, p. 165.

The following debate in the House of Lords, beginning February 10, 1766, was on the resolutions introduced by Henry Seymour Conway, the Secretary of State for the Southern Department. These resolutions upheld the authority of Parliament and denounced the riotous proceedings in the colonies. The ground was being prepared for the ministry's policy of accompanying the repeal of the Stamp Act with a Declaratory Act upholding its constitutional validity.

The Debate arose upon the first of the above Resolutions, namely, "That the King's Majesty, by and with the advice and consent of the

Lords spiritual and temporal and Commons of Great Britain in parliament assembled, had, hath, and of right ought to have, full power and authority to make laws and statutes, of sufficient force and validity to bind the colonies and people of America, subjects of the crown of Great Britain, in all cases whatsoever."

The Duke of Grafton [Secretary of State for the Northern Department], after lamenting the contrariety of opinion, on the first proposition, and observing that, in questions of this interesting nature, we ought to divest ourselves of all prejudice, or attachment to one man or another, declared his opinion to be, that the Americans were as liable to be taxed as any in Great Britain. And that therefore he should not have offered the first Resolution, but that the right had been questioned, not only by the Americans, but by persons here, some of whom were eminent, and possibly the highest in line they tread. His grace then recommended lenient measures, as thinking the Americans deluded into an opinion that England had given them up. . . .

[168] Lord Camden [Chief Justice of the Common Pleas, later Lord Chancellor under Chatham, 1766–70]—I am very unhappy the first time of speaking in this House to differ from a lord of such superior abilities and learning, but the question before your lordships concerns the common rights of mankind; it is an abstract question, and will be judged of by your lordships gravely and deliberately, without any regard to the authority of any lord who speaks on either side of the question.

My lords; he who disputes the authority of any supreme legislature treads upon very tender ground. It is therefore necessary for me in setting out to lay in my claim to your lordships, and to desire that no inference may be drawn from any thing I shall advance. I disclaim that the consequence of my reasoning will be that the colonies can claim an independence on this country, or that they have a right to oppose acts of legislature in a rebellious manner, even though the legislature has no right to make such acts. In my own opinion, my lords, the legislature had no right to make this law.

The sovereign authority, the omnipotence of the legislature, my lords, is a favourite doctrine, but there are some things they cannot do. They cannot enact any thing against the divine law, and may forfeit their right. They cannot take away any man's private property without making him a compensation. A proof of which is the many private bills, as well as public, passed every session. They have no right to condemn any man by bill of attainder without hearing him.

But though the parliament cannot take any man's private property, yet every subject must make contribution. And this he consents to do by his representatives; when the people consented to be taxed they reserved to themselves a power of giving and granting by their representatives.

The Resolution now proposed is in my [169] opinion too general, as it gives the legislature an absolute power of laying any tax upon America. . . .

Ireland was conquered originally, but was settled by the English. They tax themselves, and the parliament here has no right to tax them; Lord Hale affirms this in the before-mentioned MS. where he says, that he thinks no acts here can bind the Irish in point of subsidies.

But, my lords, even supposing the Americans have no exclusive right to tax themselves, I maintain it would be good policy to give it them.—America feels she can do better without us, than we without her.

He spoke then to the expediency, and concluded that his opinion was, that the colonies had a right to tax themselves, and the parliament not.

[170] Lord Chancellor Northington [Lord Keeper and Chancellor].—I did not think I should have troubled your lordships on the subject of this 1st Resolution, but, upon doctrines being laid down so new, so unmaintainable, and so unconstitutional, I cannot sit silent. . . .

Every government can arbitrarily impose laws on all its subjects; there must be a supreme dominion in every state; whether monarchical, aristocratical, democratical, or mixed. And all the subjects of each state are bound by the laws made by government.

But the noble lord has endeavoured to distinguish between the civil power of government and its casuistical power. Now, my lords, there is no writer on general law but what agrees in this principle, that every legislature should make laws for the benefit and safety of the whole; but suppose they make a law contrary to this principle, a resistance to such law is at the risk of life and fortune. . . .

[171] My lords, I seek for the liberty and constitution of this kingdom no farther back than the Revolution: there I make my stand. And in the reign of King William an act passed avowing the power of this legislature over the colonies.

As to the expediency of carrying the act into execution—if the noble lord means to suspend the execution, and advise the King on that head, I will tell his lordship the King cannot do it. He is sworn by his coronation oath to do the contrary; but if you should concur with his lordship as to the expediency of repeal, you will tell 12 millions of your subjects of Great Britain and Ireland, that you prefer the colonists who are got rich under their protection, and will have them at your doors, not making speeches, but using the *argumentum baculinum* [the argument of the big stick].

My lords, what have these favourite Americans done? They have called a meeting of their states, and then have entered into Resolutions by which, in my opinion, they have forfeited all their charters. . . .

My lords, the colonies are become too big to be governed by the laws they at first set out with. They have therefore run into confusion, and it will be the policy of this country to form a plan of laws for them.

If they withdraw allegiance you must withdraw protection; and then the little state of Genoa, or the kingdom or rather republic of Sweden, may soon overrun them. . . .

[177] Lord Camden [in a speech, February 24, 1766, continuing the debate on the Declaratory Act]—My lords: When I spoke last on this subject, I thought I had delivered my sentiments so fully, and supported them with such reasons, and such authorities, that I apprehended I should be under no necessity of troubling your lordships again. But I am now compelled to rise up, and to beg your further indulgence: I find that I have been very injuriously treated; have been considered as the broacher of new-fangled doctrines, contrary to the

laws of this kingdom, and subversive of the rights of parliament. My lords, this is a heavy charge, but more so when made against one stationed as I am in both capacities, as peer and judge, the defender of the law and the constitution. When I spoke last, I was indeed replied to, but not answered. In the intermediate time, many things have been said. As I was not present, I must now beg leave to answer such as have come to my knowledge. As the affair is of the utmost importance, and in its consequences may involve the fate of kingdoms, I took the strictest review of my arguments; I re-examined all my authorities; fully determined, if I found myself mistaken, publicly to own my mistake, and give up my opinion: but my searches have more and more convinced me, that the British parliament have no right to tax the Americans. I shall not therefore consider the Declaratory Bill now lying on your table; for to what purpose, but loss of time, to consider the [178] particulars of a Bill, the very existence of which is illegal, absolutely illegal, contrary to the fundamental laws of nature, contrary to the fundamental laws of this constitution? A constitution grounded on the eternal and immutable laws of nature; a constitution whose foundation and centre is liberty, which sends liberty to every subject, that is or may happen to be within any part of its ample circumference. Nor my lords, is the doctrine new, it is as old as the constitution; it grew up with it; indeed it is its support; taxation and representation are inseparable, united; God hath joined them, no British parliament can separate them; to endeavour to do it, is to stab our very vitals. . . .

My position is this—I repeat it—I will maintain it to my last hour,— taxation and representation are inseparable:—this position is founded on the laws of nature; it is more, it is itself an eternal law of nature; for whatever is a man's own, is absolutely his own; no man hath a right to take it from him without his consent, either expressed by himself or representative; whoever attempts to do it, attempts an injury; whoever does it, commits a robbery; he throws down and destroys the distinction between liberty and slavery. Taxation and representation are coeval with and essential to the constitution. . . .

[180] In short, my lords, from the whole of our history, from the earliest period, you will find that taxation and representation were always united; so true are the words of that consummate reasoner and politician Mr. Locke. I before alluded to his book; I have again consulted him; and finding what he writes so applicable to the subject in hand, and so much in favour of my sentiments, I beg your lordships' leave to read a little of this book.

"The supreme power cannot take from any man, any part of his property, without his own consent." Such are the words of this great man, and which are well worth your serious attention. His principles are drawn from the heart of our constitution, which he thoroughly understood, and will last as long as that shall last; and, to his immortal honour, I know not to what, under providence, the Revolution and all its happy effects, are more owing, than to the principles of government laid down by Mr. Locke. For these reasons, my lords, I can never give my assent to any bill for taxing the American colonies, while they

27

remain unrepresented; for as to the distinction of virtual representation, it is so absurd as not to deserve an answer; I therefore pass it over with contempt. The forefathers of the Americans did not leave their native country, and subject themselves to every danger and distress, to be reduced to a state of slavery: they did not give up their rights; they looked for protection, and not for chains, from their mother country; by her they expected to be defended in the possession of their property, and not to be deprived of it: for, should [181] the present power continue, there is nothing which they can call their own; or, to use the words of Mr. Locke, "What property have they in that, which another may, by right, take, when he pleases, to himself?"

13. The Declaratory Act

From Danby Pickering, ed., *The Statutes at Large* (Cambridge, 1762–1807). Forty-six volumes. Vol. XXVII, p. 19.
The Declaratory Act and the bill to repeal the Stamp Act received the royal assent on March 18, 1766.

An Act for the better securing the dependency of his Majesty's dominions in America upon the crown and parliament of Great Britain.

WHEREAS, several of the houses of representatives in his Majesty's colonies and plantations in America, have of late, against law, claimed to themselves, or to the general assemblies of the same, the sole and exclusive right of imposing duties and taxes upon his Majesty's subjects in the said colonies and plantations; and have, in pursuance of such claim, passed certain votes, resolutions, and or- [20] ders, derogatory to the legislative authority of parliament, and inconsistent with the dependency of the said colonies and plantations upon the crown of Great Britain: . . . be it declared . . . , That the said colonies and plantations in America have been, are, and of right ought to be, subordinate unto, and dependent upon the imperial crown and parliament of Great Britain; and that the King's majesty, by and with the advice and consent of the lords spiritual and temporal, and commons of Great Britain, in parliament assembled, had, hath, and of right ought to have, full power and authority to make laws and statutes of sufficient force and validity to bind the colonies and people of America, subjects of the crown of Great Britain, in all cases whatsoever.

II. And be it further declared . . . , That all resolutions, votes, orders, and proceedings, in any of the said colonies or plantations, whereby the power and authority of the parliament of Great Britain, to make laws and statutes as aforesaid, is denied, or drawn into question, are, and are hereby declared to be, utterly null and void to all intents and purposes whatsoever.

28

II

BRITISH ERRORS AND
AMERICAN RESISTANCE

---

14. An English Historian's View

From W. E. H. Lecky, A *History of England in the Eighteenth Century* (New York: D. Appleton, 1893). Seven volumes. Vol. IV, p. 104.
Lecky (1838–1903) was one of the chief British historians of the nineteenth century. His is a "liberal" criticism of English maladministration. His point of view has been very influential in initiating the controversy among historians about the interpretation of the events during the period of the American Revolution.

It is evident that great wisdom, moderation, and tact were needed if healthy relations were to be established between England and her colonies, and unfortunately these qualities were conspicuously absent from English councils. The downfall of the Rockingham Ministry, and the formation of a ministry of which Grafton was the nominal and Pitt the real head, seemed on the whole a favourable event. The influence and popularity of Pitt were even greater in America than in England. His acceptance of the title of Earl of Chatham, which injured him so deeply in English opinion, was a matter of indifference to the colonists; [105] and he possessed far beyond all other English statesmen the power of attracting or conciliating great bodies of men, and firing them with the enthusiasm of loyalty or patriotism. Camden, who next to Chatham was the chief English advocate of the colonial cause, was Chancellor. Conway, who moved the repeal of the Stamp Act, was one of the Secretaries of State; and Shelburne, who at the age of twenty-nine was placed over American affairs, had on the question of taxing America been on the side of Chatham and Camden. Illness, however, speedily withdrew Chatham from public affairs, and in the scene of anarchy which ensued it was left for the strongest man to seize the helm. Unfortunately, in the absence of Chatham, that man was unquestionably the Chancellor of the Exchequer, Charles Townshend.

From this time the English government of America is little more than a series of deplorable blunders. . . .

[111] It is a strange instance of the fallibility of political foresight if Townshend imagined that America would acquiesce in these [new tax] measures, that England possessed any adequate means of enforcing them, or that she could a second time recede from her demands and yet maintain her authority over the colonies. It is mournful to notice how the field of controversy had widened and deepened, and how a quarrel which might at one time have been appeased by slight mutual concessions was leading inevitably to the disruption of the Empire. England was originally quite right in her contention that it was the duty of the colonies to contribute something to the support of the army which defended the unity of the Empire. She was quite right in her belief that in some of the colonial constitutions the Executive was far too feeble, that the line which divides liberty from anarchy was often passed, and that the result was profoundly and permanently injurious to the American character. She was also, I think, quite right in ascribing a great part of the resistance of America to the disposition, so common and so natural in dependencies, to shrink as much as possible from any expense that could possibly be thrown on the mother country, and in forming a very low estimate of the character and motives of a large proportion of those ambitious lawyers, newspaper writers, preachers, and pamphleteers, who, in New England at least, were labouring with untiring assiduity to win popular applause by sowing dissension between England and her colonies. But the Americans were [112] only too well justified in asserting that the suppression of several of their industries and the monopoly by England of some of the chief branches of their trade, if they did not benefit the mother country, at least imposed sacrifices on her colonies fully equivalent to a considerable tax. They were also quite justified in contending that the power of taxation was essential to the importance of their Assemblies, and that an extreme jealousy of any encroachment on this prerogative was in perfect accordance with the tradition of English liberty. They had before their eyes the hereditary revenue, the scandalous pension list, the monstrous abuses of patronage, in Ireland, and they were quite resolved not to suffer similar abuses in America. . . . [113] A period of wild and feverish confusion followed [in the colonies]. . . .

15. The Townshend Revenue Act

From Danby Pickering, ed., *The Statutes at Large* (Cambridge, 1762–1807). Forty-six volumes. Vol. XXVII, p. 505.

The Townshend Revenue Act, passed June 29, 1767, imposed

not only several import duties on the colonies but also provided a means of collecting them, a general search warrant called a "writ of assistance." Effective November 20, 1767, this act, like the previous Stamp Act, excited great dissatisfaction in the colonies.

An act for granting certain duties in the British colonies and plantations in America . . . and for more effectually preventing the clandestine running of goods in the said colonies and plantations.

WHEREAS it is expedient that a revenue should be raised, in your Majesty's dominions in America, for making a more certain and adequate provision for defraying the charge of the administration of justice, and the support of civil government, in such provinces where it shall be found necessary; and towards further defraying the expenses of defending, protecting, and securing, the said dominions; . . . be it enacted . . . , That from and after the twentieth day of November, one thousand seven hundred and sixty seven, there shall be raised, levied, collected, and paid unto his Majesty, his heirs, and successors, for and upon the respective goods herein after mentioned, which shall be imported from Great Britain into any colony or plantation in America which now is, or hereafter may be, under the dominion of his Majesty, his heirs, or successors, the several rates and duties following; that is to say, [on glass, lead, paint, tea, and paper]. [509] . . . and that all the monies that shall arise by the said duties (except the necessary charges of raising, collecting, levying, recovering, answering, paying, and accounting for the same) shall be applied, in the first place, in such manner as is herein after mentioned, in making a more certain and adequate provision for the charge of the administration of justice, and the support of civil government, in such of the said colonies and plantations where it shall be found necessary; and that the residue of such duties shall be payed into the receipt of his Majesty's exchequer, and shall be entered separate and apart from all other monies paid or payable to his Majesty . . . ; and shall be there reserved, to be from time to time disposed of by parliament towards defraying the necessary expences of defending, protecting and securing, the British colonies and plantations in America. . . .

[512] And in order to carry the intention of the said recited acts into effectual execution, be it enacted . . . , That from and after the said twentieth day of November, one thousand seven hundred and sixty seven, such writs of assistance, to authorize and impower the officers of his Majesty's customs to enter and go into any house, warehouse, shop, cellar, or other place, in the British colonies or plantations in America, to search for and seize prohibited and uncustomed goods, in the manner directed by the said recited acts, shall and may be granted by the said superior or supreme court of justice having said jurisdiction within such colony or plantation respectively. . . .

16. Edmund Burke Criticizes Lord Grenville's Policies

From Edmund Burke, *Observations on a Late Publication intituled "The Present State of the Nation"* (1769), *Writings and Speeches of Edmund Burke* (Boston: Little, Brown, 1901). Twelve volumes. Vol. I, p. 395.

The tension that developed after 1763 between England and the colonies was, in Burke's opinion, a direct result of misgovernment within Great Britain. In his *Observations*, Burke attacked the opinions and actions of Lord Grenville, Prime Minister from 1763 to 1765. In the policies of Grenville's ministry Burke saw "the real sources of almost all the disorders which have arisen since that time."

Whoever goes about to reason on any part of the policy of this country with regard to America upon the mere abstract principles of government, or even upon those of our own ancient constitution, will be often misled. Those who resort for arguments to the most respectable authorities, ancient or modern, or rest upon the clearest maxims drawn from the experience of other states and empires, will be liable to the greatest errors imaginable. The object is wholly new in the world. It is singular; it is grown up to this magnitude and importance within the memory of man; nothing in history is parallel to it. All the reasonings about it that are likely to be at all solid must be drawn from its actual circumstances. In this new system a principle of commerce, of artificial commerce, must predominate. This commerce must be secured by a multitude of restraints very alien from the spirit of liberty; and a powerful authority must reside in the principal state, in order to enforce them. But the people who are to be the subjects of these restraints are descendants of Englishmen, and of a high and free spirit. To hold over them a government made up of nothing but restraints and penalties, and taxes in the granting of which they can have no share, will neither be wise nor long practicable. People must be governed in a manner agreeable to their temper and disposition; and men of free character and spirit must be ruled with, at least, some condescension to this spirit and this character. The British colonist must see something which will [396] distinguish him from the colonists of other nations.

Those reasonings which infer from the many restraints under which we have already laid America to our right to lay it under still more, and indeed under all manner of restraints, are conclusive—conclusive as to right, but the very reverse as to policy and practice. We ought rather to infer from our having laid the colonies under many restraints that it is reasonable to compensate them by every indulgence that can by any means be reconciled to our interest. We have a great empire to rule, composed of a vast mass of heterogeneous governments, all more or less free and popular in their forms, all to be kept in peace, and kept out of conspiracy, with one another, all to be held in subordination to this country; while the spirit of an extensive and intricate and trading interest pervades the whole, always qualifying, and often controlling, every general idea of constitution and government. It is a great and difficult object; and I wish we may possess wisdom and temper enough to manage it as we ought. Its importance is infinite. . . .

[397] This colony intercourse is a new world of commerce in a manner created; it stands upon principles of its own; principles hardly worth endangering for any little consideration of extorted revenue.

The reader sees that I do not enter so fully into this matter as obviously I might. . . . It is enough to say that before the ministers of 1765 had determined to propose the repeal of the Stamp Act in Parliament, they had the whole of the American constitution and commerce very fully before them. They considered maturely; they decided with wisdom: let me add, with firmness. For they resolved, as a preliminary to that repeal, to assert in the fullest and least equivocal terms the unlimited legislative right of this country over its colonies; and, having done this, to propose the repeal, on principles, not of constitutional right, but on those of expediency, of equity, of lenity, and of the true interests present and future of that great object for which alone the colonies were founded, navigation and commerce. . . .

If the then ministry resolved first to declare the right [the Declaratory Act], it was not from any opinion they entertained of [398] its future use in regular taxation. Their opinions were full and declared against the ordinary use of such a power. But it was plain that the general reasonings which were employed against that power went directly to our whole legislative right; and one part of it could not be yielded to such arguments without a virtual surrender of all the rest. Besides, if that very specific power of levying money in the colonies were not retained as a sacred trust in the hands of Great Britain (to be used, not in the first instance for supply, but in the last exigence for control), it is obvious that the presiding authority of Great Britain, as the head, the arbiter, and director of the whole empire, would vanish into an empty name, without operation or energy. With the habitual exercise of such a power in the ordinary course of supply, no trace of freedom could remain to America. If Great Britain were stripped of this right, every principle of unity and subordination in the empire was gone forever. Whether all this can be reconciled in legal speculation, is a matter of no consequence. It is reconciled in policy: and politics ought to be adjusted, not to human reasonings, but to human nature; of which the reason is but a part, and by no means the greatest part. . . .

[401] Upon these principles was the act repealed, and it produced all the good effect which was expected from it: quiet was restored; trade generally returned to its ancient channels; time and means were furnished for the better strengthening of government there, as well as for recovering, by judicious measures, the affections of the people, had that ministry continued, or had a ministry succeeded with dispositions to improve that opportunity. . . .

[402] Such an administration did not succeed. Instead of profiting

of that season of tranquillity, in the very next year they chose to return to measures of the very same nature with those which had been so solemnly condemned,[1] though upon a smaller scale. The effects have been correspondent. America is again in disorder; not indeed in the same degree as formerly, nor anything like it. Such good effects have attended the repeal of the Stamp Act that the colonies have actually paid the taxes; and they have sought their redress (upon however improper princi- [403] ples) not in their own violence, as formerly, but in the experienced benignity of Parliament. . . . Whether the return to the system of 1764 for raising a revenue in America, the discontents which have ensued in consequence of it, the general suspension of the assemblies in consequence of these discontents, the use of the military power, and the new and dangerous commissions which now hang over them will produce equally good effects is greatly to be doubted. Never, I fear, will this nation and the colonies fall back upon their true center of gravity, and natural point of repose, until the ideas of 1766 are resumed, and steadily pursued.

17. A Boston Riot

From *The Gentleman's Magazine*. Vol. XL (April, 1770), "Historical Chronicle," p. 189.

Saturday, 28 April, 1770. The Representation of the Affairs at Boston ["the Massacre," March 5] by the Town Committee, having been inserted in the beginning of the Magazine, the case of Capt. Preston here epitomized, will serve to show the other side of the question.

It is a matter of too great notoriety to need proofs, that the arrival of his majesty's troops in Boston was extremely obnoxious to its inhabitants. They have ever used all means in their power to weaken the regiments, and to bring them into contempt, by promoting desertions, and by grossly and falsely propagating untruths concerning them. On the arrival of the 64th and 65th, their ardour seemingly began to abate; it being too expensive to buy off so many. But the same spirit revived immediately on its being known that those regiments were ordered for Halifax. After their embarkation, one of their justices, from the seat of justice, declared, "that the soldiers must now take care of themselves, nor trust too much to their arms, for they were but a

---

[1] The Grafton-Chatham ministry followed Rockingham's. Charles Townshend was Chancellor of the Exchequer, and he promulgated the revenue acts of 1767 which imposed duties on the importation into the colonies of glass, paint, lead, paper, and tea (eds.).

handful." This was an alarming circumstance to the soldiery, since which several disputes have happened between the towns-people and the soldiers of both regiments. In general such disputes have been kept too secret from the officers. On the 2d instant, two of the 29th going through one Gray's Rope Walk, the rope-makers insultingly asked them if they would empty a vault. This unfortunately had the desired effect by provoking the soldiers, and from words they went to blows. Both parties suffered in this affray, and finally, the soldiers retired to their quarters. The insolence, as well as utter hatred of the inhabitants to the troops increased daily; insomuch, that Monday and Tuesday, the 5th and 6th instant, were privately agreed on for a general engagement; in consequence of which, several of the militia came from the country, armed, to join their friends, menacing to destroy any who should oppose them. This plan has since been discovered.

On Monday night about eight o'clock, two soldiers were attacked and beat. About nine some of the guard informed me, the town inhabitants were assembling to attack the troops, and that the bells were ringing as a signal, and not for fire, and the Beacon intended to be fired to bring in the distant people of the country. Being captain of the day, I repaired immediately to the main guard. In my way, I saw the people in great commotion. In a few minutes about 100 people passed and went toward the custom-house, where the King's money is lodged. They immediately surrounded the sentinel posted there, and with clubs and other weapons threatened to execute their vengeance on him. A Townsman assured me he heard the mob declare they would murder him. I fearing their plundering the King's chest, immediately sent a non-commissioned officer and 12 men to protect both the sentinel and the King's money, and very soon followed myself, to prevent disorder. The troops rushed thro' the people, and, by charging their bayonets in half circle, kept them at a distance. So far was I from intending death, that the troops went to the spot where the unhappy affair took place, without loading their pieces.

The mob still increased, and were more outrageous, striking bludgeons one against another, and calling out, "Come on, you Rascals, you bloody backs, you lobster scoundrels; fire if you dare; G—d damn you, fire and be damned; we know you dare not;" and much more such language was used. They advanced to the points of the bayonets, struck some of them, and even the muzzles of the pieces, and seemed to be endeavouring to close with the soldiers. Some well-behaved persons asked me if their guns were charged? I replied, yes. If I intended to order the men to fire? I answered no. While I was speaking, a soldier having received a severe blow with a stick, instantly fired. On reprimanding him, I was struck with a club on my arm, so violent a blow, that had it fallen on my head, probably it would have destroyed me. A general attack was then made on the men by heaving clubs, and snow balls, by which all our lives were in imminent danger; some persons from behind called out, "Damn your bloods, why don't you fire?" Instantly three or four of the soldiers fired, one after another, and directly after, three more in the same confusion and hurry.

The mob then ran away, except three unhappy men who instantly expired. . . . The whole of this melancholy affair was transacted in almost 20 minutes. . . .

[*190*] On examination before the justices they have sworn, that I used the word fire, and so bitter and inveterate are the malcontents against the officers and troops, that I am, though perfectly innocent, under most unhappy circumstances, having nothing in reason to expect but the loss of life in a very ignominious manner, without the interposition of his majesty's royal goodness.

18. The Boston Tea Party

From *The Gentleman's Magazine*. Vol. XLIV (January, 1774), p. 27.

SUMMARY OF THE ADVICES RELATIVE TO THE TEA-SHIPS SENT TO AMERICA.

Boston, Dec. 20 [1773]. On Tuesday last the body of the people of this and all the adjacent towns, and others from the distance of 20 miles, assembled at the Old South Meetinghouse, to enquire the reason of the delay in sending the ship Dartmouth, with the East-India tea, back to London; and having found that the owner had not taken the necessary steps for that purpose, they enjoined him at his peril to demand of the Collector of Customs a clearance for the ship, and appointed a committee of 10 to see it performed; after which they adjourned to the Thursday following, ten o'clock. They then met, and being informed by Mr. Rotch, that clearance was refused him, they enjoined him to enter a protest, and apply to the Governor for a passport by the castle, and adjourned again till three o'clock of the same day. At which time they again met, and after waiting till near sun set, Mr. Rotch came in and informed them, that he had accordingly entered his protest, and waited on the Governor for a pass, but his Excellency told him he could not, consistent with his duty, grant it until his vessel was qualified. The people, finding all their efforts to preserve the property of the East-India Company, and return it safely to London, frustrated by the tea consignees, the Collector of the Customs, and the Governor of the province, dissolved their meeting— But, behold what followed! a number of resolute men (dressed like Mohawks or Indians), determined to do all in their power to save their country from the ruin which their enemies had plotted, in less than four hours emptied every chest of tea on board the three ships, commanded by Captains Hall, Bruce, and Coffin, amounting to 342 chests, into the sea, without the least damage done to the ships or any other property. The masters and owners are well pleased that their ships are thus cleared, and the people are almost universally congratulating each other on this happy event.

Capt. Loring, in a brig from London for this place, having 58 chests of the detested tea on board, was cast ashore on the back of Cape Cod last Friday se'nnight. 'Tis expected the Cape Indians will give us a good account of the tea against our next.

We are positively informed, that the patriotic inhabitants of Lexington, at a late meeting, unanimously resolved against the use of bohea tea of all sorts, Dutch or English importation; and, to manifest the sincerity of their resolution, they brought together every ounce contained in the town, and committed it to one common bonfire.

19. The Boston Port Act

From Danby Pickering, ed., *The Statutes at Large* (Cambridge, 1762–1807). Forty-six volumes. Vol. XXX, p. 336.

The Boston Port Act, March 31, 1774, was the first of the so-called Intolerable Acts, designed to punish Boston for its lawlessness. The other acts were the Administration of Justice Act, May 20, 1774, "for the impartial administration of justice" by transferring certain trials to another province or to England, "during the term of three years"; the Massachusetts Government Act, May 20, 1774, for the purpose of permitting the royal governor to appoint his council instead of having it elected by the whole legislature; and the Quebec Act, June 22, 1774, designed to give religious freedom to the Roman Catholic majority in Canada.

An act to discontinue, in such manner, and for such time as are therein mentioned, the landing and discharging, lading or shipping, of goods, wares, and merchandise, at the town, and within the harbour of Boston, in the province of Massachuset's Bay, in North America.

Whereas dangerous commotions and insurrections have been fomented and raised in the town of Boston, in the province of Massachuset's Bay, in New England, by divers, ill-affected persons, to the subversion of his Majesty's government, and to the utter destruction of the publick peace, and good order of the said town; in which commotions and insurrections certain valuable cargoes of teas, being the property of the East India Company, and on board certain vessels lying within the bay or harbour of Boston, were seized and destroyed: And whereas, in the present condition of the said town and harbour, the commerce of his Majesty's subjects cannot be safely carried on there, nor the customs payable to his Majesty duly collected; and it is therefore expedient that the officers of his Majesty's customs should be

forthwith removed from the said town: . . . be it enacted . . . ,
That from and after the first day of June, one thousand seven hundred
and seventy four, it shall not be lawful for any person or persons whatsoever to lade, put, . . . off or from any quay, wharf, or other place,
within the said town of Boston, or in or upon any part of the bay,
commonly called The Harbour of Boston . . . into any ship, vessel,
lighter, boat, or bottom, any goods, wares, or merchandise whatsoever,
to be transported or carried into any other country, province, or [337]
place whatsoever, or into any other part of the said province of the
Massachuset's Bay, in New England; or to take up, . . . within the
said town, or in or upon any of the places aforesaid, out of any boat,
. . . any goods, . . . to be brought from any other country, province,
or place, or any other part of the said province of the Massachuset's
Bay in New England, upon pain of the forfeiture of the said goods,
. . . and of the said boat, . . . and of the guns, ammunition, tackle,
furniture, and stores, in or belonging to the same. . . .

[340] . . . until it shall sufficiently appear to his Majesty, that full
satisfaction hath been made by or on behalf of the inhabitants of the
said town of Boston to the united company of merchants of England
trading to the East Indies, for the damage sustained by the said company by the destruction of their goods sent to the said town of Boston,
. . . and until it shall be certified to his Majesty, in council, by the
governor, . . . of the said province, that reasonable satisfaction hath
been made to the officers of his Majesty's revenue, and others who
suffered by the riots and insurrections above mentioned, in the months
of November and December, in the year one thousand seven hundred
and seventy three, and in the month of January, in the year one thousand seven hundred and seventy four.

20. Burke's Speech on Conciliation

From Edmund Burke, *Speech on American Taxation* (1774),
Writings and Speeches of Edmund Burke (Boston: Little, Brown,
1901). Twelve volumes. Vol. II, p. 69.
The Townshend Acts of 1767, by which Parliament laid new
duties on a number of colonial importations in order to raise a
revenue for the maintenance of the colonial administration, produced an indignant and violent reaction in America. The British
sent troops to uphold its authority, and bloodshed occurred in
the "Boston Massacre" of 1770. Lord North's ministry immediately attempted to appease the colonists by repealing all the
Townshend duties except a small tax on tea. But by this time
the colonists felt that Parliament had no right to tax them without the consent of their own legislatures. North's government
would not withdraw the tea tax, and this refusal was one of the
causes of the Boston Tea Party of 1773. Burke, who in 1771 had

become the agent in Great Britain for the province of New York, opposed every step in this course of events. On April 19, 1774, he appealed in the House of Commons for a return to "the system of 1766" and presented further views on the matter of taxation.

How we have fared since then: what woeful variety of schemes have been adopted; what enforcing, and what repealing; what bullying, and what submitting; what doing, and undoing; what straining, and what relaxing; what assemblies dissolved for not obeying, and called again without obedience; what troops sent out to quell resistance, and, on meeting that resistance, recalled; what shiftings, and changes, and jumblings of all kinds of men at home, which left no possibility of order, consistency, vigor, or even so much as a decent unity of color in any one public measure—It is a tedious, irksome task. . . .

[71] Your ministers, in their own and his Majesty's name, have already adopted the American distinction of internal and external duties. It is a distinction, whatever merit it may have, that was originally moved by the Americans themselves; and I think they will acquiesce in it, if they are not pushed with too much logic and too little sense, in all the consequences: that is, if external taxation be understood, as they and you understand it, when you please, to be not a distinction of geography, but of policy; that it is a power for regulating trade, and not for supporting establishments. The distinction, which is as nothing with regard to right, is of most weighty consideration in practice. Recover your old ground, and your old tranquillity; try it; I am persuaded the Americans will compromise with you. When confidence is once restored, the odious and suspicious *summum jus* will perish of course. The spirit of practicability, of moderation, and mutual convenience will never call in geometrical exactness as the arbitrator of an amicable settlement. Consult and follow your experience. . . .

[72] Again, and again, revert to your old principles—seek peace and ensure it—leave America, if she has taxable matter in her, to tax herself. I am not here [73] going into the distinctions of rights, nor attempting to mark their boundaries. . . . Leave the Americans as they anciently stood, and these distinctions, born of our unhappy contest, will die along with it. They and we, and their and our ancestors, have been happy under that system. Let the memory of all actions in contradiction to that good old mode, on both sides, be extinguished forever. Be content to bind America by laws of trade; you have always done it. Let this be your reason for binding their trade. Do not burden them by taxes; you were not used to do so from the beginning. Let this be your reason for not taxing. . . . But if, intemperately, unwisely, fatally, you sophisticate and poison the very source of government, by urging subtle deductions, and consequences odious to those you govern, from the unlimited and illimitable nature of supreme sovereignty, you will teach them by these means to call that sovereignty itself in question. When you drive him hard, the boar will surely turn upon the hunters. If that sovereignty and their freedom cannot be reconciled, which will they take? They will cast your sovereignty in your face. Nobody will be

argued into slavery. Sir, let the gentlemen on the other side call forth all their ability; let the best of them get up and tell me what one character of liberty the Americans have, and what one brand of slavery they are free from, if they are bound in their property and industry by all the restraints you can imagine on commerce, and at the same time are made pack-horses of [74] every tax you choose to impose, without the least share in granting them. . . .

[75] Reflect how you are to govern a people who think they ought to be free, and think they are not. Your scheme yields no revenue; it yields nothing but discontent, disorder, disobedience; and such is the state of America, that, after wading up to your eyes in blood, you could only end just where you begun—that is, to tax where no revenue is to be found, to—My voice fails me; my inclination, indeed, carries me no further; all is confusion beyond it. . . . What is to become of the Declaratory Act, asserting the entireness of British legislative authority, if we abandon the practice of taxation?

For my part, I look upon the rights stated in that act exactly in the manner in which I viewed them on its very first proposition, and which I have often taken the liberty, with great humility, to lay before you. I look, I say, on the imperial rights of Great Britain, and the privileges which the colonists ought to enjoy under these rights, to be just the most reconcilable things in the world. The Parliament of Great Britain sits at the head of her extensive empire in two capacities. One as the local legislature of this island, providing for all things at home, immediately, and by no other instrument than the executive power. The other, and I think her nobler capacity, is what I call her imperial character; in which, as from the throne of heaven, she superintends all the several inferior legislatures, and guides and controls them all [76] without annihilating any. As all these provincial legislatures are only co-ordinate to each other they ought all to be subordinate to her; else they can neither preserve mutual peace, nor hope for mutual justice, nor effectually afford mutual assistance. It is necessary to coerce the negligent, to restrain the violent, and to aid the weak and deficient, by the overruling plenitude of her power. She is never to intrude into the place of the others whilst they are equal to the common ends of their institution. But in order to enable Parliament to answer all these ends of provident and beneficent superintendence, her powers must be boundless. . . .

[77] Such, Sir, is my idea of the constitution of the British Empire, as distinguished from the constitution of Britain; and on these grounds I think subordination and liberty may be sufficiently reconciled through the whole—whether to serve a refining speculatist or a factious demagogue I know not, but enough surely for the ease and happiness of man.

Sir, whilst we held this happy course, we drew more from the colonies, than all the impotent violence of despotism ever could extort from them. We did this abundantly in the last war; it has never been once denied; and what reason have we to imagine that the colonies would not have proceeded in supplying government as liberally if you had not stepped in and hindered them from contributing, by interrupting the channel in which their liberality flowed with so strong a course

—by attempting to take, instead of being satisfied to receive? . . .
Tyranny is a poor provider. It knows neither how to accumulate nor
how to extract.

I charge, therefore, to this new and unfortunate system the loss not
only of peace, of union, and of commerce, but even of revenue, which
its friends are contending for. It is morally certain that we have lost at
least a million of free grants since the peace. I think we have lost a
great deal more. . . .

[78] On this business of America, I confess I am serious, even to
sadness. I have had but one opinion concerning it since I sat, and before I sat, in Parliament. . . . I have in all seasons adhered to the
system of 1766 for no other reason than that I think it laid deep in
your truest interests; and that, by limiting the exercise, it fixes on the
firmest foundations a real, consistent, well-grounded authority in Parliament. Until you come back to that system, there will be no peace
for England.

21. Pitt Discusses the Quartering Act

From John Almon, *Anecdotes of the Life of . . . William Pitt,
Earl of Chatham* (London: J. S. Jordan, 1793). Three volumes.
Vol. II, p. 368.

In his speech in the House of Lords, May 26, 1774, Pitt, Earl
of Chatham, comments on the bill for quartering troops in North
America, a bill meant to assist General Lord Gage in his task of
carrying out the coercive designs of Parliament against the province of Massachusetts. This bill authorizing the quartering of soldiers on the colonists was similar to that passed in 1765.

If we take a transient view of those motives which induced the ancestors of our fellow-subjects in America to leave their native country,
to encounter the innumerable difficulties of the unexplored regions of
the western world, our astonishment at the present conduct of their
descendants will naturally subside. There was no corner of the world
into which men of their free and enterprising spirit would not fly with
alacrity, rather than submit to the slavish and tyrannical principles,
which prevailed at that period in their native country. And shall we
wonder, my Lords, if the descendants of such illustrious characters
spurn, with contempt, the hand of unconstitutional power, that would
snatch from them such dear-bought privileges as they now contend
for? Had the British Colonies been planted by any other kingdom than
our own, [369] the inhabitants would have carried with them the
chains of slavery, and spirit of despotism; but as they are, they ought
to be remembered as great instances to instruct the world, what great
exertions mankind will naturally make, when they are left to the free

exercise of their own powers. And, my Lords, notwithstanding my intention to give my hearty negative to the question now before you, I cannot help condemning, in the severest manner, the late turbulent and unwarrantable conduct of the Americans in some instances, particularly in the late riots of Boston. But, my Lords, the mode which has been pursued to bring them back to a sense of their duty to their parent state has been so diametrically opposite to the fundamental principles of sound policy, that individuals, possessed of common understanding, must be astonished at such proceedings. By blocking up the harbour of Boston, you have involved the innocent trader in the same punishment with the guilty profligates who destroyed your merchandize; and instead of making a well-concerted effort to secure [370] the real offenders, you clap a naval and military extinguisher over their harbour, and punish the crime of a few lawless depredators and their abettors upon the whole body of the inhabitants.

My Lords, this country is little obliged to the framers and promoters of this tea-tax. The Americans had almost forgot, in their excess of gratitude for the repeal of the stamp act, any interest but that of the mother country; there seemed an emulation among the different provinces, who should be most dutiful and forward in their expressions of loyalty to their real benefactor; as you will readily perceive by the following letter from Governor Bernard to a noble Lord then in office.

"The House of Representatives, (says he) from the time of opening the session to this day, has shewn a disposition to avoid all dispute with me; every thing having passed with as much good humour as I could desire. They have acted, in all things, with temper and moderation; [371] they have avoided some subjects of dispute, and have laid a foundation for removing some causes of former altercation."

This, my Lords, was the temper of the Americans; and would have continued so, had it not been interrupted by your fruitless endeavours to tax them without their consent; but the moment they perceived your intention was renewed to tax them, under a pretence of serving the East India Company, their resentment got the ascendant of their moderation, and hurried them into actions contrary to law, which, in their cooler hours, they would have thought on with horror; for I sincerely believe, the destroying of the tea was the effect of despair.

But, my Lords, from the complexion of the whole of the proceedings, I think that Administration has purposely irritated them into those late violent acts, for which they now so severely smart; purposely to be revenged on them for the victory they gained by the repeal of the stamp [372] act; a measure to which they seemingly acquiesced, but at the bottom they were its real enemies. For what other motive could induce them to dress taxation, that father of American sedition, in the robes of an East India Director, but to break in upon that mutual peace and harmony, which then so happily subsisted between them and the mother country.

My Lords, I am an old man, and would advise the noble Lords in office to adopt a more gentle mode of governing America; for the day is not far distant, when America may vie with these kingdoms, not only in arms, but in arts also. It is an established fact, that the principal towns in America are learned and polite, and understand the constitution of the empire as well as the noble Lords who are now in office; and consequently, they will have a watchful eye over their liberties, to prevent the least encroachment on their hereditary rights. . . .

[374] I will carry it to my grave, *that this country had no right under heaven to tax America.* It is contrary to all the principles of justice and civil policy, which neither the exigencies of the state, nor even an acquiescence in the taxes could justify upon any occasion whatever. Such proceedings will never meet their wished-for success; and, instead of adding to their miseries, as the bill now before you most undoubtedly does, adopt some lenient measures, which may lure them to their duty; proceed like a kind and affectionate parent over a child whom he tenderly loves; and instead of those harsh and severe proceedings, pass an amnesty on all their youthful errors; clasp them once more in your fond and affectionate arms; and I will venture [375] to affirm you will find them children worthy of their sire. But should their turbulence exist after your proffered terms of forgiveness, which I hope and expect this house will immediately adopt, I will be among the foremost of your Lordships to move for such measures as will effectually prevent a future relapse, and make them feel what it is to provoke a fond and forgiving parent! a parent, my Lords, whose welfare has ever been my greatest and most pleasing consolation.

22. A Plea for Imperial Unity

From *The Gentleman's Magazine.* Vol. XLIV (June, 1774), p. 279.

ODE FOR HIS MAJESTY'S BIRTH-DAY, JUNE 4, 1774.
By William Whitehead, Esq; Poet-Laureat.

I.

Hark!—or does the Muse's ear
Form the sounds she longs to hear?—
Hark! from yonder western main
  O'er the white wave echoing far,
Vows of duty swell the strain,
  And drown the notes of war.
The prodigal again returns,   [Boston, Mass.]
  And on his parent's neck reclines:
With honest shame his bosom burns
  And in his eye affection shines,
Shines thro' tears, at once that prove,
Crief, and joy, and filial love.

43

II.

Discord! stop that raven voice,
Lest the nations round rejoice.
Tell it not on Gallia's plain,
  Tell it not on Ebro's stream,
Tho' but transient be the pain,
  Like some delusive dream:
For soon shall Reason, calm and sage,
  Detect each vile seducer's wiles,
Shall soothe to peace mistaken rage,
  And all be harmony and smiles;
Smiles repentant, such as prove
Grief, and joy, and filial love.

III.

O prophetic be the Muse!
  May her monitory flame
Wake the soul to noble views,
  And point the path to genuine fame!
Just subjection, mild commands,
  Mutual interest, mutual love,
Form indissoluble bands,
  Like the golden chain of Jove.
Closely may they all unite!
—And see, a gleam of lustre breaks
From the shades of envious night—
—And hark, 'tis more than Fancy speaks—
They bow, they yield, they join the choral lay,
And hail, with us, our Monarch's natal day.

23. Samuel Johnson Condemns Rebellion

From Samuel Johnson, *The Patriot* (1774), *The Works of Samuel Johnson* (Troy, N.Y.: Pafraets Book Co., 1903). Sixteen volumes. Vol. XIV, p. 82.

Samuel Johnson, the celebrated lexicographer and the central literary figure of the latter half of the eighteenth century, joined in the controversy over the Americans. The following extracts are from one of his political pamphlets.

Some claim a place in the list of patriots, by an acrimonious and unremitting opposition to the court.

This mark is by no means infallible. Patriotism is not necessarily included in rebellion. A man may hate his king, yet not love his country. He that has been refused a reasonable, or unreasonable request, who thinks his merit underrated, and sees his influence declining, begins soon to talk of natural equality, the absurdity of "many made for one," the original compact, the foundation of authority, and the majesty of the people. As his political melancholy increases, he tells, and, perhaps, dreams of the advances of the [royal] prerogative, and the dangers of arbitrary power; yet his design, in all his declamation, is not to benefit his country, but to gratify his malice. . . .

[89] He that wishes to see his country robbed of its rights cannot be a patriot.

That man, therefore, is no patriot, who justifies the ridiculous claims of American usurpation; who endeavours to deprive the nation of its natural and lawful authority over its own colonies; those colonies, which were settled under English protection; were constituted by an English charter; and have been defended by English arms.

To suppose, that by sending out a colony, the nation established an independent power; that when, by indulgence and favour, emigrants are become rich, they shall not contribute to their own defence, but at their own pleasure; and that they shall not be included, like millions of their fellow-subjects, in the general system of representation; involves such an accumulation of absurdity, as nothing but the show of patriotism could palliate.

He that accepts protection, stipulates obedience. We have always protected the Americans; we may, therefore, subject them to government.

The less is included in the greater. That power which can take away life, may seize upon property. [90] The parliament may enact, for America, a law of capital punishment; it may, therefore, establish a mode and proportion of taxation.

But there are some who lament the state of the poor Bostonians, because they cannot all be supposed to have committed acts of rebellion, yet all are involved in the penalty imposed. This, they say, is to violate the first rule of justice, by condemning the innocent to suffer with the guilty.

This deserves some notice, as it seems dictated by equity and humanity, however it may raise contempt by the ignorance which it betrays of the state of man, and the system of things. That the innocent should be confounded with the guilty, is, undoubtedly, an evil; but it is an evil which no care or caution can prevent. National crimes require national punishments, of which many must necessarily have their part, who have not incurred them by personal guilt. If rebels should fortify a town, the cannon of lawful authority will endanger, equally, the harmless burghers and the criminal garrison. . . .

This infliction of promiscuous evil may, therefore, be lamented, but cannot be blamed. The power of lawful government must be maintained; and the [91] miseries which rebellion produces, can be charged only on the rebels.

24. General Gage's Proclamation

From *The Gentleman's Magazine.* Vol. XLV (January, 1775), p. 41.

Boston, Nov. 10 [1774]

This day his Excellency, General Gage, issued the following proclamation: "Whereas a number of persons unlawfully assembled at Cambridge, in the month of October last, calling themselves a Provincial Congress, did, in the most open and daring terms, assume to themselves the powers and authority of government, independent of, and repugnant to, his Majesty's government, legally and constitutionally established within this province, and tending utterly to subvert the same; and did, amongst other unlawful proceedings, take upon themselves to resolve and direct a new and unconstitutional regulation of the militia, in high derogation of his Majesty's royal prerogative; and also to elect and appoint Henry Gardner, of Stow, to be Receiver-general, in the room of Harrison Gray, Esq; then and still legally holding and executing that office; and also to order and direct the monies granted to his Majesty, to be paid into the hands of the said Henry Gardner, and not to the said Harrison Gray, Esq; and further earnestly to recommend to the inhabitants of the province, to oblige and compel the several constables and collectors to comply with and execute the said directions, contrary to their oaths, and against the plain and express rules and directions of the law: all which proceedings have a most dangerous tendency to ensnare his Majesty's subjects, the inhabitants of this province, and draw them into perjuries, riots, sedition, treason, and rebellion.

For the prevention of which evils, and the calamitous consequences thereof;

I have thought it my duty to issue this proclamation, hereby earnestly exhorting, and in his Majesty's name strictly prohibiting all his liege subjects within this province, from complying, in any degree, with the said requisitions, recommendations, directions, or resolves of the aforesaid unlawful assembly, as they regard his Majesty's highest displeasure, and would avoid the pains and penalties of the law. And I do hereby charge and command all justices of the peace, sheriffs, constables, collectors, and other officers, in their several departments, to be vigilant and faithful in the execution of their duty in their respective offices, agreeable to the well known established laws of the land; and, to the utmost of their power, by all lawful ways and means, to discountenance, discourage, and prevent a compliance with such dangerous resolves of the abovementioned, or any other unlawful assembly whatever.

Given at Boston this 10th of Nov. 1774.

Tho. Gage."

III

THE YEAR OF DECISION

***

25. A Modern Historian on the King's Responsibility

From George Otto Trevelyan, *The American Revolution* (New York: Longmans, Green, 1917). Three volumes. Vol. I, p. 222.
Trevelyan was a famous English historian, father of the equally illustrious George Macaulay Trevelyan. Like Lecky, Trevelyan is considered a "Whig" historian of the American Revolution, one who believed that the King and his ministers were responsible for the American crisis.

What purpose, human or divine, could be served by trying to dragoon such a population, so led and so minded, living along fifteen hundred miles of coast across three thousand miles of ocean, into paying a threepenny duty into the British treasury?

It was a problem striking enough to impress the Poet Laureate. Whitehead thought the moment had come for singing a word in season to the address of his Sovereign, and in 1775 he thus invoked the powers who guide the hearts of kings:—

> Beyond the vast Atlantic tide
> Extend your healing influence wide
> Where millions claim your care.
> [223] Inspire each just, each filial thought,
> And let the nations round be taught
> The British oak is there!

The advice was well meant; but it fell as flat as the lines in which it was couched. [William] Mason has commended Whitehead for insinuating sound counsel into the royal ear, in the shape of praise for wisdom and clemency which George the Third, unfortunately, had not the slightest intention of meriting. The Laureates of the eighteenth century were not of those to whom either kings or commoners looked

47

for a contribution to the stock of political wisdom; nor, (except in the case of Warton,) for any other wisdom. Mason, a stout Whig, judged favourably of Whitehead's performances; but Samuel Johnson, who liked his politics even less than his poetry, called his odes "insupportable nonsense"; and posterity, irrespective of politics, has agreed with Johnson. . . . So far as rhymes can throw light upon the relations of George the Third to the colonies, mankind will neglect Whitehead, and turn to the Birthday Ode of another bard who was not of the stuff out of which, in his day, a Poet Laureate was cut. What Robert Burns thought about the American war, and the policy of its royal author, may be seen in the fourth and fifth stanzas of "A Dream,"—which he wrote, or professed to have written, on the Fourth of June, 1786. The poem is like the best Aristophanes, on those occasions when Aristophanes was writing with a serious political purpose underlying his humour and his fancy. There is nothing in the Choruses of the Old Greek Comedy more Attic, in every essential quality, than the admonition addressed to the Prince of Wales, the advice to the young Princesses, the compliments to [224] Lord Chatham and his famous son, the allusion to the loss of America, and the homely and downright judgment passed upon those Ministers whom, during the first two and twenty years of his reign, the king had delighted to honour.

> 'Tis very true, my sovereign king,
>   My skill may weel be doubted:
> But facts are chiels that winna ding,
>   And downa be disputed.
> Your royal nest, beneath your wing,
>   Is e'en right reft and clouted;
> And now the third part o' the string,
>   An' less, will gang about it
>   Than did ae day.
>
> Far be't frae me that I aspire
>   To blame your legislation,
> Or say ye wisdom want, or fire
>   To rule this mighty nation!
> But, faith! I muckle doubt, my Sire,
>   Ye've trusted ministration
> To chaps wha in a barn, or byre,
>   Wad better fill'd their station
>   Than courts yon day.

26. A Patriotic Poem

From *The Annual Register*, 1775. P. 194.

ODE FOR HIS MAJESTY'S BIRTH-DAY, THE 4TH OF JUNE, 1775.
By Mr. Whitehead, Poet Laureat.

Ye Powers, who rule o'er states and kings,
Who shield, with sublunary wings,
　　Man's erring race, from woe,
To Britain's sons in every clime
Your blessings waft, whate'er their crime,
　　On all the winds that blow!

Beyond the vast Atlantic tide
Extend your healing influence wide,
　　Where millions claim your care:
Inspire each just, each filial thought,
And let the nations round be taught
　　The British oak is there.

Tho' vaguely wild its branches spread,
And rear almost an alien head
　　Wide-waving o'er the plain,
Let still, unspoil'd by foreign earth,
And conscious of its nobler birth,
　　The untainted trunk remain.

Where mutual interest binds the band,
Where due subjection, mild command,
　　Ensure perpetual ease,
Shall jarring tumults madly rave,
And hostile banners proudly wave
　　O'er once united seas?

No; midst the blaze of wrath divine
Heaven's loveliest attribute shall shine,
　　And mercy gild the ray:
Shall still avert impending fate;
And concord its best aera date
　　From this auspicious day.

27. Yankee Doodle

From Oscar G. T. Sonneck, *Report on the Star Spangled Banner*
. . . (Washington: U.S. Government Printing Office, 1909). P.
109.

The tune of "Yankee Doodle" was first heard in an American comic
opera produced in Philadelphia in April, 1767. Later reference to it is
found in the "Travels" of one Thomas Anburey, a British officer, in
1777. Anburey says of the name "Yankee" that "The soldiers at Boston
used it as a term of reproach, but after the affair at Bunker's Hill, the
Americans gloried in it. *Yankee Doodle* is now their paean, a favorite
of favorites . . . esteemed as warlike as the Grenadier's March. . . .
After our rapid successes, we held the Yankees in great contempt, but
it was not a little mortifying to hear them play this tune when their
army marched down to our surrender [at Yorktown]." . . .
[129] No authentic contemporary copy of the song has turned up.
Thus we can do no more than call attention to some verses that have
survived. These may be the original stanzas, or at least may have been
inspired by them. The passages are obviously satirical and are designed
to poke fun at New England country bumpkins.
Here are two short verses said to have been sung by British officers
during the Revolution.

> Yankee Doodle came to town
> For to buy a firelock:
> We will tar and feather him
> And so we will John Hancock.

> and

> Madam Hancock dreamt a dream;
> She dreamt she wanted something;
> She dreamt she wanted a Yankee King,
> To crown him with a pumpkin.

[235] *Yankee Doodle*, or *The Lexington March* (as now Christened
by the SAINTS OF NEW ENGLAND).
NB. The words to be sung thro' the Nose, & in the West Country
drawl & dialect.

> Brother Ephriam sold his Cow and bought him a Com-mission,
>   and then he went to
> Canada to Fight for the Nation; But when Ephriam he came home
>   he prov'd an arrant
> Coward, He wouldn't fight the Frenchmen there for fear of being
>   devour'd.

50

Sheep's Head and Vinegar
Butter Milk and Tansey,
Boston is a Yankee Town
Sing Hey Doodle Dandy:
First we'll take a Pinch of Snuff
And then a drink of Water
And then we'll say How do you do
And that's a Yanky Supper. . . .

Christmas is a cuming Boys
We'll go to Mother Chases,
And there we'll get a Sugar Drum
Sweeten'd with Molasses:
Heigh ho for our Cape Cod,
Heigh ho Nantasket,
Do not let the Boston wags
Fell you Oyster Basket.

Punk in Pye is very good
And so is Apple Lantern,
Had you been whipp'd as oft as I
You'd not have been so wanton:
Uncle is a Yankee Man
'I faith he pays us all off,
And he has got a Fiddle
As big as Daddy's Hog Trough.

Seth's Mother went to Lynn
To buy a pair of Breeches,
The first time Vathen put them on
He tore out all the Stitches:
Dolly Bushel – – – – – – – –
Jenny Jones she found it,
Ambrose carried it to Mill
Where Doctor Warren[1] ground it.

---

[1] Joseph Warren, physician, Revolutionary patriot and leader of Boston, delivered two stirring orations (1772, 1775) in commemoration of the "Massacre." He was president of the Massachusetts Provincial Congress until his death at the Battle of Bunker Hill (eds.).

28. Pitt Urges Withdrawal of British Troops from Boston

From John Almon, *Anecdotes of the Life of* . . . *William Pitt, Earl of Chatham* (London: J. S. Jordan, 1793). Three volumes. Vol. II, p. 389.
The following document is Lord Chatham's speech in the House of Lords on January 20, 1775, in support of his motion to withdraw the British troops from Boston, in order to prevent the possibility of any armed clash precipitating a crisis. Only eighteen peers voted for Chatham's motion; sixty-eight voted against it.

When I state the importance of the Colonies to this country, and the magnitude of danger hanging over this country, from the present plan of misadministration practised against them, I desire not to be understood to argue for a reciprocity of indulgence between England and America. I contend not for indulgence, but justice to America; and I shall ever contend, that the Americans justly owe obedience to us in a limited degree—they owe [390] obedience to our ordinances of trade and navigation; but let the line be skilfully drawn between the objects of those ordinances, and their private, internal property; let the sacredness of their property remain inviolate; let it be taxable only by their own consent, given in their provincial assemblies, else it will cease to be property. As to the metaphysical refinements, attempting to show that the Americans are equally free from obedience and commercial restraints, as from taxation for revenue, as being unrepresented here, I pronounce them futile, frivolous, and groundless.

When I urge this measure of recalling the troops from Boston, I urge it on this pressing principle, that it is necessarily preparatory to the restoration of your peace, and the establishment of your prosperity. It will then appear that you are disposed to treat amicably and equitably; and to consider, revise, and repeal, if it should be found necessary, as I affirm it will, those violent acts and declarations which have [391] disseminated confusion throughout your empire.

Resistance to your acts was necessary as it was just; and your vain declarations of the omnipotence of Parliament, and your imperious doctrines of the necessity of submission, will be found equally impotent to convince, or to enslave your fellow-subjects in America, who feel that tyranny, whether *ambitioned* by an individual part of the legislature, or the bodies who compose it, is equally intolerable to British subjects. . . .

The means of enforcing this thraldom are found to be as ridiculous and weak in [392] practice as they are unjust in principle. Indeed I cannot but feel the most anxious sensibility for the situation of General Gage, and the troops under his command, thinking him, as I do, a man of humanity and understanding; and entertaining, as I ever will, the highest respect, the warmest love, for the British troops. Their situation is truly unworthy; penned up pining in inglorious inactivity. They are an army of impotence. You may call them an army of safety and of guard; but they are in truth an army of impotence and contempt; and, to make the folly equal to the disgrace, they are an army of irritation and vexation.

But I find a report creeping abroad, that Ministers censure General Gage's inactivity: let them censure him—it becomes them—it becomes their justice and their honour. I mean not to censure his inactivity; it is a prudent and necessary inaction. But what a miserable condition is that, where disgrace is prudence, and where it is necessary to be contemptible! This tameness, however contemptible, cannot be censured, [393] for the first drop of blood shed in civil and unnatural war might be *immedicabile vulnus* [a wound past cure].

I therefore urge and conjure your Lordships immediately to adopt this conciliating measure: I will pledge myself for its immediately producing conciliatory effects, by its being thus well-timed; but if you delay till your vain hope shall be accomplished, of triumphantly dictating reconciliation, you delay for ever. . . .

[394] But our Ministers say, the Americans must not be heard. They have been condemned unheard; the discriminating hand of vengeance has lumped together innocent and guilty: with all the formalities of hostility, has blocked up the town [Boston], and reduced to beggary and famine thirty thousand inhabitants.

[395] But his Majesty is advised, that the union in America cannot last. Ministers have more eyes than I, and should have more ears; but with all the information I have been able to procure, I can pronounce it—an union, solid, permanent, and effectual. . . .

[397] I remember some years ago, when the repeal of the Stamp Act was in agitation, conversing in a friendly confidence with a person of undoubted respect and authenticity, on that subject; and he assured me with a certainty which his judgment and opportunity gave him, that these were the prevalent and steady principles of America—That you might destroy their towns, and cut them off from the superfluities, perhaps the conveniences of life; but that they were prepared to despise your power, and would not lament their loss, whilst they have—what, my Lords?—their *woods* and their *liberty*. The name of my authority, if I am called upon will authenticate the opinion irrefragably. [It was Dr. Franklin.]

If illegal violences have been, as it is said, committed in America; prepare the way, open the door of possibility, for acknowledgment and satisfaction: but proceed not to such coercion, such proscription; cease your indiscriminate inflictions; amerce not thirty thousand; oppress not [398] three millions, for the fault of forty or fifty individuals. Such severity of injustice must for ever render incurable the wounds you have already given your colonies; you irritate them to unappeasable rancour. What though you march from town to town, and from province to province; though you should be able to enforce a temporary and local submission, which I only suppose, not admit—how shall you be able to secure the obedience of the country you leave behind you in your progress, to grasp the dominion of eighteen hundred miles of continent, populous in numbers, possessing valour, liberty and resistance?

This resistance to your arbitrary system of taxation might have been foreseen: it was obvious from the nature of things, and of mankind; and above all, from the Whiggish spirit flourishing in that country. The spirit which now resists your taxation in America, is the same which formerly opposed [399] loans, benevolences, and ship-money, in England: the same spirit which called all England *on its legs*, and by the Bill of Rights vindicated the English constitution: the same spirit which established the great fundamental essential maxim of your liberties, *that no subject of England shall be taxed but by his own consent.*

This glorious spirit of Whiggism animates three millions in America; who prefer poverty with liberty, to gilded chains and sordid affluence; and who will die in defence of their rights as men, as freemen. . . . [400] There is no such thing, *no such idea in this constitution, as a supreme power operating upon property.* Let this distinction then remain for ever ascertained; taxation is theirs, commercial regulation is ours. As an American I would recognize to England her supreme right of regulating commerce [401] and navigation: as an Englishman by birth and principle, I recognize to the Americans their supreme unalienable right in their property; a right which they are justified in the defence of to the last extremity. To maintain this principle is the common cause of the Whigs on the other side of the Atlantic and on this. " 'Tis liberty to liberty engaged," that they will defend themselves, their families, and their country. In this great cause they are immoveably allied: it is the alliance of God and nature—immutable, eternal—fixed as the firmament of heaven. . . .

[404] When your Lordships look at the papers transmitted to us from America; when you consider their decency, firmness, and wisdom, you cannot but respect their cause, and wish to make it your own. For myself, I must declare and avow that in all my reading and observation —and it has been my favourite study—I have read Thucydides, and have studied and admired the master-states of the world—that for solidity of reasoning, force of sagacity, and wisdom of conclusion, under such a complication of difficult circumstances, no nation, or body of men, can stand in preference to the General Congress of Philadelphia. I trust it is obvious to your Lordships that all attempts to impose servitude upon such men, to establish despotism over such a mighty continental nation must be vain, must be fatal. We shall be forced, ultimately to retract; let us retract while we can, not when we must. I say we must [405] necessarily undo these violent oppressive acts; they must be repealed—you will repeal them; I pledge myself for it, that you will in the end repeal them; I stake my reputation on it—I will consent to be taken for an idiot if they are not finally repealed.

29. Parliament Debates the Use of Force

From William Cobbett, *The Parliamentary History of England* (London: T. C. Hansard, 1806–20). Thirty-six volumes. Vol. XVIII, p. 167.
From the debate in the House of Lords on the Earl of Chatham's motion to withdraw the troops from the colonies.

The Marquis of Rockingham observed, that as ministry had avowed an intention of sending out more troops to Boston, and as that was a measure totally repugnant to his plan of reconciliation, he was glad of an opportunity of resisting that mischievous and dangerous design of governing the colonies by force. He said that the troops which had so idly been sent thither, were by their instructions left in so disgraceful a state, that he wished them recalled with the utmost possible dispatch; and consequently he must be averse to the designs administration entertained, of further exposing our troops to shame and disgrace; and of course he joined the motion for their recall. He expressed pretty strongly his adherence to his old opinion of the propriety of the Declaratory Act, which he seemed to consider as necessary to the dominion of this country, and in no way hurtful to the freedom of America; but he reserved himself to a more proper season for debating that principle, only insisting that the congress had expressed no dissatisfaction with the Declaratory Act; and he thought it needless to give them more than they desired.

The Duke of Richmond supported Lord Chatham's motion with firmness, and answered his adversaries with accuracy and precision. He contrasted very happily the stubbornness of ministry in refusing to have the least feeling for the miseries and complaints of British subjects, while they were all awake and full of attention to the most arrogant expectations of foreign powers. . . .

[168] Lord Weymouth opposed the motion. He was for sending troops to America. . . .

The House divided: 18 contents, and 68 non-contents.

> The following extracts are representative of the opinions expressed in a debate in the House of Commons on the petitions of the London and Bristol merchants for reconciliation with America, January 23, 1775. There were, of course, numerous and lengthy debates in Parliament on the American question from this point on.

[173] Lord Clare was for not submitting to the Americans in the least, and ridiculed the opinion of those who said we had a [174] right to tax America, yet ought not to exercise it. . . . He said, if we were

resolved to sacrifice the supremacy of parliament, he would much readier consent to it on any other ground than that which the present petition would lead to, as this would be an inexhaustible source of applications of the same nature; for whenever the Americans had any point to gain, let it be ever so unreasonable, all they had to do was to refuse to pay their debts, to threaten to stop all commercial intercourse with us, and their business would be done: if therefore we were to submit, let us fairly give up the point at once; let us sooner even become their vassals, than remain open to demands which could have no bounds, and must be irresistible, when they were brought forward in the present form.

[175] Captain Luttrell. I have listened with attention to this debate, in hopes of receiving such instruction as might enable me to judge which way of acting will be most conducive to the welfare of America and this country. Sir, I am sorry to find such a variety of opinions prevail amongst us, as makes it very difficult to determine what measures are likely to prove the most salutary. . . . Sir, that the colonies are inseparably united to the imperial crown of this realm, I trust will never be denied by the friends of either clime; but though it has been asserted, America can subsist without our commerce, I believe nobody will say, she can flourish without our protection. If we abandon her to her present miserable situation, she must soon sue to us or to some other power for succour.

The following extracts are from a debate on February 20, 1775.

[323] Governor Pownall. . . . when I see that the Americans are actually resisting that government which is derived from the crown, and by the authority of parliament; when I see them opposing rights which they always acknowledged, and for asserting which, I could produce the best authority (I mean their own authority, as expressed by one of their ablest agents) when I see them arming and arraying themselves, and carrying this opposition into force by arms; seeing the question brought to an issue, not on a point of right but a trial of power; I cannot but say, that it is become necessary that this country should arm also. It is become necessary, that this government should oppose its force to force; when that force is to be employed only in maintaining the laws and constitution of the empire. These, Sir, are my reasons for acquiescing . . . in measures of force. The Americans themselves have rendered them necessary. . . . [325] At present matters are come to the last extremity—this country and America are in the situation of open and declared war; they are on the very point of striking the blow which must be the beginning of shedding of blood. . . .

[338] [In a typical balloting, 274 in the House supported the Ministry; 88 voted against it.]

[342] Mr. Temple Luttrell. . . . However grating to the ears of some individuals the subject may be, I shall take the liberty, with the

indulgence of the House, to affirm, that these measures of compelling the Americans by force of arms to acknowledge the paramount and unlimited authority of parliament, in the taxation of their property, a property created by their faculties, and by their industry, are not just, not politic, nor practicable, but a traitrous infringement on the constitution of the colonies, which rests upon the same fundamental principles that uphold the property and uphold the franchises of every native of this island. . . . [343] All persons have natural rights—a free people have legal rights, independent of parlia- [344] mentary edicts, and of which no form of government whatever can deprive them. Laws not founded on constitutional justice, are in themselves null and void; nor are the makers of them legislators, but usurpers. A very wise and learned writer, Judge Blackstone, has in his Commentaries the following passage: "If the sovereign power advance with gigantic strides and threaten desolation to a state, mankind will not be reasoned out of the feelings of humanity, nor will sacrifice their liberty by a scrupulous adherence to those political maxims, which were originally established to preserve that liberty." . . . [346] We have about seven years more of profound tranquillity with the House of Bourbon to trust to; but, from the symptoms of our domestic distraction, and the improved state of the government and finances of our neighbours, I should judge it prudent to be somewhat better provided than we are at present for an early rupture; not entirely to dismantle our ports and our coasts of soldiers and seamen, sent to immolate the martyrs to liberty of their own flesh and blood, on the distant continent of America. . . .

[347] The military coercion of America will be impracticable. What has been the fate of your famous Bills passed in the last session of the deceased parliament? I mean, Sir, the Boston Port Bill, and the Bill for altering the charter of Massachuset's Bay. America, as an earnest of her triumph over the future labours for which envy and malice may reserve her, has, like another Hercules in the cradle, already grappled with those two serpents sent for her destruction. Neither shall we be long able to sustain the unhallowed war at so remote a distance;—unexplored desarts, wood-land ambuscades, latitudes, to which few of our soldiery have been seasoned;—the southern provinces scarce to be endured in the summer months, the northern provinces not approachable in the winter season;—shipwrecks, pestilence, famine. The unrelenting invete- [348] racy and carnage of York and Lancaster, will here be joined to all the elementary hardships and maladies of a bigot crusade. . . .

[352] Lord North was for preserving the right of parliament to tax the colonies; but for transferring the exercise of that right to the colony assemblies. He was for leaving the colonies at liberty to contribute voluntarily to the alleviating the public burdens; and for reserving to parliament, a right of rejecting or increasing those voluntary aids at pleasure. Among other things, he said, if the colonies reject just conditions, they must be reduced to unconditional obedience; that such of the colonies as did not comply with the Resolution, would have the Acts rigidly enforced against them. . . .

[356] General Burgoyne. . . . Is there a man in England (I am confident there is not an officer or soldier in the King's service) who does not think the parliamentary rights of Great Britain a cause to fight for, to bleed and die for? . . . Sir, another method of evading a debate upon the true merits of this question, has been to confound the understanding. Ingenious men will run changes upon real and virtual representation, external and internal taxes, revenue and regulation, till one's head grows dizzy with distinctions, and the most gross absurdities and contradictions become, for a moment, specious. But it is not in rhetoric or sophistry to argue the great rational majority of the people of England out of the plain, simple, proposition, which is contained in the Declaratory Act of the 6th of the present King [the 6th session]. The reason of the nation has been long convinced; the trial now only is whether we have spirit to support our conviction.

Sir, if the whole body of the kingdom does not rouse at this alarm, and shake off that torpitude under which our public spirit has long shamefully languished; if every class and distinction of men do not join in this great cause; if our merchants and manufacturers do not in one instance take example from the Americans, and render it glorious by adapting it to a better cause; if they do not feel insult and affront in the suspicion, that while one country dares the interruption of commerce to effectuate her chimerical claims, the other will not exert equal fortitude to vindicate her fundamental rights; if this be our [357] wretched state, I agree that the sooner a formal surrender is made, the better; let Great Britain revert to her primitive insignificancy in the map of the world, and the congress of Philadelphia be the legislature to dispense the blessings of empire. Let us spare the blood of our subjects, let us spare the treasures of the state; but let us at the same time confess, we are no more a people. . . .

[358] The Resolution [Lord North's proposition for conciliating the differences with America] was agreed to.

30. A British Soldier in Boston

From *A British Fusilier in Revolutionary Boston: Being a Transcript from the Diary of Lieutenant Frederick Mackenzie of the Royal Welsh Fusiliers,* ed. Allen French (Cambridge, Mass.: Harvard University Press, 1926). P. 30.
About fifty years old at this time, Mackenzie was a professional soldier, adjutant to General Gage.

21st [Jan., 1775]. As there was some disturbance last night, and a quarrel between some Officers and the town Watch, the General [Gage] has ordered a Court of Enquirey, composed of five Field Officers, to examine into the cause and circumstances of it, and report thereon to him. . . .

24th Jany. The General being much displeased with the conduct of the Officers concerned in the late disturbance, and anxious to prevent just cause of complaint on the part of the Townspeople, has, in a private order, directed the Commanding Officers of Corps to assemble their Officers, and shew them the impropriety of the conduct of some of them, which has afforded the King's enemies the very advantage they seek, and given room for reflections which dishonor the Service. To point out to them the ills that must arise from their assembling to game and drink, which lays the foundation for Quarrels and Riots, and that the attacking the Watch of any Town in all [31] parts of the World, must be attended with bad consequences: for as they are appointed by Law, the Law will protect them. . . . [The Commanding Officers] are desired to inform their Officers that the Commander in Chief is determined to make the strictest enquirey into the conduct of all Officers concerned in quarrels or Riots with the Townspeople, and try them if in fault. . . .

30th. . . . We have a free intercourse with the Country, but the people are evidently making every preparation for resistance. They are taking every means to provide themselves with Arms; and [32] are particularly desirous of procuring the Locks of firelocks, which are easily conveyed out of town without being discovered by the Guards. . . .

1st February. A Garrison Court Martial assembled this day for the trial of some Soldiers for selling firelocks, and locks to the Country people. . . .

2ed Feby. . . . The townspeople encourage . . . excessive drinking, as when the Soldiers are in a State of intoxication they are frequently induced to desert. . . .

[33] Boston, 4th Feb. 1775. A Soldier of the 4th Regt who was tried a few days ago for disposing of Arms to the townspeople, has been found guilty and sentenced to receive 500 lashes. . . .

[36] 4th March. Robt Vaughan, a Soldier of the 52ed Regiment was apprehended last night at Charlestown Ferry, attempting to Desert; and this day a General Court Martial was ordered to assemble to try him for the same. . . .

6th March. . . . This day having been appointed by the Selectmen of Boston for the delivery, according to Annual Custom, of an Oration in commemoration of the 5th March 1770, on which day some Inhabitants of this town were killed and wounded, in a Riot, by the Military: at 10 o'clock the Old South Meeting was [37] opened for the purpose, and an immense concourse of people assembled therein. As this assemblage was undoubtedly intended to inflame the minds of the people, and the Troops conceived it was a great insult, under the present circumstances, to deliver an Oration on the Occasion, a great number of Officers assembled in the Church and seemed determined to take notice of, and resent any expressions made of us by the orator, reflecting on the Military. . . . The Oration, which, tho severe on the conduct of the Military, and evidently calculated to excite the resentment of the populace against them, contained nothing so violent as was expected, and was delivered without any other interruption than a few hisses from some of the Officers. . . . as soon as the Oration was ended, Mr. Saml [38] Adams came forward from a Pew . . . and moved "that the thanks of the Town should be presented to Doctor Warren for his Elegant and Spirited Oration, and that another Oration should be delivered on the 5th of March next, to commemorate *the Bloody Massacre* of the 5th of March 1770." On this several Officers began to hiss; others cried out, *"Oh! fie! Oh! fie!"* and a great bustle ensued.

31. Samuel Johnson on Taxation

From Samuel Johnson, *Taxation No Tyranny: An Answer to the Resolutions and Address of the American Congress* (1775), *The Works of Samuel Johnson* (Troy, N.Y.: Pafraets Book Co., 1903). Sixteen volumes. Vol. XIV, p. 93.

In all the parts of human knowledge, whether terminating in science merely speculative, or operating upon life, private or civil, are admitted some fundamental principles, or common axioms, which, being [94] generally received, are little doubted, and, being little doubted, have been rarely proved. . . .

Of this kind is the position, that "the supreme power of every community has the right of requiring, from all its subjects, such contributions as are necessary to the publick safety or publick prosperity," which was considered, by all mankind, as comprising the primary and essential condition of all political society, till it became disputed by those zealots of anarchy, who have denied, to the parliament of Britain the right of taxing the American colonies.

In favour of this exemption of the Americans from the authority of their lawful sovereign, and the dominion of their mother-country, very loud clamours have been raised, and many wild assertions advanced, which, by such as borrow their opinions from the reigning fashion, have been admitted as [95] arguments; and, what is strange, though their tendency is to lessen English honour and English power, have been heard by Englishmen, with a wish to find them true. . . .

To be prejudiced is always to be weak; yet there are prejudices so near to laudable, that they have been often praised, and are always pardoned. To love their country has been considered as virtue in men, whose love could not be otherwise than blind, because their preference was made without a comparison; but it has never been my fortune to find, either in ancient or modern writers, any honourable mention of those, who have, with equal blindness, hated their country.

These antipatriotick prejudices are the abortions of folly impregnated by faction, which, being produced against the standing order of nature, have not strength sufficient for long life. They are born only to scream and perish, and leave those to contempt or detestation, whose kindness was employed to nurse them into mischief. . . .

[96] But we are soon told, that the Americans, how- [97] ever wealthy, cannot be taxed; that they are the descendants of men who left all for liberty, and that they have constantly preserved the principles and stubbornness of their progenitors; that they are too obstinate for persuasion, and too powerful for constraint; that they will laugh at argument, and defeat violence; that the continent of North America contains three millions, not of men merely, but of whigs, of whigs fierce for liberty, and disdainful of dominion; that they multiply with the fecundity of their own rattlesnakes, so that every quarter of a century doubles their numbers.

Men accustomed to think themselves masters do not love to be threatened. This talk is, I hope, commonly thrown away, or raises passions different from those which it was intended to excite. Instead of terrifying the English hearer to tame acquiescence, it disposes him to hasten the experiment of bending obstinacy, before it is become yet more obdurate, and convinces him that it is necessary to attack a nation thus prolifick, while we may yet hope to prevail. When he is told, through what extent of territory we must travel, to subdue them, he recollects how far, a few years ago, we travelled in their defence. When it is urged, that they will shoot up, like the hydra, he naturally considers how the hydra was destroyed. . . .

[100] But terrours and pity are not the only means by which the taxation of the Americans is opposed. There are those, who profess to use them only as auxiliaries to reason and justice; who tell us, that to tax the colonies is usurpation and oppression, an invasion of natural and legal rights, and a violation of those principles which support the constitution of English government.

This question is of great importance. That the Americans are able to bear taxation, is indubitable; that their refusal may be overruled, is highly probable; but power is no sufficient evidence of truth. Let us examine our own claim, and the objections of the recusants, with caution proportioned to the event of the decision, which must convict one part of robbery, or the other of rebellion.

A tax is a payment, exacted by authority, from [101] part of the community, for the benefit of the whole. From whom, and in what proportion such payment shall be required, and to what uses it shall be applied, those only are to judge to whom government is intrusted. In the British dominions taxes are apportioned, levied, and appropriated by the states assembled in parliament.

Of every empire all the subordinate communities are liable to taxation, because they all share the benefits of government, and, therefore, ought all to furnish their proportion of the expense.

This the Americans have never openly denied. That it is their duty to pay the costs of their own safety, they seem to admit; nor do they refuse their contribution to the exigencies, whatever they may be, of the British empire; but they make this participation of a publick burden a duty of very uncertain extent, and imperfect obligation, a duty temporary, occasional, and elective, of which they reserve to themselves the right of settling the degree, the time, and the duration; of judging when it may be required, and when it has been performed.

They allow to the supreme power nothing more than the liberty of notifying to them its demands or its necessities. Of this notification they profess to think for themselves, how far it shall influence their counsels; and of the necessities alleged, how far they shall endeavour to relieve them. They assume the exclusive power of settling not only the mode, but the quantity, of this payment. They are ready to cooperate with all the other [102] dominions of the king; but they will cooperate by no means which they do not like, and at no greater charge than they are willing to bear.

This claim, wild as it may seem; this claim, which supposes dominion without authority, and subjects without subordination, has found among the libertines of policy, many clamorous and hardy vindicators. The laws of nature, the rights of humanity, the faith of charters, the danger of liberty, the encroachments of usurpation, have been thundered in our ears, sometimes by interested faction, and sometimes by honest stupidity. . . .

[106] The colonies of England differ no otherwise from those of other nations, than as the English constitution differs from theirs. All government is ultimately and essentially absolute, but subordinate societies may have more immunities, or individuals greater liberty, as the operations of government are differently conducted. An Englishman in the common course of life and action feels no restraint. [107] An English colony has very liberal powers of regulating its own manners, and adjusting its own affairs. But an English individual may, by the supreme authority, be deprived of liberty, and a colony divested of its powers, for reasons of which that authority is the only judge.

In sovereignty there are no gradations. There may be limited royalty, there may be limited consulship, but there can be no limited government. There must, in every society, be some power or other, from which there is no appeal, which admits no restrictions, which pervades the whole mass of the community, regulates and adjusts all subordination, enacts laws or repeals them, erects or annuls judicatures, extends or contracts privileges, exempts itself from question or control, and bounded only by physical necessity.

By this power, where it subsists, all legislation and jurisdiction is animated and maintained. From this all legal rights are emanations, which, whether equitably or not, may be legally recalled. It is not infallible, for it may do wrong; but it is irresistible, for it can be resisted only by rebellion, by an act which makes it questionable, what shall be thenceforward the supreme power.

An English colony is a number of persons, to whom the king grants a charter, permitting them to settle in some distant country, and enabling them to constitute a corporation enjoying such powers as the charter grants, to be administered in such forms as the charter prescribes. As a corporation, they make laws for themselves; but as a corporation, [108] subsisting by a grant from higher authority, to the control of that authority they continue subject. . . .

[109] Our colonies, . . . however distant, have been hitherto, treated as constituent parts of the British empire. The inhabitants incorporated by [110] English charters are entitled to all the rights of Englishmen. They are governed by English laws, entitled to English dignities, regulated by English counsels, and protected by English arms; and it seems to follow, by consequence not easily avoided, that they are subject to English government, and chargeable by English taxation. . . .

[113] But hear, ye sons and daughters of liberty, the sounds which the winds are wafting from the western continent. The Americans are telling one another, what, if we may judge from their noisy triumph, they have but lately discovered, and what yet is a very important truth: "That they are entitled to life, liberty, and property; and that they have never ceded to any sovereign power whatever a right to dispose of either without their consent."

While this resolution stands alone, the Americans are free from singularity of opinion; their wit has not yet betrayed them to heresy. While they speak as the naked sons of nature, they claim but what is claimed by other men, and have withheld nothing but what all withheld. They are here upon firm ground, behind entrenchments which can never be forced.

Humanity is very uniform. The Americans have this resemblance to Europeans, that they do not always know when they are well. They soon quit the fortress, that could neither have been mined by sophistry, nor battered by declamation. Their next resolution declares, that "Their ancestors, who first settled the colonies, were, at the time of their emi- [114] gration from the mother-country, entitled to all the rights, liberties, and immunities of free and natural-born subjects within the realm of England."

This, likewise, is true; but when this is granted, their boast of original rights is at an end; they are no longer in a state of nature. These lords of themselves, these kings of me, these demigods of independence sink down to colonists, governed by a charter. If their ancestors were subjects, they acknowledged a sovereign; if they had a right to English privileges, they were accountable to English laws; and, what must grieve the lover of liberty to discover, had ceded to the king and parliament, whether the right or not, at least, the power of disposing, "without their consent, of their lives, liberties, and properties." It, therefore, is required of them to prove, that the parliament ever ceded to them a dispensation from that obedience, which they owe as natural-born subjects, or any degree of independence or immunity, not enjoyed by other Englishmen. . . .

[132] When subordinate communities oppose the decrease of the general legislature with defiance thus audacious, and malignity thus acrimonious, nothing remains but to conquer or to yield; to allow their claim of independence, or to reduce them, by force, to submission and allegiance. . . .

[137] The argument of the irregular troops of controversy, stripped

of its colours, and turned out naked to the view, is no more than this. Liberty is the birthright of man, and where obedience is compelled, there is no liberty. The answer is equally simple. Government is necessary to man, and where obedience is not compelled, there is no government.

If the subject refuses to obey, it is the duty of authority to use compulsion. Society cannot subsist but by the power, first of making laws, and then of enforcing them. . . .

[140] The dean of Gloucester [Dean Tucker] has proposed, and seems to propose it seriously, that we should, at once, release our claims, declare them masters of themselves, and whistle them down the wind. His opinion is, that our gain from them will be the same, and our expense less. What they can have most cheaply from Britain, they will still buy; what they can sell to us at the highest price, they will still sell.

It is, however, a little hard, that, having so lately fought and conquered [the French] for their safety, we should govern them longer. By letting them loose before the [141] war, how many millions might have been saved. One wild proposal is best answered by another. Let us restore to the French what we have taken from them. We shall see our colonists at our feet, when they have an enemy so near them. Let us give the Indians arms, and teach them discipline, and encourage them, now and then, to plunder a plantation. Security and leisure are the parents of sedition.

While these different opinions are agitated, it seems to be determined by the legislature, that force shall be tried. Men of the pen have seldom any great skill in conquering kingdoms, but they have strong inclination to give advice. I cannot forbear to wish, that this commotion may end without bloodshed, and that the rebels may be subdued by terrour rather than by violence; and, therefore, recommend such a force as may take away, not only the power, but the hope of resistance, and, by conquering without a battle, save many from the sword. . . .
It has been proposed, that the slaves should be set free, an act, which, surely, the lovers of liberty cannot but commend. If they are furnished with firearms for defence, and utensils for husbandry, and settled in some simple form of government within the country, they may be more grateful and honest than their masters. . . .

[143] We are told, that the subjection of Americans may tend to the diminution of our own liberties; an event, which none but very perspicacious politicians are able to foresee. If slavery be thus fatally con- [144] tagious, how is it that we hear the loudest yelps for liberty among the drivers of negroes? . . .

32. James Boswell's Letter

From James Boswell, *Life of Samuel Johnson*, ed. George Birk-beck Hill (New York: Harper & Bros., 1891). Four volumes. Vol. II, p. 334. [First published in 1791.]

"To James Boswell, Esq.   [January 21, 1775]
 . . . I am going to write about the Americans. If you have picked up any hints among your lawyers, who are great masters of the law of nations, or if your own mind suggests any thing, let me know. But mum, it is a secret." . . .

[336] "Mr. Boswell to Dr. Johnson.   Edinburgh, Jan. 27, 1775.
 . . . You rate our lawyers here too high, when you call them great masters of the law of nations. . . .

As for myself, I am ashamed to say I have read little and thought little on the subject of America. I will be much obliged to you, if you will direct me where I shall find the best information of what is to be said on both sides. It is a subject vast in its present extent and future consequences. The imperfect hints which now float in my mind, tend rather to the formation of an opinion that our government has been precipitant and severe in the resolutions taken against the Bostonians. Well do you know that I have no kindness for that race. But nations, or bodies of men, should, as well as individuals, have a fair trial, and not be condemned on character alone. Have we not express contracts with our colonies, which afford a more certain foundation of judge-ment, than general political speculations on the mutual rights of States and their provinces or colonies? Pray let we know immediately what to read, and I shall diligently endeavor to gather for you any thing that I can find. Is Burke's speech on American taxation published by himself? Is it authentick? I remember to have heard you say, that you had never considered East-Indian affairs; though, surely, they are of much im-portance to Great-Britain. Under the recollection of this, I shelter myself from the reproach of ignorance about the Americans. If you write upon the subject I shall certainly understand it. But, since you seem to expect that I should know something of it, without your in-struction, and that my own mind should suggest something, I trust you will put me in the way." . . .

[356] The doubts which, in my correspondence with him, I had ventured to state as to the justice and wisdom of the conduct of Great-Britain towards the American colonies, while I at the same time re-quested that he would enable me to inform myself upon that momen-tous subject, he had altogether disregarded; and had recently published a pamphlet, entitled, *Taxation no Tyranny; an answer to the Resolu-tions and Address of the American Congress*

He had long before indulged most unfavourable sentiments of our fellow-subjects in America. For, as early as 1769, I was told by Dr. John Campbell, that he had said [357] of them, "Sir, they are a race of convicts, and ought to be thankful for any thing we allow them short of hanging."

Of this performance I avoided to talk with him; for I had now formed a clear and settled opinion, that the people of America were well warranted to resist a claim that their fellow-subjects in the mother-country should have the entire command of their fortunes, by taxing them without their own consent; and the extreme violence which it breathed, appeared to me so unsuitable to the mildness of a Christian philosopher, and so directly opposite to the principles of peace which he had so beautifully recommended in his pamphlet respecting Falkland's Islands, that I was sorry to see him appear in so unfavourable a light. Besides, I could not perceive in it that ability of argument, or that felicity of expression, for which he was, upon other occasions, so eminent. Positive assertion, sarcastical severity, and extravagant ridicule, which he himself reprobated as a test of truth, were united in this rhapsody.

That this pamphlet was written at the desire of those who were then in power, I have no doubt; and, indeed, he [358] owned to me, that it had been revised and curtailed by some of them.

33. Burke Pleads for Peace

From Edmund Burke, *Speech on Moving Resolutions for Conciliation with the Colonies* (House of Commons, March 22, 1775), *Writings and Speeches of Edmund Burke* (Boston: Little, Brown, 1901). Twelve volumes. Vol. II, p. 105.

New repressive measures were passed by Parliament in 1775 as colonial resistance stiffened and the First Continental Congress assembled at Philadelphia. Powerless and in despair, Burke witnessed the events that were destroying the unity that he so passionately desired to preserve. Even now Burke said that "To reconcile British superiority with American liberty shall be my great object. . . . I am far from thinking that both, even yet, may not be preserved." On the first resolution offered by Burke the votes in favor were 78, those against 270. The other resolutions were not put to vote. This balloting may be regarded as the final answer of the House of Commons to all attempts to save the American colonies except by force.

The proposition is peace. Not peace through the medium of war; not peace to be hunted through the [106] labyrinth of intricate and endless negotiations; not peace to arise out of universal discord, fomented from principle, in all parts of the empire, not peace to depend on the juridical determination of perplexing questions, or the precise marking the shadowy boundaries of a complex government. It is simple peace, sought in its natural course and in its ordinary haunts. . . .

[108] I mean to give peace. Peace implies reconciliation; and where there has been a material dispute, reconciliation does in a manner always imply concession on the one part or on the other. In this state of things I make no difficulty in affirming that the proposal ought to originate from us. Great and acknowledged force is not impaired, either in effect or in opinion, by an unwillingness to exert itself. The superior power may offer peace with honor and with safety. Such an offer from such a power will be attributed to magnanimity. But the concessions of the weak are the concessions of fear. . . .

The capital leading questions on which you must this day decide are these two: First, whether you [109] ought to concede; and secondly, what your concession ought to be. . . . Sir, to enable us to determine both on the one and the other of these great questions with a firm and precise judgment, I think it may be necessary to consider distinctly the true nature and the peculiar circumstances of the object which we have before us. . . .

The first thing that we have to consider with regard to the nature of the object is the number of people in the colonies. I have taken for some years a good deal of pains on that point. I can by no calculation justify myself in placing the number below two millions of inhabitants of our own European blood and color—besides at least 500,000 others, who form no inconsiderable part of the strength and opulence of the whole. . . .

[110] I put this consideration of the present and the growing numbers in the front of our deliberation because, Sir, this consideration will make it evident to a blunter discernment than yours that no partial, narrow, contracted, pinched, occasional system will be at all suitable to such an object. . . . It will prove that some degree of care and caution is required in the handling such an object; it will show that you ought not, in reason, to trifle with so large a mass of the interests and feelings of the human race. You could at no time do so without guilt; and be assured you will not be able to do it long with impunity.

But the population of this country, the great and growing population, though a very important consideration, will lose much of its weight if not combined with other circumstances. The commerce of your colonies is out of all proportion beyond the numbers of the people. . . .

[113] The trade with America alone is now within less than £500,000 of being equal to what this great commercial nation, England, carried on at the beginning of this century with the whole world! . . . But, it will be said, is not this American trade an unnatural protuberance, that has drawn the juices from the rest of the body? The reverse. It is the very food that has nourished every other part into its

present magnitude. Our general trade has been greatly augmented, and augmented more or less in almost every part to which it ever extended, but with this material difference: that of the six millions which in the beginning of the century constituted the whole mass of our export commerce the colony trade was but one twelfth part; it is now (as a part of sixteen millions) considerably more than a third of the whole. This is the relative proportion of the importance of the colonies at these two periods: and all reasoning concerning our mode of treating them must have this proportion as its basis, or it is a reasoning weak, rotten, and sophistical. . . .

[116] I pass, therefore, to the colonies in another point of view: their agriculture. This they have prosecuted with such a spirit that, besides feeding plentifully their own growing multitude, their annual export of grain, comprehending rice, has some years ago exceeded a million in value. . . . At the beginning of the century some of these colonies imported corn from the mother country. For some time past the Old World has been fed from the New. The scarcity which you have felt would have been a desolating famine, if this child of your old age, with a true filial piety, with a Roman charity, had not put the full breast of its youthful exuberance to the mouth of its exhausted parent. . . .

[120] In this character of the Americans a love of freedom is the predominating feature which marks and distinguishes the whole; and as an ardent is always a jealous affection, your colonies become suspicious, restive, and untractable whenever they see the least attempt to wrest from them by force, or shuffle from them by chicane, what they think the only advantage worth living for. This fierce spirit of liberty is stronger in the English colonies, probably, than in any other people of the earth, and this from a great variety of powerful causes; which, to understand the true temper of their minds, and the direction which this spirit takes, it will not be amiss to lay open somewhat more largely.

First, the people of the colonies are descendants of Englishmen. England, Sir, is a nation which still, I hope, respects, and formerly adored, her freedom. The colonists emigrated from you when this part of your character was most predominant; and they took this bias and direction the moment they parted from your hands. They are therefore not only devoted to liberty, but to liberty according to English ideas and on English principles. . . . It happened, you know, Sir, that the great contests for freedom in this country were from the earliest times chiefly upon the question of taxing. . . . [121] On this point of taxes the ablest pens and most eloquent tongues have been exercised, the greatest spirits have acted and suffered. . . . They took infinite pains to inculcate, as a fundamental principle, that in all monarchies the people must in effect themselves, mediately or immediately, possess the power of granting their own money, or no shadow of liberty could subsist. The colonies draw from you, as with their lifeblood, these ideas and principles. Their love of liberty, as with you, is fixed and attached on this specific point of taxing. . . .

[122] If anything were wanting to this necessary operation of the form of government, religion would have given it a complete effect.

Religion, always a principle of energy, in this new people is no way worn out or impaired; and their mode of professing it is also one main cause of this free spirit. The people are Protestants, and of that kind which is the most adverse to all implicit submission of mind and opinion. This is a persuasion not only favorable to liberty, but built upon it. . . . [123] All Protestantism, even the most cold and passive, is a sort of dissent. But the religion most prevalent in our northern colonies is a refinement on the principle of resistance; it is the dissidence of dissent, and the protestantism of the Protestant religion. This religion, under a variety of denominations agreeing in nothing but in the communion of the spirit of liberty, is predominant in most of the northern provinces, where the Church of England, notwithstanding its legal rights, is in reality no more than a sort of private sect, not composing, most probably, the tenth of the people. . . .

Sir, I can perceive, by their manner, that some gentlemen object to the latitude of this description, because in the southern colonies the Church of England forms a large body, and has a regular establishment. It is certainly true. There is, however, a circumstance attending these colonies which, in my opinion, fully counterbalances this difference and makes the spirit of liberty still more high and haughty than in those in the northward. It is that in Virginia and the Carolinas they have a vast multitude of [124] slaves. Where this is the case in any part of the world, those who are free are by far the most proud and jealous of their freedom. Freedom is to them not only an enjoyment, but a kind of rank and privilege. . . . I do not mean, Sir, to commend the superior morality of this sentiment, which has at least as much pride as virtue in it; but I cannot alter the nature of man. The fact is so; and these people of the southern colonies are much more strongly, and with a higher and more stubborn spirit, attached to liberty, than those to the northward. . . .

Permit me, Sir, to add another circumstance in our colonies which contributes no mean part towards the growth and effect of this untractable spirit: I mean their education. In no country, perhaps, in the world is the law so general a study. The profession itself is numerous and powerful, and in most provinces it takes the lead. The greater number of the deputies sent to the Congress were lawyers. But all who read, and most do read, endeavor to obtain some smattering in that science. I hear that they have sold nearly as many of Blackstone's Commentaries in America as in England. . . . [125] This study renders men acute, inquisitive, dexterous, prompt in attack, ready in defense, full of resources. In other countries, the people, more simple, and of a less mercurial cast, judge of an ill principle in government only by an actual grievance; here they anticipate the evil, and judge of the pressure of the grievance by the badness of the principle. They augur misgovernment at a distance, and snuff the approach of tyranny in every tainted breeze.

The last cause of this disobedient spirit in the colonies is hardly less powerful than the rest, as it is not [126] merely moral, but laid deep in the natural constitution of things. Three thousand miles of ocean lie between you and them. No contrivance can prevent the effect of this distance in weakening government. Seas roll, and months pass, between the order and the execution; and the want of a speedy explanation of a single point is enough to defeat a whole system. . . .

Then, Sir, from these six capital sources, of descent, of form of government, of religion in the [127] northern provinces, of manners in the southern, of education, of the remoteness of situation from the first mover of government—from all these causes a fierce spirit of liberty has grown up. It has grown with the growth of the people in your colonies, and increased with the increase of their wealth: a spirit that, unhappily meeting with an exercise of power in England, which, however lawful, is not reconcilable to any ideas of liberty, much less with theirs, has kindled this flame that is ready to consume us. . . .

[130] Sir, I would state that, as far as I am capable of discerning, there are but three ways of proceeding relative to this stubborn spirit which prevails in your colonies and disturbs your government. These are: to change that spirit, as inconvenient, by removing the causes; to prosecute it, as criminal; or to comply with it, as necessary. I would not be guilty of an imperfect enumeration; I can think of but these three. Another has, indeed, been started—that of giving up the colonies [Dean Tucker's opinion]; but it met so slight a reception that I do not think myself obliged to dwell a great while upon it. . . .

The first of these plans—to change the spirit, as in- [131] conven-ient, by removing the causes—I think is the most like a systematic proceeding. . . .

[133] I think it is nearly as little in our power to change [134] their republican religion as their free descent, or to substitute the Roman Catholic as a penalty, or the Church of England as an improvement. The mode of inquisition and dragooning is going out of fashion in the Old World, and I should not confide much to their efficacy in the New. The education of the Americans is also on the same unalterable bottom with their religion. You cannot persuade them to burn their books of curious science, to banish their lawyers from their courts of law, or to quench the lights of their assemblies by refusing to choose those persons who are best read in their privileges. It would be no less impracticable to think of wholly annihilating the popular assemblies in which these lawyers sit. The army, by which we must govern in their place, would be far more chargeable to us, not quite so effectual, and perhaps, in the end, full as difficult to be kept in obedience.

With regard to the high aristocratic spirit of Virginia and the south-ern colonies, it has been proposed, I know, to reduce it by declaring a general enfranchisement of their slaves. This project has had its advo-cates and panegyrists; yet I never could argue myself into any opinion of it. Slaves are often much attached to their masters. A general wild offer of liberty would not always be accepted. History furnishes few instances of it. It is sometimes as hard to persuade slaves to be free as it is to compel freemen to be slaves; and in this auspicious scheme we should have both these pleasing tasks on our hands at once. But when we talk of enfranchisement, do we not perceive that the American mas-ter may enfranchise, too, and arm servile hands in defense of freedom? —a measure to which other people have [135] had recourse more than

70

once, and not without success, in a desperate situation of their affairs. . . .

But let us suppose all these moral difficulties got over. The ocean remains. You cannot pump this dry; and as long as it continues in its present bed, so long all the causes which weaken authority by distance will continue. . . .

If, then, Sir, it seems almost desperate to think of any alterative course for changing the moral causes (and not quite easy to remove the natural) which produce prejudices irreconcilable to the late exercise of our authority, but that the spirit infallibly will continue, and, continuing, will produce such effects as now embarrass us—the second mode under consideration is to prosecute that spirit in its overt acts, as criminal. . . . [136] It looks to me to be narrow and pedantic to apply the ordinary ideas of criminal justice to this great public contest. I do not know the method of drawing up an indictment against a whole people. . . .

Perhaps, Sir, I am mistaken in my idea of an empire, as distinguished from a single state or kingdom. But my idea of it is this: that an empire is the aggregate of many states under one common head, whether this head be a monarch or a presiding republic. It does, in such constitutions, frequently happen (and nothing but the dismal, cold, dead uniformity of servitude can prevent its happening) that the subordinate parts have many local privileges and immunities. Between these privileges and the su- [137] preme common authority the line may be extremely nice. Of course disputes—often, too, very bitter disputes, and much ill blood—will arise. . . .

[139] In this situation, let us seriously and coolly ponder. What is it we have got by all our menaces, which have been many and ferocious? What advantage have we derived from the penal laws we have passed, and which, for the time, have been severe and numerous? What advances have we made towards our object by the sending of a force which, by land and sea, is no contemptible strength? Has the disorder abated? Nothing less. When I see things in this situation, after such confident hopes, bold promises, and active exertions, I cannot, for my life, avoid a suspicion that the plan itself is not correctly right.

If, then, the removal of the causes of this spirit of American liberty be, for the greater part, or rather entirely, impracticable; if the ideas of criminal process be inapplicable, or, if applicable, are in the highest degree inexpedient, what way yet remains? No way is open but the third and last—to comply with the American spirit as necessary, or, if you please, to submit to it as a necessary evil.

If we adopt this mode, if we mean to conciliate and concede, let us see of what nature the concession ought to be. To ascertain the nature of our concession, we must look at their complaint. The colonies complain that they have not the characteristic mark and seal of British freedom. They complain that they are taxed in a Parliament in which they are not represented. If you mean to satisfy them at all, you must satisfy them with regard to this complaint. . . .

[141] My idea, therefore, without considering whether we yield as matter of right, or grant as matter of favour, is *to admit the people of*

our colonies into an interest in the Constitution, and, by recording that ad- [142] mission in the journals of Parliament, to give them as strong an assurance as the nature of the thing will admit, that we mean forever to adhere to that solemn declaration of systematic indulgence. . . .

[179] If America gives you taxable objects on which you lay your duties *here*, and gives you, at the same time, a surplus by a foreign sale of her commodities to pay the duties on these objects which you tax at home, she has performed her part to the British revenue. But with regard to her own internal establishments, she may, I doubt not she will, contribute in moderation; I say in moderation, for she ought not to be permitted to exhaust herself. She ought to be reserved to a war, the weight of which, with the enemies that we are most likely to have, must be considerable in her quarter of the globe. There she may serve you, and serve you essentially.

For that service, for all service, whether of revenue, trade or empire, my trust is in her interest in the British Constitution. My hold of the colonies is in the close affection which grows from common names, from kindred blood, from similar privileges, and equal protection. These are ties which, though light as air, are as strong as links of iron. Let the colonies always keep the idea of their civil rights associated with your government; they will cling and grapple to you, and no force under heaven will be of power to tear them from their allegiance. But let it be once understood that your government may be one thing, and their privileges another; that these two things may exist without any mutual relation; the cement is gone; the cohesion is loosened; and every thing hastens to decay and dissolution. . . . [180] Deny them this participation in freedom, and you break that sole bond which originally made, and must still preserve, the unity of the empire. Do not entertain so weak an imagination as that your registers and your bonds, your affidavits and your sufferances, your cockets and your clearances, are what form the great securities of your commerce. Do not dream that your letters of office, and your instructions, and your suspending clauses, are the things that hold together the great contexture of this mysterious whole. These things do not make your government. Dead instruments, passive tools as they are, it is the spirit of the English communion that gives all their life and efficacy to them. It is the spirit of the English Constitution, which, infused through the mighty mass, pervades, feeds, unites, invigorates, vivifies every part of the empire, even down to the minutest member. . . .

[181] All this, I know well enough, will sound wild and chimerical to the profane herd of those vulgar and mechanical politicians, who have no place among us; a sort of people who think that nothing exists but what is gross and material, and who, therefore, far from being qualified to be directors of the great movement of empire, are not fit to turn a wheel in the machine. But to men truly initiated and rightly taught, these ruling and master principles, which, in the opinion of such men as I have mentioned, have no substantial existence, are in truth every thing and all in all. Magnanimity in politics is not seldom the truest wisdom; and a great empire and little minds go ill together.

34. From Lexington to Bunker Hill

From *The Annual Register*, 1775. "History of Europe," p. 124.

[February.] A circular letter from the secretary of state for the American department, forbidding, in the king's name, and under pain of his displeasure, the election of deputies for the ensuing general congress, was productive of no manner of effect; the elections every where took place, even in the province of New York. . . . [125] Boston continued very quiet. To which the injunctions of the different congresses perhaps contributed as much, as the ships of war that crowded the harbour, or the force that was stationed in the town. The calm was, however, precarious and fallacious on both sides. Combustible matter had been gathered in abundance. More was in preparation, and the least spark was likely to kindle a general conflagration. . . .

The people, since the acts for casting away their charter, and for protecting the soldiery from any trial in the province, considered themselves as put under military government. Every motion of that body became suspected, and was in their eyes an exertion of [126] the most odious and most dreadful tyranny. This appearance of resistance seems, on the other side, to have greatly irritated the military, for from this time they appear to have lived upon worse terms with the inhabitants of Boston than they had hitherto done; some general and wanton insults, as well as particular outrages having been complained of. But the crisis was now fast approaching, in which all lesser evils and calamities were to be lost and forgotten in the contemplation of those of a great and serious nature.

[The British expeditions to Lexington and Concord are described and the events narrated in some detail. Excerpts from the narrative are given.] It is said and believed, that this expedition had another object in view, which was to seize on the persons of Messrs. Hancock and Adams, those great and obnoxious leaders of the faction which opposed the new system of government. . . .

[Concerning the skirmish at Lexington, the historian comments:] Upon their arrival at Lexington, about five in the morning, they found the company of militia, belonging to that town, assembled on a green near the road; upon which an officer in the van called out, *Disperse, you rebels; throw down your arms, and disperse:* the soldiers at the same time running up with loud huzzas, some scattering shots were first fired, and immediately succeeded by a general discharge, by which eight of the militia were killed and wounded.

Thus was the first blood drawn in this unhappy civil contest. Great pains were taken on each side to shew the other to have been the aggressor upon this occasion. A matter of little consequence, in a political view, as things were now too far advanced to leave room for a probable hope of any other than such a final issue. . . .

[128] By the nearest calculation that can be made, there were from 1800 to 2000 of the best troops in the service (being about half the force that was then stationed at Boston) employed upon this expedition. The event sufficiently shewed how ill informed those were who had so often asserted at home, that a regiment or two could force their way through any part of the continent, and that the very sight of a grenadier's cap, would be sufficient to put an American army to flight.

Upon this occasion, each side charged the other with the most inhuman cruelties. Civil wars produce many such charges; but we have good reason, and some authority for believing, that these accounts, if at all true on either side, were much exaggerated. . . .

[133] [The American army invests the British forces in Boston. For June 12 the *Register* historian comments:] About the same time General Gage issued a proclamation, by which a pardon was offered in the king's name, to all those who should forthwith lay down their arms, and return to their respective occupations and peaceable duties, excepting only from the benefit of the pardon, Samuel Adams and John Hancock, whose offences were said to be of too flagitious a nature to admit of any other consideration than that of condign punishment. All those who did not accept of the proffered mercy, or who should protect, assist, supply, conceal, or correspond with them, to be treated as rebels and traitors. . . . It is needless to observe, that this proclamation had as little effect as any of those that preceded it. Hancock was about that time chosen president of the continental congress.

This proclamation was looked upon as the preliminary to immediate action. Accordingly, from that moment both sides held themselves in readiness for it. [The account of the Battle of Bunker Hill follows.] . . .

[135] Thus ended the hot and bloody affair of Bunker's-Hill [*sic*], in which we had more men and officers killed and wounded, in proportion to the number engaged, than in any other action which we can recollect. The whole loss in killed and wounded, amounted to 1054, of whom 226 were killed; of these, 19 were commissioned officers. . . . [136] All these circumstances concur in shewing the hard and dangerous service in which they [the King's troops] were engaged. The battle of Quebec, in the late war, with all its glory, and the vastness of the consequences of which it was productive, was not so destructive to our officers, as this affair of a retrenchment cast up in a few hours. It was a matter of grievous reflection, that those brave men, many of whom had nobly contributed their share when engaged against her natural enemies, to extend the military glory of their country into every quarter of the globe, should now have suffered so severely, in only a prelude to this unhappy civil contest. . . .

[137] They [the Americans] now exulted, that their actions had thoroughly refuted those aspersions which had been thrown upon them in England, of a deficiency in spirit and resolution. . . .

35. On American Affairs, May–July, 1775

From *The Gentleman's Magazine.* Vol. XLV (May, 1775), p. 249.

At Boston, as Gen. Gage, by his moderation [250] and prudent conduct, has been able to preserve the strictest discipline among his troops, so the civil magistrates, on their part, have been equally vigilant in restraining the excesses of the common people. The complaints that have been justly founded have in general been redressed, and, except the ordinary irregularities occasioned by liquor, no material injury has been done by the soldiers to the inhabitants, nor by the inhabitants to the soldiers, except by refusing them supplies. But this pacific temper will probably soon have an end. When the succours arrive, the intentions of government cannot be long concealed. Some insults have already been offered, which the injured parties have prudently overlooked. On the 16th of March (the day the provincial congress had recommended for fasting and prayer), a party of the 4th regiment, when the people were assembling, pitched two markee-tents within ten yards of their place of worship, and, with three drums and three fifes, kept beating and playing during the whole time of divine service. On the 17th, Col. Hancock's fine seat near the Common was maltreated, the fences broken down, and the enclosures defaced; and, on the 18th, the Neck-guard seized 13,425 musket-cartridges, with 3000 lb weight of ball, private property, which the General refused to restore on the application of the owner. These are the preludes, perhaps, to hostilities of a more serious nature, which will lead to the discovery of the intentions of the ministry in transporting to America so formidable a force.

From *The Gentleman's Magazine.* Vol. XLV (June, 1775), p. 262.

HIS EXCELLENCY GEN. GAGE'S ANSWER TO THE FOREGOING LETTER [BY GOVERNOR JONATHAN TRUMBULL, CONNECTICUT].

Boston, May 3, 1775.

Sir,

. . . [263] That troops should be employed for the purpose of protecting the magistrates in the execution of their duty, when opposed with violence, is not a new thing in the English or any other government. That any acts of the British parliament are unconstitutional or oppressive, I am not to suppose; if any such there are, in the apprehension of the people of this province, it had been happy for them, if they had sought relief only in the way which the constitution, their reason, and their interest, pointed out. . . .

The intelligence you seem to have received, relative to the late excursion of a body of troops into the country [reference to the Battles of Lexington and Concord], is altogether injurious and contrary to the true state of facts; the troops disclaim, with indignation, the barbarous outrages of which they are accused, so contrary to their known humanity. I have taken the greatest pains to discover if any were committed, and have found examples of their tenderness both to the young and the old, but no vestige of cruelty or barbarity. It is very possible, that, in firing into houses from whence they were fired upon, old people, women or children, may have suffered; but if any such thing has happened, it was in their defence, and undesigned. . . . The leaders here have taken pains to prevent any account of this affair getting abroad, but such as they have thought proper to publish themselves; and to that end the post has been stopped, the mails broke open, and letters taken out; and by these means the most injurious and inflammatory accounts have been spread throughout the continent, which has served to deceive and inflame the minds of the people.

When the resolves of the Provincial Congress breathed nothing but war; when those two great and essential prerogatives of the King, the levying of troops, and disposing of the public monies, were wrested from him; and when magazines were forming by an assembly of men, unknown to the constitution, for the declared purpose of levying war against the King; you must acknowledge it was my duty, as it was the dictate of humanity, to prevent, if possible, the calamities of civil war, by destroying such magazines. This, and this alone, I attempted. . . .

You enquire, Is there no way to prevent this unhappy dispute from coming to extremities? Is there no alternative, but absolute submission, or the desolations of war? I answer, I hope there is; the King and parliament seem to hold out terms of reconciliation, consistent with the honour and interest of Great-Britain, and the rights and privileges of the colonies; they have mutually declared their readiness [264] to attend to any real grievances of the colonies. . . . I must add, likewise, the resolution of the 27th of February, on the grand dispute of taxation and revenue, leaving it to the colonies to tax themselves, under certain conditions. Here is, surely, a foundation for an accommodation, to people who wish a reconciliation, rather than a destructive war, between countries so nearly connected by the ties of blood and interest; but I fear that the leaders of this province have been, and still are, intent only on shedding blood. . . .

Tho. Gage

From *The Gentleman's Magazine.* Vol. XLV (June, 1775), p. 293.

ACCOUNT OF THE PROCEEDINGS OF THE AMERICAN COLONISTS, SINCE THE PASSING OF THE BOSTON PORT-BILL.

[On the Battle at Lexington:] . . . and such was the cruelty and barbarity of the rebels, that they scalped and cut off the ears of some of the wounded men, who fell into their hands.

It is not known what number of the rebels were killed and wounded; but, it is supposed, that their loss was very considerable. . . .

Of the many affidavits that have been published by the Provincials, with a view to fix the commencement of hostilities on the King's troops, that of this gentleman [Lieutenant Gould] appears to be of the greatest importance, as it sets the affair at the bridge, which has been greatly misrepresented, in the most impartial point of view. [Part of his affidavit follows:] [294] . . . from whence we proceeded to Lexington. On our arrival at that place we saw a body of provincial troops armed, to the number of about sixty or seventy men. On our approach they dispersed, and soon after firing began; but which party fired first I cannot exactly say, as our troops rushed on shouting and huzzaing previous to the firing, which was continued by our troops so long as any of the Provincials were to be seen. . . . I myself was wounded at the attack of the bridge [at Concord], and am now treated with the greatest humanity, and taken all possible care of, by the Provincials, at Medford. . . .

This unhappy affair has had amazing effect throughout every part of America. The city of New York, which was looked upon as the most moderate, is now become the most violent.

From *The Gentleman's Magazine.* Vol. XLV (July, 1775), p. 331.

A proclamation issued by his Excellency the Hon. Thomas Gage, Esq; Governor and Commander in Chief, in and over his Majesty's Province of Massachusetts-Bay, and Vice-Admiral of the same. . . .

[332] The minds of men having been . . . gradually prepared for the worst extremities, a number of armed persons, to the amount of many thousands, assembled on the 19th of April last, and from behind walls and lurking holes attacked a detachment of the King's troops, who, not expecting so consummate an act of phrenzy, unprepared for vengeance, and willing to decline it, made use of their arms only in their own defense. Since that period, the rebels, deriving confidence from impunity, have added insult to outrage; have repeatedly fired upon the King's ships and subjects with cannon and small arms. . . . The actions of the 19th of April are of such notoriety as must

baffle all attempts to contradict them; and the flames of buildings and other property from the islands and adjacent country, for some weeks past, spread a melancholy confirmation of the subsequent assertions.

In this exigency of complicated calamities, I avail myself of the last effort within the bounds of my duty, to spare the effusion of blood, to offer, and I do hereby, in his Majesty's name, offer and promise his most gracious pardon to all persons who shall forthwith lay down their arms, and return to the duties of peaceable subjects, excepting only from the benefit of such pardon, *Samuel Adams* and *John Hancock*, whose offences are of too flagitious a nature to admit of any other consideration than that of *condign punishment*.

And to the end that no person within the limits of this proffered mercy may plead ignorance of the consequences of refusing it, I, by these presents, proclaim, not only the persons above named and excepted, but also all their adherents, associates and abettors, meaning to comprehend in those terms, all and every person and persons, of what class, denomination, or description soever, who have appeared in arms against the King's government, and shall not lay down the same as aforementioned; and likewise all such as shall so take arms after the date hereof, or who shall in any wise protect or conceal, such offenders, or assist them with money, provision, cattle, arms, ammunition, carriages, or any other necessary for subsistence or offence; or shall hold secret correspondence with them by letter, message, signal, or otherwise;—to be rebels and traitors, and as such to be treated. . . . [He then declared martial law and extended his protection to the loyalists from "the parricides of the constitution."]

Given at Boston, this twelfth day of June, in the fifteenth year of the reign of his Majesty George the Third, by the Grace of God, of Great-Britain, France, and Ireland, King, Defender of the Faith, &c. Annoque Domini, 1775.

Thomas Gage
Thomas Flucker, Secretary

36. The King's Proclamation of Rebellion

From Peter Force, *American Archives*, Fourth Series (Washington: U.S. Government Printing Office, 1837–46). Six volumes. Vol. III, p. 240.
News of the King's Proclamation of Rebellion, August 23, 1775, arrived in America on October 31, 1775. Before that date, two days after the Battle of Bunker Hill, John Dickinson, a moderate in Congress, submitted a final petition for peace. This petition, passed by Congress on July 8, was taken to England by Richard Penn, brother of Governor Penn of Pennsylvania, but the King ignored it.

A Proclamation, By The King,
For Suppressing Rebellion and Sedition.
George R.

Whereas many of our subjects in divers parts of our colonies and plantations in *North America*, misled by dangerous and ill designing men, and forgetting the allegiance which they owe to the power that has protected and supported them; after various disorderly acts committed in disturbance of the publick peace, to the obstruction of lawful commerce, and to the oppression of our loyal subjects carrying on the same; have at length proceeded to open and avowed rebellion, by arraying themselves in a hostile manner, to withstand the execution of the law, and traitorously preparing, ordering and levying war against us: And whereas, there is reason to apprehend that such rebellion hath been much promoted and encouraged by the traitorous correspondence, counsels and comfort of divers wicked and desperate persons within this Realm: To the end therefore, that none of our subjects may neglect or violate their duty through ignorance thereof, or through any doubt of the protection which the law will afford to their loyalty and zeal, we have thought [241] fit, by and with the advice of our Privy Council, to issue our Royal Proclamation, hereby, declaring, that not only all our Officers, civil and military, are obliged to exert their utmost endeavours to suppress such rebellion, and to bring the traitors to justice, but that all our subjects of this Realm, and the dominions thereunto belonging, are bound by law to be aiding and assisting in the suppression of such rebellion, and to disclose and make known all traitorous conspiracies and attempts against us, our crown and dignity; and we do accordingly strictly charge and command all our Officers, as well civil as military, and all others our obedient and loyal subjects, to use their utmost endeavours to withstand and suppress such rebellion, and to disclose and make known all treasons and traitorous conspiracies which they shall know to be against us, our crown and dignity; and for that purpose, that they transmit to one of our principal Secretaries of State, or other proper officer, due and full information of all persons who shall be found carrying on correspondence with, or in any manner or degree aiding or abetting the persons now in open arms and rebellion against our Government, within any of our Colonies and Plantations in *North America*, in order to bring to condign punishment the authors, perpetrators and abettors of such traitorous designs.

Given at our Court at St. James's the twenty-third day of August, one thousand seven hundred and seventy-five, in the fifteenth year of our reign.

God save the King.

37. On American Affairs, September–December, 1775

From *The Gentleman's Magazine*. Vol. XLV (September, 1775), p. 445.

ACCOUNT OF THE PROCEEDINGS OF THE AMERICAN COLONISTS.

From the inactivity of the armies in America, the public have been led to hope, that a plan of accommodation is now under consideration, in order to restore peace, and effectually remove every cause of future contention between the parent-state and her colonies; but, how flattering soever such hopes may be to those who have the prosperity of the whole British empire only in view, there is a spirit of malignancy discernible in the leaders of the contending parties that will not easily be subdued on either side. From this observation it needs not the gift of second sight to foretel, that no plan of reconciliation will ever be formed that will content the present Ministry and the present Continental Congress. The preparations on both sides for shedding human blood is alarming to a very high degree; but, what is still worse, inveteracy against each other begins to shew itself. The Colonists, who, hitherto, in all their remonstrances and petitions, in all their addresses and appeals, have paid a becoming deference to the parent-state (in words at least), begin now to throw aside that dutiful regard which seemed to be the leading principle that influenced their conduct, and to assume another air in their deliberations, and speak in terms that denounce defiance. In this situation, when the minds of a people are inflamed and irritated, if no gentle palliatives are applied, but, on the contrary, preparations made to crush, rather than overcome them by the more manly exercise of moderation, what is to be expected, but that, when the pillars of the fabric were made to totter, the mighty giant by whom they were shaken should perish in the ruins!

It is not by the violent and rash outrages of the multitude that the temper of a people is to be estimated; but by the deliberate and determined resolutions of those whom the voluntary, uninfluenced suffrages of their fellow-subjects have pointed out as the wisest, steadiest, and least prejudiced men amongst them; and not from these alone, but from the general concurrence of the free and independent landholders and citizens, who cordially join in executing what the others unite in planning; so that one spirit and one mind appear to animate the whole. Hence it is, that the General Congress, presuming upon the strength of that unanimity by which the Colonies are linked together, have ventured to direct the standard of opposition to be displayed, and to risk the decision of the present controversy to the longest sword.

In the mean time, it should seem, that a very considerable number of men of property in the parent-state, jealous for the honour of their country, and piqued at the rebellious spirit so universally prevalent in America, are daily joining in supplicating his Majesty to maintain and affect the authority of the British legislature, and in tendering their lives and fortunes to enable his Majesty to pursue such measures as may be found necessary to punish rebellion wherever it may appear. Such is the general state of the present contest, of which, ruinous as it must end, each party seems determined to abide the issue.

Matters are therefore hastening to a crisis; the armies are already in the field, and much distress is felt by individuals. . . .

Even the freedom of speech, which every Englishman enjoys without restraint, is denied in America to natives of the country—The voice of the multitude is the only voice that is to be heard; and the penalty of opposing it, if not tarring and feathering, is generally expulsion.

From *The Gentleman's Magazine.* Vol. XLV (October, 1775), p. 476.

The following addresses, among many others lately presented to the King, are selected as specimens of the opposite modes of treatment recommended to his Majesty, with respect to the Americans on the present critical occasion.

[Address of London Merchants against the Americans signed by 941 merchants and traders, pp. 476–77. Petition of London Merchants in Favour of the Americans signed by 1171 merchants and traders, pp. 477–78. Address of the Corporation of Bristol against the Americans signed by 901 persons, p. 478. Petition of Bristol Merchants in Favour of the Americans (number of signers not given), pp. 478–80. Address of London Liverymen against the Americans signed by 1029 Liverymen, pp. 501–2.]

From *The Gentleman's Magazine.* Vol. XLV (November, 1775), p. 543.

ACCOUNT OF THE PROCEEDINGS OF THE AMERICAN COLONISTS.

. . . If the Provincials mean only to maintain their constitutional liberties, they should act upon the defensive. Neither conquest nor plunder should be their object [a reference to the American invasion of Canada]. A firmness in maintaining what they think their just claims should mark their conduct. The rights of Englishmen cannot be denied them; nor can they avail themselves of these rights without a due submission to the parent state. The so much desired reconciliation is not so difficult a task to accomplish as people in general apprehend. . . .

If the Americans contend for any thing, and if they know what is worth contending for, it is A PERMANENT CONSTITUTION. It is to hold that which their ancestors acquired for them, and which has been confirmed to them by long continued usage. If they contend for more, it is a just reason why they should be constrained to accept of less; but if they keep within the just bounds of their fundamental grants, justice requires that they should be permitted to enjoy them. . . .

[545] It should seem that the Government was at no time better disposed to a reconciliation than at present; and that the Colonies were at no time readier to accept of reasonable terms.

From *The Gentleman's Magazine*. Vol. XLV (December, 1775), p. 561.

To Mr. John Wesley.

Sir,

I have read your calm address to the Americans [in which Rev. Mr. Wesley supported the English government] with much surprize and concern. That a man, after a long life devoted to the awful concerns of religion, and of a rigidity of morals strikingly contrasted to the times, should in his old age step forth a champion in political controversy, is a paradox only to be solved by a reflection on the general motives of such compositions. They exhibit a proof, Mr. Wesley, that the most perfect of men have hopes on earth as well as in the heavens; and indeed you have the moderation and the sincerity not to forbid us to believe so. . . .

[562] Can it be hoped, Mr. Wesley, that men acting upon the known and established systems of human policy, irritated to enthusiasm in the contention for every thing that is dear, will turn aside to listen to your Address? . . . [563] The forms of our free government have outlasted the ends for which they were instituted, and have become a mere mockery of the people for whose benefit they should operate; and in such deplorable aeras, an ultimate appeal rests in human nature, in human policy, and in human experience in the many, whose advantages are the ultimate ends of all government: and although men have seldom virtue enough to new model a constitution on an equitable basis, they will always have spirit in the end to overturn a corrupt one. Nor is there that scene of misery which you prognosticate to be expected, from even a total separation of America, or its formation into a Republic, if this country forces it by injustice into measures not originally imagined or proposed. . . .

[564] But upon what tenure do Americans hold their properties as freemen, if without the wholesome deliberations of their own delegates, who can be singly judges of American interests, they are to be bound by acts of parliament which mutilate and destroy property? Of what use are their assemblies, and their popular representatives, if they are only to be the instrument of outward oppression, and not the protectors of inward strength and independence? . . .

The constitution has been deceived. The Americans have discovered that the Monarch and the legislature are become one. They have considered an act of the British parliament as only the inhalation of the royal breath, and an equal infringement on British and American rights, which from analogy must ever suffer together. They think they are defending both; and the event will in the end discover who have been the least wise, if not who have been the least just.

And now, Mr. Wesley, I take my leave of you. You have forgot the precept of your Master, that God and Mammon cannot be served together. You have one eye on a pension, and the other upon heaven; one hand stretched out to the King, and the other raised up to God. I pray that the first may reward you, and that the last may forgive you.

AMERICUS

From *The Gentleman's Magazine.* Vol. XLV (December, 1775), p. 597.

ACCOUNT OF THE PROCEEDINGS OF THE AMERICAN COLONISTS.

Affairs respecting America continue to wear a most unpromising appearance. It is now the declared design of Government to employ the whole national force, in case the obstinacy of the confederated Provinces is not to be overcome by the terms held forth by Administration, in order to compel them to acknowledge the supremacy of the British Legislature, and to extort their submission. . . .

The levity with which this reference has been treated, and the readiness with which very many worthy citizens have been induced to encourage Government to endeavour at once to crush rebellion in the bud, and to extinguish by one decisive stroke that turbulent spirit of opposition to acts of the British Parliament, which has long been observable throughout America, must in a great measure be owing to the facility with which they have been made to believe these Colonists are to be reduced. But though this is thought an easy task in the closet, it may meet with many mortifying obstructions in the field. The nature of the contest, and the locality where it is to be maintained, are serious considerations, and, when placed in the balance against the advantages arising from the resources of Government, must be allowed their due weight. A variety of contingencies may occur to defeat the best-concerted plans of reduction before they can be carried into execution at 3000 miles distance.

IV

THE WAR AGAINST
AMERICAN INDEPENDENCE:
"A GREAT NATIONAL CAUSE"

---

38. A Political Poem

From *The Annual Register*, 1776. P. 204.

Addressed to the Rev. Dean Tucker
Said to be written by Soame Jenyns, Esq;

AMERICA

Crown'd be the man with lasting praise,
    Who first contriv'd the pin
To loose mad horses from the chaise,
    And save the necks within.

[205]   See how they prance, and bound, and skip,
    And all controul disdain!
They bid defiance to the whip,
    And tear the silken rein.

Awhile we try if art or strength
    Are able to prevail;
But, hopeless, when we find at length
    That all our efforts fail,

With ready foot the spring we press,
    Out jumps the magic plug,
Then, disengag'd from all distress,
    We sit quite safe and snug.

The pamper'd steeds, their freedom gain'd,
　　Run off full speed together;
But, having no plan ascertain'd,
　　They run they know not whither.

Boys, who love mischief and a course,
　　Enjoying the disaster,
Bawl, stop 'em! stop 'em! till they're hoarse,
　　But mean to drive them faster.

Each, claiming now his nat'ral right,
　　Scorns to obey his brother;
So they proceed to kick and bite,
　　And worry one another.

Hungry at last, and blind, and lame,
　　Bleeding at nose and eyes,
By suff'rings grown extremely tame,
　　And by experience wise,

With bellies full of liberty,
　　But void of oats and hay,
They both sneak back, their folly see,
　　And run no more away.

Let all who view th' instructive scene,
　　And patronize the plan,
Give thanks to Glo'ster's honest Dean,
　　For Tucker, thou'rt the man!

39. A Loyalist Song

From *Songs and Ballads of the American Revolution*, ed. Frank
Moore (New York: D. Appleton, 1856). P. 128.
　　Moore writes: "This song must have been very popular with
the loyalists, as four different editions were published in broad-
sides, during the two years following its first appearance, in the
'Halifax Journal,' a short time subsequent to the evacuation of
Boston." Moore dates it 1776.

BURROWING YANKEES

Ye Yankees who, mole-like, still throw up the earth,
And like them, to your follies are blind from your birth;
Attempt not to hold British troops at defiance,
True Britons, with whom you pretend an alliance.

Mistake not; such blood ne'er run in your veins,
'Tis no more than the dregs, the lees, or the drains:
Ye affect to talk big of your hourly attacks;
Come on! and I'll warrant, we'll soon see your backs.

[129] Such threats of bravadoes serve only to warm
The true British hearts, you ne'er can alarm;
The Lion once rous'd, will strike such a terror,
Shall show you, poor fools, your presumption and error.

And the time will soon come when your whole rebel race
Will be drove from the lands, nor dare show your face:
Here's a health to great George, may he fully determine,
To root from the earth all such insolent vermin.

40. The Expense of Colonies

From Adam Smith, *An Inquiry into the Nature and Causes of
the Wealth of Nations* (London: Bell, 1896). Two volumes.
Vol. II, p. 488. [First edition, 1776.]
Adam Smith (1723–90) wrote the outstanding treatise on
economics of the period. His *Wealth of Nations* originated the
study of political economy as a separate department of scientific
inquiry. It is still greatly influential because of Smith's advocacy
of free trade and individual enterprise. Smith was also a learned
moral philosopher and professor at the University of Glasgow.
He was elected to Johnson's famous club and appointed as a
commissioner of customs at the high salary of £600 a year.

It is not contrary to justice that both Ireland and America should
contribute towards the discharge of the public debt of Great Britain.
That debt has been contracted in support of the government established by the Revolution [of 1688], a government to which the protestants of Ireland owe, not only the whole authority which they at
present enjoy in their own country, but every security which they possess for their liberty, their property, and their religion; a government
to which several of the colonies of America owe the liberty, security,
and property which they have ever since enjoyed. That public debt
has been contracted in the defence, not of Great Britain alone, but of
all the different provinces of the empire; the immense debt contracted
in the late war in particular [the Seven Years War], and in a great
part of that contracted in the war before, were both properly contracted
in defence of America. . . .
[489] No oppressive aristocracy has ever prevailed in the colonies.

Even they, however, would, in point of happiness and tranquillity, gain considerably by a union with Great Britain. It would, at least, deliver them from those rancorous and virulent factions which are inseparable from small democracies, and which have so frequently divided the affections of their people, and disturbed the tranquillity of their governments, in their form so nearly democratical. In the case of a total separation from Great Britain, which, unless prevented by a union of this kind, seems very likely to take place, those factions would be ten times more virulent than ever. Before the commencement of the present disturbances, the coercive power of the mother country had always been able to restrain those factions from breaking out into anything worse than gross brutality and insult. If that coercive power were entirely taken away, they would probably soon break out into open violence and bloodshed. . . .

[490] Great Britain seems to be at least as oeconomical as any of her neighbours. The military establishment which she maintains for her own defence in time of peace, is more moderate than that of any European state which can pretend to rival her either in wealth or in power. None of those articles, therefore, seem to admit of any considerable reduction of expence. The expence of the peace establishment of the colonies was, before the commencement of the present disturbances, very considerable, and is an expence which may, and if no revenue can be drawn from them, ought certainly to be saved altogether. This constant expence in time of peace, though very great, is insignificant in comparison with what the defence of the colonies has cost us in time of war. The last war, which [491] was undertaken altogether on account of the colonies, cost Great Britain, it has already been observed, upwards of ninety millions. The Spanish war of 1739 was principally undertaken on their account; in which, and in the French war that was the consequence of it, Great Britain spent upwards of forty millions, a great part of which ought justly to be charged to the colonies. In those two wars the colonies cost Great Britain much more than double the sum which the national debt amounted to before the commencement of the first of them. Had it not been for those wars that debt might, and probably would by this time, have been completely paid; and had it not been for the colonies, the former of those wars might not, and the latter certainly would not have been undertaken. It was because the colonies were supposed to be provinces of the British empire, that this expence was laid out upon them. But countries which contribute neither revenue nor military force towards the support of the empire, cannot be considered as provinces. They may perhaps be considered as appendages, as a sort of splendid and showy equipage of the empire. But if the empire can no longer support the expence of keeping up this equipage, it ought certainly to lay it down; and if it cannot raise its revenue in proportion to its expence, it ought, at least, to accommodate its expence to its revenue. If the colonies, notwithstanding their refusal to submit to British taxes, are still to be considered as provinces of the British empire, their defence in some future war may cost Great Britain as great an expence as it ever has done in any former war. The rulers of Great Britain have, for more

than a century past, amused the people with the imagination that they possessed a great empire on the west side of the Atlantic. This empire, however, has hitherto existed in imagination only. It has hitherto been, not an empire, but the project of an empire; not a gold mine, but the project of a gold mine; a project which has cost, and which continues to cost, and which, if pursued in the same way as it has been hitherto, is likely to cost, immense expence, without likely to bring any profit; for the effects of the monopoly of the colony trade, it has been shewn, are, to the great body of the people, mere loss instead of profit. It is [492] surely now time that our rulers should either realize this golden dream, in which they have been indulging themselves, perhaps, as well as the people; or, that they should awake from it themselves and endeavour to awaken the people. If the project cannot be completed, it ought to be given up. If any of the provinces of the British empire cannot be made to contribute towards the support of the whole empire, it is surely time that Great Britain should free herself from the expence of defending those provinces in time of war, and of supporting any part of their civil or military establishments in time of peace, and endeavour to accommodate her future views and designs to the real mediocrity of her circumstances.

41. The Cost of Keeping the Colonies

Josiah Tucker, Dean of Gloucester, *A Series of Answers to Certain Popular Objections against Separating from the Rebellious Colonies* (Gloucester: R. Raikes, 1776). P. 85.

Josiah Tucker (1712–99) had a high reputation for his knowledge of trade. His tracts on the American troubles made him famous, although at the time his policy pleased nobody in England.

. . . every Man now plainly sees, that we shall never be able to retain the *Americans* in [86] due and constitutional Subjection (even supposing that we conquered them in the present war) but at such an Expense both of Men, and Money, as would, in the Event prove our Ruin.

Josiah Tucker, Dean of Gloucester, *An Humble Address and Earnest Appeal to those Respectable Personages in Great Britain and Ireland, who . . . Are the Ablest to Judge, and the Fittest to Decide, Whether a Connection, or a Separation from the Continental Colonies of America Be Most for the National Advantage* . . . (London: T. Cadell, 1776). P. 4.

Great Britain and her Colonies are at open War: And the proper and important Question arising from such a Fact is the following, What is to be done at the present crisis?

Three Schemes have been proposed; the Parliamentary,—Mr. Burke's,—and my own.

The Parliamentary Scheme is,—To maintain *vi et armis* the Supremacy of the Mother-Country over her Colonies, in as full and ample a Manner, as over any Part of the British Dominions.

[5] Mr. Burke's is, . . . To resign or relinquish the Power of the British Parliament over the Colonies, and to erect each Provincial Assembly into an independent American Parliament;—subject nevertheless to the King of Great-Britain, with his usual prerogatives:—For which Favour of acknowledging the same Sovereign, the Colonists are to be complimented with the most precious Rights, Privileges, and Advantages of British Subjects:— . . . as to their contributing any Proportion, either of Men or Money, to the Public Expence, and in Return for those Favours:—All this is entirely left to their own innate Goodness and Generosity, to do just as they please.

My Scheme (which Mr. Burke, in his last Speech of March 22, 1775, is pleased to term a *childish* one) is,—To separate totally from the Colonies, and to reject them from being Fellow-Members, and joint Partakers with us in the Privileges and Advantages of the British Empire, because they refuse to submit to the Authority and Jurisdiction of the British Legislature:—Offering at the same Time to enter into Alliances of Friendship, and Treaties of Commerce with them, as with any other sovereign, independent States.

42. On American Affairs, March–May, 1776

From *The Gentleman's Magazine.* Vol. XLVI (March, 1776), p. 136.

No other material advices from America have since our last been suffered to transpire. It is not to be supposed, however, that the Americans have continued inactive. Convinced that they have now nothing to trust to but implicit submission, or effectual resistance, they have, doubtless before this time, determined which to adopt; but in a crisis so delicate, and so important, we will not hazard a conjecture which of the two they have made their choice. If resistance, the contest will be bloody; if submission, the contest is at an end: and, by the present temper of administration, there are no real grievances of which the Colonies have just reason to complain, but what Government are ready to redress. The authority of the following paper will justify [137] this opinion. It was communicated to the General Congress in the name, though it has since been affirmed without the knowledge of Lord North, and by that Congress believed to be written by Mr. Grey Cooper, Under-Secretary to the Treasury. The paper is as follows:

"That it is earnestly hoped by all the real friends of the Americans, that the terms expressed in the Resolution of the 20th of February, 1775, will be accepted by all the Colonies who have the least affection for their King and country, or a just sense of their own interests.

"That these terms are honourable for Great Britain, and safe for the Colonies.

"That, if the Colonies are not blinded by faction, these terms will remove every grievance relative to taxation, and be the basis of a Compact between the Colonies and the Mother-Country.

"That the people in America ought, on every consideration, to be satisfied with them.

"That no farther relaxation can be admitted.

"The temper and spirit of the nation are so much against concessions, that if it were the intention of administration, they could not carry the question.

"But administration have no such intention, as they are fully and firmly persuaded that further concessions would be injurious to the Colonies as well as to Great Britain.

"That there is not the least probability of a change in administration.

"That they are perfectly united in opinion, and determined to pursue the most effectual measures, and to use the whole force of the kingdom, if it be found necessary, to reduce the rebellious and refractory Provinces and Colonies.

"There is so great a spirit in the nation against the Congress, that the people will bear the temporary distresses of a stoppage of the American trade.

"They may depend on this to be true."

From *The Gentleman's Magazine*. Vol. XLVI (April, 1776), p. 141.

It was this day [March 28, 1776] reported, with great probability of truth, that, as Government had refused to treat with the present Congress, the Americans have come to a resolution to call a new Congress, the Delegates to be appointed by their Assemblies, and not one of the old Members to be in, and that Government has actually appointed Commissioners to treat with them, and are to go express before Lord Howe sails. If this should prove true, a reconciliation between the Colonies and the Mother Country may soon be expected to take place.

From *The Gentleman's Magazine*. Vol. XLVI (May, 1776), p. 218.

[FROM THE KING'S SPEECH CLOSING PARLIAMENT]

My Lords and Gentlemen,

We are engaged in a great national cause, the prosecution of which must inevitably be attended with many difficulties and much expence: but when we consider that the essential rights and interests of the whole empire are deeply concerned with the issue of it, and can have no safety or security but in that constitutional subordination for which we are contending, I am convinced that you will not think any price too high for the preservation of such objects.

I will still entertain a hope, that my rebellious subjects may be awakened to a sense of their errors, and that, by a voluntary return to their duty, they will justify me in bringing about the favourite wish of my heart, the restoration of harmony, and the reestablishment of order and happiness in every part of my dominions. But, if a due submission should not be obtained from such motives and such dispositions on their part, I trust that I shall be able, under the blessing of Providence, to effectuate it by a full exertion of the great force with which you have intrusted me.

43. A British Officer on the American Declaration of Independence

From Stephen Kemble, *Kemble Papers* (New York: Collections of the New York Historical Society, Vol. XVI, 1884). P. 81.

Kemble, born in New Jersey in 1740, was Deputy Adjutant-General of the British forces in North America from 1773 to 1779 under Generals Thomas Gage, Sir William Howe, and Sir Henry Clinton.

Sunday, July 14th [1776]. This day a Flag of Truce [containing an Act of Oblivion] sent by Lord Howe to New York was stopped by the rebels off Red Hook; it carried a Letter for Mr. Washington, which was not received as the Title was not thought honorable enough, being only directed to Geo: Washington, Esqr. . . . From appearances think the Rebels will not listen to any proffers for an Accommodation; their declaration of Independancy [*sic*] is a convincing proof that they will oppose every mode for a Reconciliation unless on their own terms.

44. On American Affairs, July–December, 1776

From *The Gentleman's Magazine.* Vol. XLVI (July, 1776), p. 330.

. . . there is no reasonable ground to conclude . . . that it is either the wish or intention of the moderate and sensible part of the Americans to withdraw their obedience from the parent-state. On the contrary, all America, by which we would be understood to mean a large majority of the industrious inhabitants of that continent, think it their greatest happiness to be considered as the free subjects of a Sovereign of the Brunswick line, by whom alone they can hope to be confirmed in their civil and religious rights, to have their complaints candidly considered, and their grievances redressed; . . . Why, then, should we not hope that the King's troops will be received as friends, and that, instead of the destroying sword, the Generals do carry with them the olive-branch, and that the first news we receive may announce the preliminaries of peace.

From *The Gentleman's Magazine.* Vol. XLVI (August, 1776), p. 377.

In the preceding part of this Magazine [pp. 361–62] the reader will find the Declaration of Independency issued by the American Congress, with a recapitulation of the grievances which have forced them into that desperate measure. Whether those grievances were real or imaginary, or whether they did or did not deserve a parliamentary inquiry, we will not presume to decide. The ball is now struck, and time only can shew where it will rest.

From *The Gentleman's Magazine.* Vol. XLVI (September, 1776), p. 403.

THOUGHTS ON THE LATE DECLARATION
OF THE AMERICAN CONGRESS.

The declaration is without doubt of the most extraordinary nature both with regard to sentiment and language, and considering that the motive of it is to assign some justifiable reasons of their separating themselves from Great Britain, unless it had been fraught with more truth and sense, might well have been spared, as it reflects no honour upon either their erudition or honesty.

We hold, they say, these truths to be self-evident: That all men are created equal. In what are they created equal? Is it in size, strength, understanding, [404] figure, moral or civil accomplishments, or situation of life? Every plough-man knows that they are not created equal in any of these. All men, it is true, are equally created, but what is this to the purpose? It certainly is no reason why the Americans should turn rebels because the people of Great Britain are their fellow-creatures, i.e. are created as well as themselves. It may be a reason why they should not rebel, but most indisputably is none why they should. They therefore have introduced their self-evident truths, either through ignorance, or by design, with a self-evident falsehood: since I will defy any American rebel, or any of their patriotic retainers here in England, to point out to me any two men, throughout the whole World, of whom it may with truth be said that they are created equal.

The next of their self-evident truths is, that all men are endowed by their Creator with certain unalienable rights (the meaning of which words they appear not at all to understand); among which are life, liberty, and the pursuit of happiness. Let us put some of these words together. All men are endowed by their Creator with the unalienable right of life. How far they may be endowed with this unalienable right I do not yet say, but, sure I am, these gentry assume to themselves an unalienable right of talking nonsense. Was it ever heard since the introduction of blunders into the world that life was a man's right? Life or animation is of the essence of human nature, and is that without which one is not a man, and therefore to call life a right, is to betray a total ignorance of the meaning of words. A living man, i.e. a man with life, hath a right to a great many things; but to say that a man with life hath a right to be a man with life is so purely American, that I believe the texture of no other brain upon the face of the earth will admit the idea. Whatever it may be, I have tried to make an idea out of it, but own I am unable. . . .

The next assigned cause and ground of their rebellion is, that every man hath an unalienable right to liberty; and here the words, as it happens, are not nonsense, but then they are not true: slaves there are in America, and where there are slaves, there liberty is alienated.

If the Creator hath endowed man with an unalienable right to liberty, no reason in the world will justify the abridgment of that liberty, and a man hath a right to do every thing that he thinks proper without controul or restraint: and upon the same principle there can be no such things as servants, subjects, or government of any kind whatsoever. In a word, every law that hath been in the world since the formation of Adam, gives the lye to this self-evident truth, (as they are pleased to term it,) because every law, divine or human, that is or hath been in the world, is an abridgment of man's liberty. . . .

An Englishman

From *The Gentleman's Magazine.* Vol. XLVI (September, 1776), p. 429.

Letters, seemingly authentic, inform that the 4th of July was set apart, throughout the Colonies, by order of the American Congress, as a day of fasting and prayer, preparatory to their dedicating their country to God. This is the more probable, as they have all along prefaced their operations with an appeal to the Divine Being; but the account of the ceremony of laying a Crown on the Bible, and dividing it into 13 parts, wants confirmation. . . .

[430]   PROCEEDINGS OF THE AMERICAN COLONIES

Every thing at present wears a gloomy appearance; and should the summer be suffered to elapse without a change of circumstances, little good can be expected from a winter's campaign in that country, where the severity of the weather, and the want of the comforts of necessary refreshment, will cut off more men than the destroying sword.

But much is yet to be expected from the formidable force of Gen. Howe, when aided by the fleet commanded by his brother! Be it so; yet the undertaking is confessedly desperate, and consequently the success doubtful; and should it miscarry, what a carnage! what confusion! what consternation will it not spread, not among the troops only, the immediate sufferers, but through the whole extent of this infatuated nation! What exultation to our enemies abroad, and what humiliation to our friends! In this critical moment of national danger, when our All is at hazard, is it criminal to utter the word *reconciliation!* Must he be marked as an enemy to his Sovereign, and his country, who wishes to unite the hearts and affections of a brave and loyal people in one common cause! RECONCILIATION! How is that to be effected? The answer is (negatively), Not by the sword, for that will never effect it. The people who have been represented without courage, without discipline, without experience, without commanders, without engineers, and without the means of defence, have, upon trial, been found possessed of all these advantages. The country that was to have been ransacked from one end to the other with 5000 veterans, is already hardly accessible in any part to 50,000 of the best troops the world can produce, headed by Generals, who should they fall, where are their equals to supply their loss? Where then is the hope of reduction by force?

From *The Gentleman's Magazine.* Vol. XLVI (October, 1776), p. 450.

Mr. Urban,

I think it may fairly be presumed, that the gentleman, upon whose strictures I am animadverting, sets no very high value on his own natural rights because he does what he can to destroy them. He would prove, if he could, that men are not created equal: and enquires, 'Is it in size, strength, understanding, figure, moral or civil accomplishments? Every ploughman (says he) knows that they are not created equal in any of these.' But I ask, whoever affirmed they were? Nevertheless, as, originally, any one man had as much right to reign and rule over another man, as that other man had to reign and rule over him, it is certainly in this sense (the sense of the declaration) a self-evident TRUTH, that all men were created equal. . . .

He would prove too, if he could, that men have no right to life, liberty, and the pursuit of happiness. Let him not therefore complain, nor make resistance, should any one attempt to deprive him of life or liberty: and should his task-master command him to hew wood and draw water, let him not murmur; for, according to his notion, no man has a right to pursue his own plan of happiness.

This gentleman, I presume, can demonstrate, that, since the world was made, there never existed any such thing as oppression among mankind. Indeed, if his arguments are good, he has already done it: for certainly there can be no oppression where there are no natural rights. True it is, the phrase used in the declaration is *unalienable* rights: and surely unalienable they are, if natural:—rights which men have received from God, together with their nature, are inseparable from it. . . .

Unalienable means, according to this witty gentleman, that which cannot be transferred to another. If he had been wise, he would have known, that to *alienate*, strictly speaking, signifies to *estrange from* or to *take away*: and that certainly a thing may be taken [451] away from a man, which yet cannot be transferred to another. . . . Like a consummate logician, he adds,—'To say that a man with life hath a right to be a man with life, is so purely American, that I believe the texture of no other brain upon the face of the earth will admit the idea.' In reply I will only observe, that as, according to his account, a man with life has no *right* to be a man with life, if, at any time, a highwayman should happen to pistol this gentleman, in so doing, by his way of reasoning, the highwayman will do him no *wrong*.

To prove that mankind have no unalienable right to enjoy liberty, this gentleman argues thus: 'Slaves there are in America, and where there are slaves, there liberty is alienated.' But, surely, tho' I should ever be so unhappy as to lose my liberty, it will not follow that I have no right to it. Does not all the world know that great numbers have a right to enjoy what is yet with-holden from them? . . .

Further, to prove the matter more fully, he affirms, that every law, which has been in the world since the formation of Adam, gives the lye to this self evident truth, as the congress are pleased to term it: (viz. that every man has an unalienable right to liberty:) because, says he, 'every law, divine or human, that is or hath been in the world, is an abridgement of liberty.'—Divine laws have nothing to do here.—As for human laws, if they take away *liberty* they neither do nor can take away the *right* to it. Nothing, however, can be more certain than that, if the existence of human laws will prove that mankind have no right to liberty, this gentleman (clever as he is) will be a little puzzled to shew any reason why he ought not to be a slave; and, indeed, if he were, seeing he is so zealous an advocate for slavery, in my judgment, he would deserve as little pity as any other slave. . . .

Yours, &c.
PHILANDER

From *The Gentleman's Magazine.* Vol. XLVI (December, 1776), p. 547.

STRICTURES ON PHILANDER'S DEFENCE OF THE AMERICAN CONGRESS

Mr. Urban,

. . . The Englishman [*Gent. Mag.*, September, 1776] has said nothing, that I know of, against men's natural rights; but only that all laws, human and divine, give the lye to the American assertion, because they were formed purposely to abridge these rights; that is, in some cases to *alienate* them. God himself has set the example of alienating, where necessary, those rights he gave us with our natures.

The Congress, it seems, have pleaded, in excuse for having established a merciless tyranny, that it is *a self-evident truth that all men are created equal.* To defend this absurdity, their interpreter tells us, that by *all men* is here meant only those *original* men who lived in a state of Nature, and of those one man had as much right to reign or rule as another.—But what has this far-fetched case to do with a people in a state of Society? And even, if it *was* applicable, it is no *self-evident* truth, nor, I believe, any truth at all; for it is likely (I think most likely) that men were at first created with different capacities and mental powers, some formed to rule, and others to obey:—in which sense we might properly say, with the Son of Sirach, that, "in the divisions of the nations of the whole earth, God set a ruler over every people." . . .

We will suppose, then, that our enemies understand the word *alienate*, as their interpreter asserts, in the sense of *taking away;*—the *Englishman* also is *wise* enough to understand it in the same sense. Liberty, says he, may be taken away, for there are slaves in America. I will add, that the *right* too may be taken away, for there are slaves on the river Thames; all of them legally, and some at least justly, deprived of freedom. The grave gentleman's objection to this is *monstrous;*—human laws, if they take away liberty, neither do nor CAN take away the right to it:—an idea subversive of all subordination, magistracy, justice, and every legal controul, by which alone societies, and indeed all the *rights* of mankind, are supported. As for divine laws, with one dash of the pen he renders them perfectly nugatory, by saying that they have "nothing to do with the abridgement of liberty." He is angry, perhaps, that they have so much to do *here*, since they are so *pointedly* against American conduct.

But I will tell the angry gentleman, that a man may really have the *things themselves*, and yet have alienated or parted with his *right* to them. A rebel, a traytor, for instance, may be *a man with life*; and the same may he said of the highwayman who pistols my merry friend the *Englishman*. A *man with liberty*, likewise, may not have a *right* to be *a man with liberty*; if, for instance, he obstinately avows his resolution of committing the above crimes:—and, as to the last instance, I cannot but think, that, if a man was breaking into a chamber-window at High Wycomb, with an intention of Cuckolding my grave antagonist *Philander*, he would *not* be justified in so doing merely because he thought, with the Americans, that he had an *unalienable right to the pursuit of happiness!*

Such are the *ostensible* reasons which our enemies give for becoming *self-evident* parricides (and *self-evident* fools too, by throwing away the lives, liberties, and happiness which they had). They have other latent reasons which I cannot now consider such as their *unalienable* right of avarice, and their *unalienable* right of ambition, etc. But there is one really plausible reason given by our enemies for their rebellion (and but one that I know of), and that is, "that they have a right to their property, *unalienable*, but by an assembly in which they are *represented*." As this is a matter of the highest importance, I may perhaps take the liberty of considering it in a future letter.

Patrio-Mastix

45. British Forces in America

From *The Annual Register*, 1776. P. 166.

[Howe's army totaled about 35,000, if the different sections could have been united at the beginning of the campaign:] . . . This force . . . was truly formidable, and such as no part of the New World had ever seen before. Nor was it, perhaps, exceeded by any army in Europe of an equal number, whether considered with respect to the excellency of the troops, the abundant military stores and warlike materials, or the goodness and number of artillery of all sorts with which it was provided. It was, besides, supported by a very numerous fleet, particularly well adapted to the nature of the service.

V

BRITISH CONFUSION AND
AMERICAN VICTORY

---

46. A Poet's Plea for Peace

From *The Annual Register*, 1777. P. 196.

ODE FOR THE NEW-YEAR, 1777
Written by W. Whitehead, Esq.

. . . Enough of slaughter have ye known,
Ye wayward children of a distant clime;
   For you we heave the kindred groan,
We pity your misfortune and your crime.
   Stop, parricides, the blow,
   O find another foe!
And hear a parent's dear request,
Who longs to clasp you to her yielding breast.

   What change would ye require? What form
     Ideal, floats in fancy's sky?
Ye fond enthusiasts, break the charm,
     And let cool reason clear the mental eye.
     On Britain's well-mix'd state alone
     True liberty has fix'd her throne,
Where law, not man, an equal rule maintains:
Can freedom e'er be found where many a tyrant reigns?

     United, let us all those blessings find,
     The God of nature meant mankind.
       Whate'er of error, ill redrest,
       Whate'er of passion, ill represt,

Whate'er the wicked have conceived,
And folly's heedless sons believ'd,
Let all lie buried in oblivion's flood,
And our great cement be, the public good.

47. On American Affairs, January–November, 1777

From *The Gentleman's Magazine*. Vol. XLVII (January, 1777), p. 25.

Arts made use of by the American Leaders to spirit the People to take up Arms against the Mother Country, from a Sermon preached before the University of Oxford, by Myles Cooper, LL.D., President of King's College, New York, and Fellow of Queen's, Oxford.

["This Gentleman," the editor remarks, "was driven from America, and narrowly escaped with Life."]

. . . If it be right in a sovereign state to attempt the forcible suppression of a wicked and unprovoked rebellion, after all persuasive methods have failed, then this war is just and necessary. If it be right in a Prince to afford protection to his loyal and best subjects, against the tyranny and oppression of his worst and most disloyal, then the war is just, necessary, and laudable; for even in these revolted provinces there are still thousands and ten thousands of his Majesty's subjects, of inflexible loyalty, who could be induced by no menaces or persecutions to bow the knee to the *Baal of Independency*, or to swerve at all from the duties of allegiance. In this number are included a large proportion of the men of property, the greater part of the members of the Church of England, and in several of the colonies, all its Clergy without exception, to say nothing of others. These, from the beginning, have been the objects of republican rage, and fanatic malignity. . . .

One important object of this war, as hath been intimated, and which proves it to be a *just* one, is to protect those loyalists, who have been thus persecuted for adhering to their allegiance, and to restore them to their legal rights, and, till now, undoubted possessions. For these purposes the sword is unsheathed, and the battle set in array. It is with a view that such *monstrous* "wickedness of the wicked may come to an end," (to use the language of my text,) and that "the just may be established"; or, in the words of the Royal Proclamation, that the King's "loyal subjects within his colonies and provinces in North America, may be delivered from the violence, injustice, and tyranny of those daring rebels, who have assumed to themselves the exercise of arbitrary power." Never was there a more worthy object of military exertion; never was the power of any nation better employed.

From *The Gentleman's Magazine*. Vol. XLVII (February, 1777), p. 76.

Mr. Urban,

It is curious and not unentertaining to see how doctors (I mean doctors of divinity) differ.

Doctor Miles Cooper, in his Fast Sermon, at Oxford, p. 12., says thus:—

"It is indeed difficult to assign any reasons that will justify the rebellion of subjects against the sovereign authority. *Submission to the higher powers* is at least enjoined upon Christians under the severest penalty. But were Christianity altogether out of the question, yet the insurrection of subjects against their rightful governors, is condemned by those laws which are fundamental to society."

Doctor John Butler, on the other hand, in his Fast Sermon before the House of Commons, says thus, p. 7.—

"No man, who breathes the air of this country, and feels the benefit of it, would abruptly, or too severely, censure any exercise of liberty. There was a time when lawful resistance was treated as a contradiction in terms; thanks to some great names, who have speculated upon the rights of mankind [77] and some greater worthies who have struggled for them; we have discovered that resistance may not only be necessary, but that it may be lawful, that it may even be meritorious."

Now, from these two paragraphs, several pleasant observations might be made. I shall only observe, that if Dr. John Butler be right, then Dr. Miles Cooper is NOBODY. . . . And if Dr. Miles Cooper tells truth, then Dr. John Butler tells (I would not use a coarse word) its opposite. . . .

"*Who shall decide, when doctors disagree?*" Not I truly; these points are too profound for me; let those deep judges, your fierce Whigs, and staunch Tories, determine such difficult matters. I am no party-man, and only propose these disquisitions to the examination of the politician, and for the amusement of the curious. . . .

L.R.

From *The Gentleman's Magazine*. Vol. XLVII (April, 1777), p. 168.

Mr. Urban,

. . . I appeal to every candid breast, upon examining American measures, whether it is not morally impossible but they must have aimed at independence all along: besides, their only plausible pretence is a distant fear that they might in future be oppressed by not being represented. Should this time ever have arrived, and redress been denied, which is next to impossible, they would then have been stronger in themselves, they would have had all honest men (no mean party, I hope,) on their side, and should they deem this an advantage, they might then have resisted without violation of religion and conscience. . . .

American rebellion, compared to a war with France or Spain, is as the murther of a deserving parent to what is called an affair of honour. But this revolt, he [Philander] asserts, has been owing entirely to ourselves!——I repress the sentiments of indignation, which every honest man must feel on such an occasion. Let us hear, however, how this writer attempts to throw off the blame from the unnatural offspring. He gives us three reasons:—the first is that the petition [the Olive Branch Petition] brought by Mr. Penn was rejected. What I remember of this petition, besides its specious pretences, is, that the very outset of it appeared to be industriously affronting to their Sovereign; that they profess in the body of it, that they had *taken up arms*; and for fear it should miss of its aim, it was signed by two persons at that time proclaimed traitors!

Secondly, we have withdrawn our protection, &c.——This is too silly to dwell upon. There is always a point in such cases, where tenderness and compassion must end; and folly and madness would begin, should we continue protection to inveterate and causeless rebels.

Thirdly, we have employed foreign troops—the only mischief of which is, as far as I can see, that we did not pay these rebels the compliment of consulting them about the means of punishing their own unparalleled baseness. . . .

Patrio-Mastix

From *The Gentleman's Magazine.* Vol. XLVII (November, 1777), p. 527.

POLITICAL CHARACTER OF THE AMERICANS
(FROM THE PA. PACKET)

The People of America, with respect to their political characters, may be divided into the five following classes: 1) Rank tories. 2) Moderate men. 3) Timid whigs. 4) Furious whigs. 5) Staunch whigs.

I. The rank tories are advocates for unconditional submission to Great Britain. They rejoice in every misfortune that befalls the United States. They fabricate lies to deceive and intimidate the people of America. They prefer money stamped with the mark of the beast, and at the same time they employ their utmost ingenuity to depreciate the money issued by the Congress and by conventions. They sicken at the names of the Congress and of General Washington. They esteem no arts too base to injure or betray their friends of America. They are in love with slavery and have no more relish for the sweets of liberty than they have for the enjoyment of the kingdom of heaven.

II. The moderate men are advocates for the situation of the colonies in the year 1763. They are influenced either, 1. by a connection with men who hold offices under the old governments; or, 2dly, by the fondness for those luxuries which were introduced among us by our connection with Great Britain; or 3dly, by an attachment to the pomp and hierarchy of the church of England. In this respect they resemble the children of Israel, who say of themselves, "We remember the filth which we did eat in Egypt freely; the cucumbers and the melons, and the leeks, and the onions, and the garlic; but now our soul is dried away: there is nothing at all besides this manna before our eyes." Numbers xi. 5, 6. They think freedom too dear when purchased with the temporary loss of tea, coffee, sugar, wine and rum. Good mutton, beef, bread, milk, and the fruits of our earth, which are the produce of our country, appear "as nothing at all in their eyes." Lastly, it is characteristic of a moderate man to hate the people of New England, and to love all rank tories.

III. The timid whigs speak of the power of Britain as if the Supreme Being had delegated his omnipotence to that island. They entertain a false idea of the power and resources of America. The loss of a few riflemen in a skirmish, or of a fort, or a village, induce them to conclude that the contest is over, and that America is subdued. They have no objections to independence, provided we are able to maintain it. They are perpetually harping upon the expense of the war. After the loss of a village, or a fort, they refuse to take continental money, and fly into some obscure corner of the country for safety; but upon the news of a victory they come forth, appear stout, and wonder that any man should ever be afraid of the power of Britain. One timid whig admitted into the councils of America does more mischief than ten rank tories. Avarice is generally the source of his timidity.

IV. The furious whigs injure the cause of liberty as much by their violence as the timid whigs do by their fears. They think the destruction of Howe's army of less consequence than the detection and punishment of the most insignificant tory. They think the common forms of justice should be suspended towards a tory criminal; and that a man who only speaks against our common defence, should be tomahawked, scalped, and roasted alive. Lastly, they are all cowards, and skulk under the cover of an office, or a sickly family, when they are called to oppose our enemy in the field. Woe to that state or community that is governed by this class of men.

V. The staunch whigs are friends to liberty from principle. They are undismayed with misfortunes, and are not usually elated with trifling advantages over our enemies. They are implacable in their hatred to the court of Britain. They prefer the annihilation of the continent to reconciliation, and they had rather renounce their existence than their beloved independency. They have an unshaken faith in the divine justice, and they esteem it a mark of equal folly and impiety to believe that Great Britain can ever subdue America. They are friends to order and good government, and are both just and merciful in the exercise of power. Lastly, they esteem the loss of property, of friends, and even of life itself, as nothing when compared with the loss of liberty. Let America look to this class of men alone for her salvation in the cabinet and the field.

48. Pitt Defends the Rebels Again

From John Almon, *Anecdotes of the Life of . . . William Pitt, Earl of Chatham* (London: J. S. Jordan, 1793). Three volumes. Vol. II, p. 431.
During the whole of the year 1776 Chatham was detained in the country by disease. It was not until May 20, 1777, that he again appeared in Parliament. He came wrapped in flannels and supported upon crutches.

The gathering storm might break; it has already opened and in part burst. . . . If an end be not put to this war, there is an end to this country. . . . They are rebels; but what are they rebels for? Surely not for defending their unquestionable rights? What have these rebels done heretofore? I remember when they raised four regiments on their own bottom, and took Louisbourg from the veteran troops of France. But their excesses have been great. I do not mean their panegyric; but must observe in attenuation, the erroneous and infatuated counsels, which have prevailed—the door to mercy and justice has been shut against them. . . . [432] America has carried us through four wars, and will now carry us to our death, if things were not taken in time.

49. Samuel Johnson's Opinions on Slavery, Taxation, and Parliament

From James Boswell, *Life of Samuel Johnson*, ed. George Birkbeck Hill (New York: Harper & Bros., 1891). Four volumes. Vol. III, p. 227. [First published in 1791.]

[*From the year 1777*]

After supper I accompanied him to his apartment, and at my request he dictated to me an argument in favour of the negro who was then claiming his liberty, in an action in the Court of Sessions in Scotland. He had always been very zealous against slavery in every form, in which I, with all [228] deference, thought that he discovered 'a zeal without knowledge.' Upon one occasion, when in company with some very grave men at Oxford, his toast was, 'Here's to the next insurrection of the negroes in the West Indies.' His violent prejudice against our West Indian and American settlers appeared whenever there was an opportunity. Towards the conclusion of his *Taxation no Tyranny*, he says, 'how is it that we hear the loudest *yelps* for liberty among the drivers of negroes?' . . .

[233] I unluckily entered upon the controversy concerning the right of Great-Britain to tax America, and attempted to argue in favour of our fellow-subjects on the other side of the Atlantick. I insisted that America might be very well governed, and made to yield sufficient revenue by the means of *influence*, as exemplified in Ireland, while the people [234] might be pleased with the imagination of their participating in the British constitution, by having a body of representatives, without whose consent money could not be exacted from them. Johnson could not bear my thus opposing his avowed opinion, which he had exerted himself with an extreme degree of heat to enforce; and the violent agitation into which he was thrown, while answering, or rather reprimanding me, alarmed me so, that I heartily repented of my having unthinkingly introduced the subject. I myself, however, grew warm, and the change was great, from the calm state of philosophical discussion in which we had a little before been pleasingly employed.

I talked of the corruption of the British Parliament, in which I alleged that any question, however unreasonable or unjust, might be carried by a venal majority; and I spoke with high admiration of the Roman Senate, as if composed of men sincerely desirous to resolve what they should think best for their country. My friend would allow no such [235] character to the Roman Senate; and he maintained that the British Parliament was not corrupt, and that there was no occasion to corrupt its members; asserting, that there was hardly ever any question of great importance before Parliament, any question in which a man might not very well vote either upon one side or the other. He said there had been none in his time except that respecting America.

50. Burgoyne's Surrender and Thoughts of Stopping the War

From *The Annual Register*, 1777. P. 176.
The following excerpt deals with General Burgoyne's expedition and surrender.

. . . undertaken with the most confident hopes, and for some time pursued with very flattering appearances of success. It was supposed the principal means for the immediate reduction of the colonies; but it has only served, in conjunction with other operations, which in the first instance have succeeded better, to demonstrate the difficulties attending the subjugation of a numerous people at a great distance, in an extensive country marked with strong lines, and abounding in strong natural defences, if the resources of war are not exceedingly deficient, and that the spirit of the people is in any degree proportioned to their situation. It may now, whatever it was in the beginning, be a matter of doubt, whether any superiority of power, of wealth, and of discipline, will be found to over-ballance such difficulties.

It would not be easy at present, as many things necessary to be known have not yet been fully explained, and improper, as the whole is still a subject of public investigation, to attempt forming any judgment upon the general plan or system of this campaign. The general conduct of the war this year has already undergone much censure; and undoubtedly, the sending of the grand army at such a distance to the southward, whilst the inferior was left struggling with insurmountable difficulties in the north, when it would seem that their junction or cooperation, would have rendered them greatly superior to any force which could have been possibly brought to oppose their progress, seems, in this view of things, not to be easily accounted for.

51. In Favor of Stopping Hostilities

From John Almon, *Anecdotes of the Life of . . . William Pitt, Earl of Chatham* (London: J. S. Jordan, 1793). Three volumes. Vol. II, p. 448.
  The following excerpts are from Chatham's speech delivered in the House of Lords, November 20, 1777, the occasion being the debate on the King's Address at the opening of the new parliamentary session. Burgoyne's surrender was not yet known in England, but the military news was unfavorable. Chatham's amendment to the Address to the Throne concerning American affairs was defeated by a vote of 97 to 24.

My Lords, this ruinous and ignominious situation, where we cannot act with success, nor suffer with honour, calls upon us to remonstrate in the strongest and loudest language of truth to rescue the ear of Majesty from the delusions which surround it. The desperate state of our arms abroad is in part known: no man thinks more highly of them than I do: I love and honour the English troops: I know their virtues and their valor: I know they can achieve anything except impossibilities: and I know that the conquest of English America is an impossibility. You cannot, I venture to say it, you CANNOT conquer America. Your armies last war effected everything that could be effected; and what was it? It cost a numerous army under the command of a most able gene- [449] ral, now a noble Lord [Lord Amherst] in this House, a long and laborious campaign, to expel five thousand Frenchmen from French America. My Lord, you *cannot conquer America.* What is your present situation there? We do not know the worst; but we know that in three campaigns we have done nothing, and suffered much. Besides the sufferings, perhaps *total loss* of the Northern force; the best appointed army that ever took the field, commanded by Sir William Howe, has retired from the American lines; he was obliged to relinquish his attempt, and, with great delay and danger, to adopt a new and distant plan of operations. We shall soon know, and in any event have reason to lament, what may have happened since. As to conquest, therefore, my Lords, I repeat [450] it is impossible. You may swell every expense, and every effort still more extravagantly; pile and accumulate every assistance you can buy or borrow; traffic and barter with every little pitiful German Prince that sells and sends his subjects to the shambles of a foreign country; your efforts are for ever vain and impotent—doubly so from this mercenary aid on which you rely; for it irritates, to an incurable resentment, the minds of your enemies—to overrun them with the sordid sons of rapine and of plunder; devoting them and their possessions to the rapacity of hireling cruelty! If I were an American, as I am an Englishman, while a foreign troop was landed in my country, I never would lay down my arms; never! never! never! . . .

[452] My Lords, no man wishes for the due dependence of [453] America on this country more than I do. To preserve it, and not confirm that state of independence into which *your measures* hitherto have *driven* them, is the object which we ought to unite in attaining. The Americans, contending for their rights against the arbitrary exactions, I love and admire; it is the struggle of free and virtuous patriots: but contending for independency and total disconnection from England, as an Englishman, I cannot wish them success: for, in a due constitutional dependency, including the ancient supremacy of this country in regulating their commerce and navigation, consists the mutual happiness and prosperity both of England and America. She derived assistance and protection from us; and we reaped from her the most important advantages:—She was, indeed, the fountain of our wealth, the nerve of our strength, the nursery and basis of our naval power. It is our duty, therefore, my Lords, if we wish to save our country, most seriously to endeavour the recovery of these most beneficial subjects: and in this perilous crisis, perhaps the present moment may be [454] the only one in which we can hope for success: for in their negotiations with France, they have, or think they have, reason to complain: though it be notorious that they have received from that power important supplies and assistance of various kinds, yet it is certain they expected it in a more decisive and immediate degree. America is in ill humour with France, on some points that have not entirely answered her expectations: let us wisely take advantage of every possible moment of reconciliation. Besides, the natural disposition of America herself still leans towards England—to the old habits of connection and mutual interest that united both countries. This *was* the established sentiment of all the Continent; and still, my Lords, in the great and principal part, the sound part of America, this wise and affectionate disposition prevails; and there is a very considerable part of America yet sound—the middle and the southern provinces.

Some parts may be factious and blind to their true interests; but if we express a wise and benevolent disposition to communicate with them [455] those immutable rights of nature, and those constitutional liberties, to which they are equally entitled with ourselves, by a conduct so just and humane, we shall confirm the favourable and conciliate the adverse. I say, my Lords, the rights and liberties to which they are equally entitled, with ourselves, but no more. I would participate to them every enjoyment and freedom which the colonizing subjects of a free state can possess, or wish to possess; and I do not see why they should not enjoy every fundamental right in their property, and every original substantial liberty, which Devonshire or Surrey, or the county I live in, or any other county in England, can claim; reserving always, as the sacred right of the mother-country, the due constitutional dependency of the Colonies. The inherent supremacy of the State in regulating and protecting the navigation and commerce of all her subjects, is necessary for the mutual benefit and preservation of every part, to constitute and preserve the prosperous arrangement of the whole Empire.

[456] The sound parts of America, of which I have spoken, must be sensible of these great truths and of their real interests. America is not in that state of desperate and contemptible rebellion, which this country has been deluded to believe. It is not a wild and lawless banditti, who having nothing to lose, might hope to snatch something from public convulsions; many of their leaders and great men have a great stake in this great contest:—the gentleman who conducts their armies, I am told, has an estate of four or five thousand pounds a year; and when I consider these things, I cannot but lament the inconsiderate violence of our penal acts, our declarations of treason and rebellion, with all the fatal effects of attainder and confiscation. . . .

[458] You cannot conciliate America by your present measures; you cannot subdue her [459] by your present, or by any measures. . . . What then, can you do? You cannot conquer, you cannot gain, but you can address, you can lull the fears and anxieties of the moment into an ignorance of the danger that should produce them. But, my Lords, the time demands the language of truth: we must not now apply the flattering unction of servile compliance, or blind complaisance. In a just and necessary war, to maintain the rights or honour of my country, I would strip the shirt from my back to support it. But in such a war as this, unjust in its principles, impracticable in its means, and ruinous in its consequences, I would not contribute a single effort, nor a single shilling. I do not call for vengeance on the heads of those who have been guilty; I only recommend them to make their retreat: let them walk off; and let them make haste, or they may be assured that speedy and condign punishment will overtake them. . . .

[462] My Lords, to encourage and confirm that innate [American] inclination to this country, [463] founded on every principle of affection, as well as consideration of interest—to restore that favourable disposition into a permanent and powerful reunion with this country— to revive the mutual strength of the empire; again, to awe the House of Bourbon, instead of meanly truckling, as our present calamities

compel us, to every insult of French caprice and Spanish punctilio—
to reestablish our commerce—to re-assert our rights and our honour—
to confirm our interests, and renew our glories for ever (a consumma-
tion most devoutly to be endeavoured! and which, I trust, may yet arise
from reconciliation with America)—I have the honour of submitting
to you the following amendment, which I move to be inserted after
the two first paragraphs of the Address:—

'And that this House does most humbly advise and supplicate his
Majesty to be pleased to cause the most speedy and effectual measures
to be taken for restoring peace in America; and that no time may be lost
in proposing an immediate cessation of hostilities there, in order to the
opening a treaty for the final settlement [464] of the tranquillity of
these invaluable provinces, by a removal of the unhappy causes of this
ruinous civil war; and by a just and adequate security against the return
of the like calamities in times to come. And this House desire to offer
the most dutiful assurances to his Majesty, that they will, in due time,
cheerfully co-operate with the magnanimity and tender goodness of
his Majesty for the preservation of his people, by such explicit and
most solemn declarations and provisions of fundamental and irre-
vocable laws, as may be judged necessary for the ascertaining and fixing
for ever the respective rights of Great Britain and her colonies.' [The
amendment was negatived.]

52. On the Military Situation in America, 1777

From Frederic Harrison, *Chatham* (New York: Macmillan, 1905).
P. 233.

When the news of Burgoyne's surrender came at the end of 1777,
Chatham defended the general and his army, and justly declared them
to have "been sacrificed to the ignorance, temerity, and incapacity of
ministers." He revived his protest against the use of Indians—"a
pollution of our national character; a stigma which all the waters of the
Delaware and Hudson would never wash away." He challenged the
ministers to recall the mercenaries and to disband the savages—to
withdraw our troops entirely. On the motion for an adjournment of
the House for six weeks, he again spoke on 11th December 1777. He
insisted that the hereditary Council of the nation should not take
holiday when the nation was in mourning. Nay more, it was in imminent peril—"Safe no longer than its enemies think proper to permit." He reviewed the state of our naval and military defences, and
exposed their weakness. "They told you in the beginning, that 15,000
men would traverse America, with scarcely the appearance of interruption. Two campaigns have passed since they gave us this assurance;

treble that number has been employed; and one of your armies, which composed two-thirds of the force by which America was to be subdued, has been totally destroyed, and is now led captive through those provinces you call rebellious. Those men whom you called cowards, poltroons, runaways and knaves, are become victorious over your veteran troops; and, in the midst of victory and the flush of conquest, have set ministers an example of moderation and magnanimity."

53. A Satire on the Democratic Enemy

From *Songs and Ballads of the American Revolution,* ed. Frank Moore (New York: D. Appleton, 1856). P. 196.

The Rebels
1778

Ye brave, honest subjects, who dare to be loyal
And have stood the brunt of every trial
    Of hunting-shirts and rifle-guns:
Come listen awhile, and I'll sing you a song;
I'll show you those Yankees are all in the wrong,
Who, with blustering look and most awkward gait,
'Gainst their lawful sovereign dare for to prate,
    With their hunting-shirts and rifle-guns.

[197] The arch-rebels, barefooted tatterdemalions,
In baseness exceed all other rebellions,
    With their hunting-shirts and rifle-guns.
To rend the empire, the most infamous lies
Their mock-patriot Congress do always devise;
Independence, like the first of rebels, they claim
But their plots will be damned in the annals of fame,
    With their hunting-shirts and rifle-guns.

Forgetting the mercies of Great Britain's king,
Who saved their forefathers' necks from the string;
    With their hunting-shirts and rifle-guns.
They renounce allegiance and take up their arms,
Assemble together like hornets in swarms.
So dirty their backs and so wretched their show
That carrion-crow follows wherever they go,
    With their hunting-shirts and rifle-guns.

With loud peals of laughter, your sides, sirs, would crack
To see General Convict and Colonel Shoe-black,
  With their hunting-shirts and rifle-guns.
See cobblers and quacks, rebel priests and the like,
Pettifoggers and barbers, with sword and with pike,
[198] All strutting, the standard of Satan beside,
And honest names using, their black deeds to hide.
  With their hunting-shirts and rifle-guns.

This perjured banditti now ruin this land,
And o'er its poor people claim lawless command,
  With their hunting-shirts and rifle-guns.
Their pasteboard dollars prove a common curse;
They don't chink like silver and gold in our purse.
With nothing their leaders have paid their debts off;
Their honor's dishonor, and justice they scoff,
  With their hunting-shirts and rifle-guns.

For one lawful ruler, many tyrants we've got,
Who force young and old to their wars, to be shot,
  With their hunting-shirts and rifle-guns.
Our good king, God speed him! never used men so;
We then could speak, act, and like freemen could go;
But committees enslave us, our Liberty's gone,
Our trade and church murdered, our country's undone,
  By hunting-shirts and rifle-guns.

Come take up your glasses, each true loyal heart,
And may every rebel meet his due desert,
  With his hunting-shirt and rifle-gun.
[199] May Congress, Conventions, those damn'd inquisitions,
Be fed with hot sulphur, from Lucifer's kitchens,
May commerce and peace again be restored,
And Americans own their true sovereign lord!
  Then oblivion to shirts and rifle-guns.
            God save the King!

54. On General Washington

From *The Gentleman's Magazine*. Vol. XLVIII (August, 1778), p. 368.

PARTICULARS OF THE LIFE AND CHARACTER OF GENERAL
WASHINGTON, EXTRACTED FROM A LETTER IN LLOYD'S
EVENING POST OF AUG. 17, SIGNED AN OLD SOLDIER

A late celebrated patriot said in Parliament, that Mr. Washington was an independent gentleman of £5000 per annum, clear estate. Many such things are said. It is not usual, however, in that country, to estimate men's fortunes by their annual incomes; in fact, owing to many circumstances not necessary here to recite, it is hardly possible this should be done with any precision. His estate, even under his excellent management, never was, one year with another, worth £500 per annum. There are an hundred men [369] in Virginia who have better estates than Mr. Washington; nay, five hundred. . . . His appointment soon after to the command of one of the Provincial regiments, and his very decent conduct in that command, are facts of sufficient notoriety. One circumstance, perhaps, not so generally known, may be mentioned. The very first engagement in which he was ever concerned, was against his own countrymen. He unexpectedly fell in, in the woods, with a party of the other Virginia regiment in the night, and fifty men were killed before the mistake was found out. The blame was laid (and possibly with great justness) on the darkness of the night. It is remarkable, however, that the same misfortune befell him in his last action at German Town; the blame was then also laid on a darkness occasioned by a thick fog. . . .

It is not to be denied, that he was not then much liked in the army; but it is not less true that no very good reasons were ever given for his being disliked. I attributed it (and I hope I may be allowed to have some pretensions to judge of it, having served with him in that very campaign) to his being a tolerably strict disciplinarian; a system which ill suited with the impatient spirits of his headstrong countrymen, who are but little used to restraint. Method and exactness are the fort of his character; he gave a very strong proof of this in this very service.

He is not a generous, but a just man; and having, from some idea of propriety, made it a point neither to gain nor lose as an individual in the war [against the French], he kept to his purpose, and left the service without either owing a shilling, or being a shilling richer for it.

After his resignation he lived entirely as a country gentleman, distinguished by his skill and industry in improvements in agriculture. He was a member of the House of Burgesses; respectable, but not shining.

At the time of the stamp-act, and during the commencement of the present troubles, he took such a part only as most of his compeers did; save only, that being more industrious, and probably less violent, than most of them, he carried the scheme of manufacturing to a greater height than almost any other man.

When it was determined by some restless men in the northern colonies to raise an army, they soon foresaw that it would be impossible to effect this without the concurrence of their southern fellow-colonies; they fixed their eyes, in particular, on Virginia, which having long been called his Majesty's ancient dominion, the people, naturally ostentatious, were proud to be considered as taking the lead. They were artfully indulged and humoured in this pardonable instance of human vanity. Mr. Randolph, a Virginian, was made President of the Congress, and Mr. Washington, Commander in Chief; both of them very honest and well-meaning men. Their honesty betrayed them; for it is an undoubted fact, that they would never have accepted of those posts, if they had not entertained the just and strongest suspicions of the unwarrantable views of their northern brethren. Alas! they considered not how difficult, and even impossible it would be for them, after having once passed the strait line of rectitude, to stop short of the utmost wrong. Their seducers were systematic; and having now prevailed on them, in one great instance, to fly in the face of Government, they knew their game too well not to manage so as to cut off all hopes of a retreat. Things were pushed to so desperate an extremity, that safety was now to be found only in going on; the relinquishment of independency, circumstanced as affairs then were, and were contrived to be, would certainly have meant to have relinquished also the first ground of the quarrel, the right of taxation.

All this may appear paradoxical, but it is nevertheless perfectly consistent with the genuine workings of human nature, and these Americans are not singular in having acted the part I am describing. It is an undoubted fact, that Washington and Randolph (who then acted in concert, and [370] who then also greatly influenced the Colony of Virginia, and, of course, the whole Continent) were, at the time I am speaking of, as adverse to independency, as (for I would express myself strongly) the heads of the northern faction were bent upon it. . . .

Placed at the head of an army and country, which, at least, were great and glorious in the American accounts of them, it is not to be wondered at that Mr. Washington soon began to feel his consequence. His ruling passion is military fame. Nature has certainly given him some military talents, yet it is more than probable he never will be a great soldier. There are insuperable impediments in his way. He is but of slow parts, and these are totally unassisted by any kind of education. Now, though such a character may acquit itself with some sort of eclat, in the poor, pitiful, unsoldier-like war in which he has hitherto been employed, it is romantic to suppose he must not fail, if ever it should be his lot to be opposed by real military skill. He never saw any actual service, but the unfortunate action of Braddock. He never read a book in the art of war of higher value than Bland's Exercises; and it has already been noted, that he is by no means of bright or shining parts. If, then, military knowledge be not unlike all other; or, if it be not totally useless as to all the purposes of actual war, it is impossible that ever Mr. Washington should be a great soldier. In fact, by the mere dint and bravery of our army alone, he has been beaten whenever he has engaged; and that this is left to befall him again, is a problem which, I believe, most military men are utterly at a loss to solve.

It should not be denied, however, that, all things considered, he really has performed wonders. That he is alive to command an army, or that an army is left him to command, might be sufficient to ensure him the reputation of a great General, if British Generals any longer were what British Generals used to be. In short, I am of the opinion of the Marquis de la Fayette, that any other General in the world than General Howe would have beaten General Washington; and any other General in the world than General Washington would have beaten General Howe.

I am, &c

An Old Soldier

55. Boswell and Johnson on America in 1778

From James Boswell, *Life of Samuel Johnson*, ed. George Birk-beck Hill (New York: Harper & Bros., 1891). Four volumes. Vol. III, p. 250. [First published in 1791.]

[From the year 1778]

"What do you say to *Taxation no Tyranny*, now, after Lord North's declaration, or confession, or whatever else his conciliatory speech should be called? I never differed from you in politicks but upon two points,—the Middlesex Election, and the Taxation of the Americans by the British *Houses of Representatives*. There is a *charm* in the word *Parliament*, so I avoid it. As I am a steady and a warm Tory, I regret that the King does not see it to be better for him to receive constitutional supplies from his American subjects by the voice of their own assemblies, where his Royal Person is represented, than through the medium of his British subjects. I am persuaded that the power of the Crown, [251] which I wish to increase, would be greater when in contact with all its dominions, than if 'the rays of regal bounty' were to 'shine' upon America through that dense and troubled body, a modern British Parliament. But, enough of this subject; for your angry voice at Ashbourne upon it, still sounds aweful 'in my mind's *ears*.' I ever am, my dear Sir, your most affectionate humble servant,

James Boswell."

56. Pitt's Final Attempt to Save the Empire

From John Almon, *Anecdotes of the Life of . . . William Pitt,*
Earl of Chatham (London: J. S. Jordan, 1793). Three volumes.
Vol. II, p. 509.
The following is an extract from Chatham's last speech, House
of Lords, April 7, 1778. The occasion was a motion by the Duke
of Richmond, a Rockingham Whig, setting forth the bad management of the war and advising his Majesty to withdraw immediately his forces from America and to effect a reconciliation with
the revolted provinces. Chatham, who believed that the motion
contained an implied recognition of American independence, was
strongly opposed to it. When the Duke of Richmond had concluded his reply, Chatham tried to answer but his strength failed
him and he fell back in convulsions. The debate was immediately
adjourned and the dying statesman carried to a house in Down-
ing Street, then to his own home where he died a few days later.

He began by lamenting that his bodily infirmities had so long, and
especially at so important a crisis, prevented his attendance [510] on
the duties of Parliament. He declared that he had made an effort
almost beyond the powers of his constitution to come down to the
House on this day (perhaps the last time he should ever be able to
enter its walls) to express the indignation he felt at an idea which he
understood was gone forth, of yielding up the sovereignty of America!
My Lords, continued he, I rejoice that the grave has not closed
upon me; that I am still alive to lift up my voice against the dismemberment of this ancient and most noble monarchy! Pressed down as
I am by the hand of infirmity, I am little able to assist my country in
this most perilous conjuncture; but, my Lords, while I have sense and
memory, I will never consent to deprive the royal offspring of the
House of Brunswick, the heirs of the Princess Sophia, of their fairest
inheritance. Where is the man that will dare to advise such a measure?
My Lords, his Majesty succeeded to an empire as great in extent as its
reputation was [511] unsullied. Shall we tarnish the lustre of this nation by an ignominious surrender of its rights and fairest possessions?
Shall this great kingdom, that has survived whole and entire the
Danish depredations, the Scottish inroads, and the Norman conquest;
that has stood the threatened invasion of the Spanish armada, now fall
prostrate before the House of Bourbon? Surely, my Lords, this nation
is no longer what it was! Shall a people, that seventeen years ago was
the terror of the world, now stoop so low as to tell its ancient inveterate enemy, take all we have, only give us peace? It is impossible!
I wage war with no man, or set of men. I wish for none of their
employments; nor would I co-operate with men who still persist in
unretracted error: or who, instead of acting on a firm decisive line of
conduct, halt between two opinions, where there is no middle path.

In God's name, if it is absolutely necessary to declare either for peace or war, and the former [512] cannot be preserved with honour, why is not the latter commenced without hesitation? I am not, I confess, well informed of the resources of this kingdom; but I trust it is still sufficient to maintain its just rights, though I know them not. My Lords, any state is better than despair. Let us at least make one effort; and if we must fall, let us fall like men!

57. The Trend of Public Opinion

From James Boswell, *Life of Samuel Johnson*, ed. George Birkbeck Hill (New York: Harper & Bros., 1891). Four volumes. Vol. IV, p. 94. [First published in 1791.]

[From the year 1781]

Sir Philip defended the [Parliamentary] Opposition to the American war ably and with temper, and I joined him. He said, the majority of the nation was against the ministry. JOHNSON. ". . . As to the American war, the *sense* of the nation is *with* the ministry. The majority of those who can *understand* is with it; the majority of those who can only *hear*, is against it; and as those who can only hear are more numerous than those who can understand, and Opposition is always loudest, a majority of the rabble will be for Opposition."

This boisterous vivacity entertained us; but the truth in my opinion was, that those who could understand the best were against the American war, as almost every man now is, when the question has been coolly considered. . . .

[136] One day, when I told him that I was a zealous Tory, but not enough "according to knowledge," and should be obliged to him "for a reason," he was so candid, and expressed himself so well, that I begged of him to repeat what he had said, and I wrote down as follows:—

OF TORY AND WHIG

"A wise Tory and a wise Whig, I believe, will agree. Their principles are the same, though their modes of thinking are different. A high Tory makes government unintelligible: It is lost in the clouds. A violent Whig makes it impracticable: he is for allowing so much liberty to every man, that there is not power enough to govern any man. The prejudice of the Tory is for establishment; the prejudice of the Whig is for innovation. A Tory does not wish to give more real power to Government; but that [137] Government should have more reverence. Then they differ as to the Church. The Tory is not for giving more legal power to the Clergy, but wishes they should have a considerable influence, founded on the opinion of mankind; the Whig is for limiting and watching them with a narrow jealousy."

58. The Defeat of Cornwallis and the Debate on Peace

From *The Gentleman's Magazine.* Vol. LII (January, 1782), p. 8.

Extract of a Letter from Sir Henry Clinton to the Right Hon. Lord George Germain, one of his Majesty's Principal Secretaries of State, received on the 16th instant by Lord Dalrymple, who arrived in the Swallow Packet, which left New-York the 17th of November.

. In my last dispatch I had the honour to acquaint your Lordship with my fears respecting the fate of the army in Virginia.

It now gives me the deepest concern to inform you, that they were but too well founded, as your Lordship will perceive by Lord Cornwallis's letter to me of the 20th ult. a copy of which, and the papers accompanying it, being inclosed for your information. . . .

Copy of a letter from Lieut.-Gen. Earl Cornwallis to Sir Hen. Clinton, dated York-Town, in Virginia, Oct. 20, 1781.

I have the mortification to inform your Excellency, that I have been forced to give up the posts of York and Gloucester, and to surrender the troops under my command, by capitulation, on the 19th inst. as prisoners of war to the combined forces of America and France. . . .

From *The Gentleman's Magazine.* Vol. LII (February, 1782), p. 92.

The following extracts are parliamentary reports from the "Historical Chronicle," a section in *The Gentleman's Magazine.*

Feb. 4. . . . Speaking of peace, Ld Shelburne desired it might be remembered, that on that day, the 4th of February, he averred in his place, whenever propositions of peace were laid before that House, ministers would get up and say, that America was of very little consequence—its trade was of no value, and therefore it was to be given up. This, said his Lordship, will be the language of the Cabinet, after expending above a hundred millions of money, and as many thousand lives, in defence of that on which they set no value. . . .

[93] Feb. 11. His Grace the D. of Chandos moved in the H. of Peers for all such correspondence, &c. as passed between his Majesty's ministers and the commanders in America in 1781, relative to the capture of the army under the command of E. Cornwallis. It passed in negative. . . .

Feb. 22. Gen. Conway moved in the H. of C. "That an humble address be presented to his Majesty, that he will be graciously pleased to take into his royal consideration the many calamities that have befallen his people, in consequence of the present war; and that, in conformity to the gracious assurances from the Throne, of his Majesty's ardent wish to restore peace to his kingdoms, he will be pleased to give directions to his ministers not to pursue any longer the impracticable object of reducing his Majesty's revolted Colonies, by force, to their allegiance, by a war on the continent of America, and to assure his Majesty, that his faithful Commons will most cheerfully concur with him in such measures as may be found necessary to accelerate the blessing of returning peace." The numbers for carrying on the war were 194; against it 193. Majority only *One*.

From *The Gentleman's Magazine*. Vol. LII (March, 1782), p. 142.

Feb. 22. Gen. Conway brought forward his promised motion, which see p. 93 [of the previous issue above].

This motion, the general observed, was the more interesting, as ministers well knew there was a disposition at this time in America to treat of peace; and that there were persons now, or lately had been, at no great distance, properly authorized to treat of terms. He desired to know of the new Secretary, how they had been received?

Mr. Ellis replied, that he was not aware of any propositions for peace, nor did he know of any persons properly authorized to make them. He was against the motion, not because he did not ardently wish for peace; but because the motion would infallibly tend to counteract its own intention. He owned, that circumstances were greatly changed, and that measures must yield to circumstances. The war in America, he thought, must be contracted; but not abandoned. France must be humbled, or no peace could be secure. He was against the motion; so were all the members nearly connected with government; and when the question was moved, the numbers were 193 Ayes, and only 194 Noes. Majority 1.

[143] Feb. 27. . . . The House of Peers went into committee on the D. of Chandos's motion for enquiring into the cause of the surrender of the army under Ld Cornwallis.

Ld Townshend objected to that enquiry, while Sir H. Clinton and Ld Cornwallis were absent. . . .

Gen. Conway took occasion to renew his motion for addressing his Majesty to put a stop to the American war, a motion, he said, which, while he had a heart to feel, or a tongue to speak, he would never cease to press. He was, he said, the more encouraged in his present attempt by what had fallen from two members deservedly of great weight in that House (Mr. R——y and the Ld Adv. of S—l—d) who had declared themselves converts to the impracticability of subduing America by force. . . .

[144] The object of the motion, he said, was in his mind very clearly expressed. It went to advise his Majesty to order his ministers to renounce the war on the Continent of America for the impracticable object of reducing the Colonies by force. In other words, to abandon an "offensive war;" but gentlemen affect not to understand what is meant by an offensive war, than which nothing can be clearer to common sense; an offensive war is a war in which attempts are made by an army to possess themselves of what they had not before; a defensive war is to keep what they have gotten. Upon this principle could any one mistake the real meaning of his motion? He had not said a syllable of withdrawing our troops from the places which they now actually held; he would advise no such measure, but, on the contrary, condemn it.

After sporting a little with ministers, he reverted to the necessity of coming to a speedy determination of the American war, lest by delay the opportunity of making peace might be lost. At this very moment, whilst he was speaking, he was afraid that a dreadful blow was preparing against some vital part of the empire; for he was given to understand, that a fleet of 40 sail of the line, partly French and partly Spanish, had lately put to sea, for the purpose of some great expedition, from which we had every thing to dread. The state of those powers who composed the Armed Neutrality furnished us also with reasons for the greatest apprehension. In short, nothing, he said, could preserve the empire from that ruin into which ministers were plunging it but a vote of that House. . . .

[145] The Attorney General said, that if gentlemen really wished to have peace with America, the present resolution was not the way to obtain it. It would first be necessary to have a truce, that the enmity and ill blood which the war had occasioned might have time to subside; and even to have a truce, there were several laws that barred Government from either peace or truce till those laws were repealed; he therefore would move that the farther consideration of the motion should be adjourned to that day fortnight. This passed in the negative, 234 to 215, and the General's motion then passed without a division. . . .

Feb. 28. The Attorney General moved in the House of Commons to bring in a Bill to enable his Majesty to conclude a peace or truce with the revolted Colonies in America, which was agreed to. . . .

[147] March 8. Lord John Cavendish moved three resolutions in the House of Commons, which he said were not to be controverted. This he did with a view to investigate the cause of our present calamities, without which it would be impossible to find out or apply a remedy. The first thing that struck him was the profusion with which the supplies had been granted. The sums already voted for the present disastrous war amounted to One Hundred Millions; the taxes

for interest only, to upwards of Three Millions. In the last glorious war we had been led from victory to victory, from conquest to conquest, by the aid of our colonies and the sums voted amounted to no more than 70 millions. At the end of the last war the whole world was at our feet, and there was not in the world a navy but our own. In the present war we have purchased nothing but losses and disgrace; America gone, Minorca is no more, our dominions in the West Indies nearly annihilated, while our navy is everywhere inferior to that of the enemy. This being premised he stated his resolutions.

His first resolution was, That it appears to this House, that, in the prosecution of the present ruinous war, from the year 1775 to 1782, one hundred millions have been expended by this country.

The second resolution. That we have lost of our ancient dominions in America 13 provinces, excepting the parts now occupied by our armies in New York, Savannah, Charles Town, and Hallifax; and also our new acquired possession, East Florida. In the West Indies several of our most valuable islands, while the remainder are threatened with the most immediate danger from the inferiority of our fleets; and in Europe the island of Minorca.

The third, That we are actually at war with America, France, Spain, and Holland, without one single ally.

The fourth, That such a melancholy national situation must be ascribed to want of foresight in the first instance, and subsequent mismanagement in ministers. . . .

[Lord North's ministry resigned March 20.]

59. Free States According to International Law

From William M. Malloy, *Treaties, Conventions, International Acts, Protocols and Agreements Between the United States of America and Other Powers, 1776–1909* (Washington: U.S. Government Printing Office, 1910). Two volumes. Vol. I, p. 587.

The following extract is taken from the Treaty of Paris, 1783. This is the treaty that ended the war with the colonies in America.

. . . ARTICLE I.

His Britannic Majesty acknowledges the said United States, viz. New Hampshire, Massachusetts Bay, Rhode Island and Providence Plantations, Connecticut, New York, New Jersey, Pennsylvania, Delaware, Maryland, Virginia, North Carolina, South Carolina, and Georgia, to be free, sovereign, and independent States; that he treats with them as such, and for himself, his heirs and successors, relinquishes all claims to the Government, proprietary and territorial rights of the same, and every part thereof. . . .

VI

EPILOGUE

---

60. Good Riddance to America

From Josiah Tucker, Dean of Gloucester, *Four Letters on Important National Subjects* (Gloucester: R. Raikes, 1783). P. 7. See document 41 for comment on Tucker.

As to America, and the Resistance which this honourable Fraternity have so strenuously excited throughout that Country, I am as glad of the general Event, though not of the particular Circumstances attending it, as the most flaming Republicans.—I say, I am glad, that America had declared herself independent of us, though for Reasons very opposite to theirs. America, I have proved beyond the Possibility of a Confutation, ever was a Millstone hanging about the Neck of this Country, to weigh it down: And as we ourselves had not the Wisdom to cut the Rope, and to let the Burthen fall off, the Americans have kindly done [8] it for us. The only Thing to be lamented, which never can be lamented enough, was, that as soon as this ungrateful People had refused to pass a public Vote for contributing any Thing, or in any Mode, towards the general Expence of the Empire, but on the contrary, had entered into Combinations to forbid the Importation of our Manufactures, we had not taken them at their Word, and totally cast them off. Had we done this, it would have been happy for us; nay, it would have been happy for them too: Because this would have saved both them and us that Blood and Treasure, which have been so profusely lavished for many Years, without answering any one End whatever:—Unless indeed the raising of a few American Upstarts to be American Princes,—the enriching of a few Cormorants, and Contractors here in Britain,—and the placing of some of the more distinguished Members of the aforementioned pa- [9] triotic Fraternity on ministerial Thrones can be thought to have been Objects sufficient to compensate such portentous Losses.

61. Thoughts of a Patriot Poet

From *The Poetical Works of William Cowper*, ed. William Benham (London: Macmillan, 1893). P. 202.

The Task, Cowper's informal and personal descriptive-didactic poem, was perhaps the most popular literary work of the eighteenth century, long within reach of almost everyone in school and at home. Probably begun in July, 1783, it was completed in September, 1784, and published in 1785. The following selection is from Book II, entitled "The Time-Piece."

England, with all thy faults, I love thee still,   206
My country! and, while yet a nook is left
Where English minds and manners may be found,
Shall be constrain'd to love thee. Though thy clime
Be fickle, and thy year, most part, deform'd   210
With dripping rains, or wither'd by a frost,
I would not yet exchange thy sullen skies
[203] And fields without a flow'r, for warmer France
With all her vines; nor for Ausonia's groves
Of golden fruitage, and her myrtle bow'rs.
To shake thy senate, and from heights sublime
Of patriot eloquence to flash down fire
Upon thy foes, was never meant my task;
But I can feel thy fortunes, and partake
Thy joys and sorrows with as true a heart   220
As any thund'rer there. And I can feel
Thy follies, too; and with a just disdain
Frown at effeminates, whose very looks
Reflect dishonour on the land I love.
How, in the name of soldiership and sense,
Should England prosper, when such things as smooth
And tender as a girl, all-essenc'd o'er
With odours, and as profligate as sweet;
Who sell their laurel for a myrtle wreath,
And love when they should fight,—when such as these   230
Presume to lay their hand upon the ark
Of her magnificent and awful cause?
Time was when it was praise and boast enough
In ev'ry clime, and travel where we might,
That we were born her [England's] children; praise enough
To fill th' ambition of a private man,
That Chatham's language was his mother tongue,
And Wolfe's great name compatriot with his own.
Farewell those honours, and farewell with them
The hope of such hereafter! They have fall'n   240
Each in his field of glory: one in arms,

And one in council—Wolfe upon the lap
Of smiling Victory that moment won,
And Chatham, heart-sick of his country's shame!
They made us many soldiers. Chatham still
Consulting England's happiness at home,
Secur'd it by an unforgiving frown
If any wrong'd her. Wolfe, where'er he fought,
Put so much of his heart into his act,
That his example had a magnet's force,   250
And all were swift to follow whom all lov'd.
Those suns are set. Oh, rise some other such!
Or all that we have left is empty talk
Of old achievements, and despair of new. . . .
True, we have lost an empire—let it pass.   263
True, we may thank the perfidy of France,
[204] That pick'd the jewel out of England's crown,
With all the cunning of an envious shrew.
And let that pass,—'twas but a trick of state! . . .

62. A Tribute to George Washington and His Policy of Neutrality

From William Cobbett, *The Parliamentary History of England*
(London: T. C. Hansard, 1806–20). Thirty-six volumes. Vol.
XXX, p. 1274.
The King's Speech had referred to the war with France and to
the necessity of perseverance in the national exertions for victory.
In the House of Commons, January 21, 1794, Charles James Fox
moved an amendment to the Address of Thanks for the Speech
from the Throne advising his Majesty to take the earliest means
of making peace on such terms as might be prudent to insist on,
and expressing the hope that no obstacle would arise to such a
peace from any considerations respecting the form of government
which might prevail in France. During the War of Independence,
Fox was one of America's warmest supporters and he here holds
Washington up as a model of capable leadership.

Sir, I cannot help alluding to the president of the United States,
General Washington, a character whose conduct has been so different
from that which has been pursued by the ministers of this country.
How infinitely wiser must appear the spirit and principles manifested
in his late address to congress than the policy of modern European
courts! Illustrious man, deriving honour less from the splendour of
his situation than from the dignity of insignificance, and all the
potentates of Europe (excepting the members of our own royal
family) become little and contemptible! He has had no occasion to

have recourse to any tricks of policy or arts of alarm; his authority has been sufficiently supported by the same means by which it was acquired, and his conduct has uniformly been characterised by wisdom, moderation, and firmness. Feeling gratitude to France for the assistance received from her in that great conquest which secured the independence of America, he did not chuse to give up the system of neutrality. Having once laid down that line of conduct, which both gratitude and policy pointed out as most proper to be pursued, not all the insults or provocation of the French minister, Genet, could turn him from his purpose. Entrusted with the welfare of a great people, he did not allow the misconduct of another, with respect to himself, for one moment to withdraw his attention from their interests. He had no fear of the jacobins; he felt no alarm from their principles, and considered no precaution as necessary in order to stop their progress. [1275] The people over whom he presided he knew to be acquainted with their rights and their duties. He trusted to their own good sense to defeat the effect of those arts which might be employed to inflame or mislead their minds; and was sensible that a government could be in no danger while it retained the attachment and confidence of its subjects—attachment, in this instance, not blindly adopted, confidence not implicitly given, but arising from the conviction of its excellence, and the experience of its blessings. I cannot, indeed, help admiring the wisdom and the fortune of this great man; by the phrase 'fortune,' I mean not in the smallest degree to derogate from his merit. But, notwithstanding his extraordinary talents and exalted integrity, it must be considered as singularly fortunate, that he should have experienced a lot, which so seldom falls to the portion of humanity, and have passed through such a variety of scenes without stain and without reproach. It must, indeed, create astonishment, that, placed in circumstances so critical, and filling for a series of years a station so conspicuous, his character should never once have been called in question; that he should in no one instance have been accused either of improper insolence, or of mean submission in his transactions with foreign nations. For him it has been reserved to run the race of glory, without experiencing the smallest interruption to the brilliancy of his career. But, Sir, if the maxims now held out were adopted, the man who now ranks as the assertor of his country's freedom, and the guardian of its interests and its honour, would be deemed to have betrayed that country, and entailed upon himself indelible reproach. How, Sir, did he act when insulted by Genet? Did he consider it as necessary to avenge himself for the misconduct or madness of an individual, by involving a whole continent in the horrors of war? No; he contented himself with procuring satisfaction for the insult, by causing Genet to be recalled; and thus at once consulted his own dignity and the interests of his country. Happy Americans! while the whirlwind spreads desolation over one quarter of the globe, you remain protected from its baneful effects, by your own virtues and the wisdom of your government! Separated from Europe by an immense ocean, you feel not the effects of those prejudices and passions, which convert the boasted seats of [1276] civilization into scenes of horror and bloodshed! You profit by the folly and madness of contending nations, and afford in your more congenial clime an asylum to those blessings and virtues which they wantonly contemn, or wickedly exclude from their bosom! Cultivating the arts of peace under the influence of freedom, you advance by rapid strides to opulence and distinction; and if by any accident you should be compelled to take part in the present unhappy contest; if you should find it necessary to avenge insult, or repel injury, the world will bear witness to the equity of your sentiments and the moderation of your views, and the success of your arms will, no doubt, be proportioned to the justice of your cause!

63. Columbia, A Republican Symbol

From *The Complete Poetical Works of Robert Burns* (Boston: Houghton Mifflin Co., 1897). P. 158.

Ode for General Washington's Birthday [1794]

. . . 'Tis Liberty's bold note I swell:
   Thy harp, Columbia, let me take!
See gathering thousands, while I sing,
A broken chain, exulting, bring
    And dash it in a tyrant's face,
    And dare him to his very beard,
    And tell him he no more is fear'd,
      No more the despot of Columbia's race!   10
   A tyrant's proudest insults brav'd,
They shout a People freed! They hail an Empire sav'd!

Where is man's godlike form?   [Washington]
   Where is that brow erect and bold,
   That eye that can unmov'd behold
The wildest rage, the loudest storm
That e'er created Fury dared to raise?
Avaunt! thou caitiff, servile, base,   [Lord North]
   That tremblest at a despot's nod,
   Yet, crouching under the iron rod,   20
Canst laud the arm that struck th' insulting blow!
[159]   Art thou of man's Imperial line?
Dost boast that countenance divine?
   Each skulking feature answers: No!
But come, ye sons of Liberty,
Columbia's offspring, brave as free,
In danger's hour still flaming in the van,
Ye know, and dare maintain the Royalty of Man! . . .

VII

MEMOIRS AND CORRESPONDENCE

64. Francis Bernard, Letters, 1765–68

From Francis Bernard, *Select Letters on the Trade and Government of America* (London: T. Payne, 1774). P. v.
  Sir Francis Bernard (1711?–79), Governor of New Jersey from 1758 to 1760 and then of Massachusetts Bay from 1760 to 1769, faithfully upheld the views of the home government and thereby engaged in numerous disputes with the Massachusetts General Court (assembly). Eventually Governor Bernard was recalled to England, being *persona non grata* in America. His problems as government official are described in his letters to William Wildman, second Viscount Barrington (1717–93), successively Chancellor of the Exchequer, Treasurer of the Navy, and Secretary at War, holding the last post from 1765 to 1778.

[From the Preface] . . . these letters were dictated by a love of both Countries [Britain and America], and an earnest desire that they should be united in mutual affection as they are in mutual interest. This will [*vi*] depend in a great measure upon the Connexion of the Colonies with the *imperial* state. This can be maintained no otherwise than by a subordination of the former as *Dependent* states, to the latter as the *Imperial* sovereign. *Imperium in imperio* is a monster in politics which cannot subsist. The notions of policy which have been adopted in *America* since the stamp-act have a final tendency to separate the Colonies from the Mother Country; an event which, as I have said before, can be desirable by neither; as the consequences of it will probably be the Ruin of both. . . .

[30]   Boston, Nov. 23, 1765
  . . . It must have been supposed that such an innovation as a Parliamentary taxation would cause a great alarm, and meet with much opposition in most parts of America: it was quite new to the people, and had no visible bounds set to it; the Americans declared that they

would not submit to it, before the Act passed; and there was the greatest probability that it would require the utmost power of Government to carry it into execution. Whereas, at this time, the governments were weak and impotent to an amazing degree; the governors and officers of the Crown in several of the chief provinces entirely dependent upon the people for subsistence; the popular scale so much weightier than the Royal, that it required address and management, and frequent temporising, to preserve a tolerable balance; the persons of the governors and crown officers quite defenceless, and exposed to the violence of the people, without any possible resort for protection. Was this a time to introduce so great a novelty as a Parliamentary inland taxation into America?

Nor was the time less favorable to the Equity of such a taxation. . . . It should be considered, that the American governments themselves have, in the prosecution of the late war, contracted very large debts; which it will take some years to pay off, and in the meantime [31] occasion very burdensome taxes for that purpose only. . . .

Since the insurrections against the stamp act, the Americans have found the governments so contemptibly weak, and the people so superior to royal authority, that they are not a little elated upon their triumphs over the defenceless officers of the crown; and seem to be resolved, that their idea of their relation to Great Britain, however extravagant, various, and inconsistent, shall be the standard to it: so that it is to be feared, that it will cost much time and treasure to bring America to that degree of submission which the Parliament will think necessary to require of them.

The question will not be, Whether there shall be a stamp act or not, but whether [32] America shall or shall not be subject to the legislature of Great Britain. It is my opinion that all the political evils in America rise from the want of ascertaining the relation between Great Britain and the American colonies. Hence it is, that ideas of that relation are formed in Britain and America so very repugnant and contradictory to each other. In Britain the American governments are considered as corporations empowered to make bye-laws, existing only during the pleasure of Parliament; who hath never yet done anything to confirm their establishments, and hath at any time a power to dissolve them. In America, they claim (I mean in the public papers) to be perfect states, no otherwise dependent upon Great Britain than by having the same King; which, having complete legislatures within themselves, are no way subject to that of Great Britain; which in such instances as it has heretofore exercised a legislative power over them, has usurped it. In a difference so very wide who shall determine? the Parliament of Great Britain? No, say the Americans (I mean the violent of them); that would be to make them judges in their own cause. Who then? the King? He is bound by charters, or constitutions equal to charters, and cannot declare against his own grants. So, at this rate, there is no superior tribunal to determine upon the rights and privileges of the American colonies. . . .

[33] So much is America altered by the late financial acts, that a new system of policy, and of a more refined kind than was wanted

heretofore, has now become needful. The patchwork government of America will last no longer: the necessity of a parliamentary establishment of the governments [34] of America upon fixed constitutional principles, is brought on with a precipitation which could not have been foreseen but a year ago; and is become more urgent by the very incidents which make it more difficult. The circumstance of the Americans justifying their [dis]obedience by their not being represented, points out a method to enforce their obedience upon their own principles. Take them at their word: let them send representatives at the present time, and for the present purposes: thirty for the continent, and fifteen for the islands [the West Indies], would be sufficient. In this Parliament, the Colonies being actually represented, let the affair of the American governments be canvassed to the bottom; and let a general, uniform system of government be formed and established by Act of Parliament, by which the Americans according to their own principles will be bound; and let the relation of America to Great Britain be determined and ascertained by a solemn recognition: so that the rights of the American governments, and their subordination to that of Great Britain, may no longer be a subject of doubt and disputation. When this great work is done, the American representatives may be dismissed, and left to attend their own legislatures, which will then know the bounds of their own authority. . . . Ireland affords an example of the usefulness of this work, and the manner of doing it. . . .

[38]   Dec. 14, 1765
. . . A further delay of a Parliamentary regulation of the American governments, and above all, ascertaining the nature of their subordination, will, I fear, make the business irretrievable. When the Americans have actually acquired the power of defying the Parliament, which some of them vainly pretend [39] to now, a separation will soon follow. The weak patchwork government of this country [America] has no power to defer such an event one hour after the people have resolved upon it. . . .

[42]   Feb. 28, 1766
. . . The Stamp Act is become in itself a matter of indifference; it is swallowed up in the importance of the effects of which it has been the cause. The taxing the Americans by the Parliament, has brought their very subjection to the Crown of Great Britain in question. . . . [43] The people [of America] have felt their strength, and flatter themselves that it is much greater than it is; and will not, of their own accord, submit readily to anything they do not like: and there is no internal principle of policy which can by any means restore the power of Government, and enforce a due subordination. . . .

[53]   Jan. 28, 1768
I understand that it is a prevailing opinion on your side the ocean, that America, if let alone, will come to herself, and return to the same sense of duty and obedience to Great Britain which she professed be-

fore. But it seems to me, that discerning and considerate men on this side the water expect no such thing. If indeed the ill temper of the Americans had arose from accidental causes, and exercised itself without meddling with fundamental principles, the cause ceasing, the effects might also cease; and the subject of complaint being removed, a perfect and durable conciliation might be restored.

But when the dispute has been carried so far as to involve in it matters of the highest importance to the imperial Sovereignty; when it has produced questions which the Sovereign State cannot give up, and the Dependent States insist upon as the terms of a reconciliation; when the Imperial State has so far given way as to let the Dependent States flatter themselves that their pretensions are admissible; whatever terms of Reconciliation time, accident or design may produce, if they are deficient in settling the true Relation of Great Britain to her Colonies, and ascertaining the bounds of the Sovereignty of [54] the one, and the Dependence of the other, Conciliation will be no more than a suspension of animosity; the seeds of which will be left in the ground ready to start up again whenever there shall be a new occasion for the Americans to assert their independence of the authority of Parliament; that is, whenever the Parliament shall make ordinances which the Americans shall think not for their interest to obey. . . .

65. James Boswell, Letters, 1775–80

From *The Letters of James Boswell*, ed. Chauncey Brewster Tinker (Oxford: Clarendon Press, 1924). Two volumes. Vol. I, p. 213.
    The work of James Boswell (1740–95) in English biography, his *Life of Samuel Johnson*, is considered the supreme achievement in that genre. Boswell, unlike the subject of his study, was Scotch, and, unlike most of his countrymen, sided with the Americans. The footnotes in the following selection are Tinker's.

To the Reverend William Temple, Grantham, 18 March 1775.
    . . . As to American affairs, I have really not studied the subject. It is too much for me perhaps; or I am too indolent or frivolous. From the smattering which newspapers have given me, I have been of different minds several times. That I am a Tory, a lover of power in monarchy, and a discourager of much liberty in the people I avow. But it is not clear to me that our colonies are compleatly our subjects. I am puzzled with the charters. At any rate, the measures of Administration seem to have been [214] ill digested and violent. I should hope that things may now take a good turn. I can figure Britain and the colonies in a most agreable [sic] state, like a father and son who are both sensible and spirited men, who can make mutual allowances, and

who, having a kindness for each other, study to promote a common interest. But selfishness and narrowness of comprehension destroys men and nations. . . .

[216] To the Reverend William Temple, London, 4 April 1775.
 . . . Franclin [sic] has written upon stilling the waves of the ocean by oil, as I see you would quiet the turbulent Americans by lenient measures. Your soft admonitions would at any time calm the tempest of my soul. . . .

[233] To the Reverend William Temple, Edinburgh, 19 June 1775.
 . . . The word *fruit* makes me recollect that Mr. Hume said Burke's *Speech on Reconciliation with the Colonies,* which I lent to him, had a great deal of flower, a great deal of leaf, and a little fruit. Yesterday I met Mr. Hume at Lord Kames's, in the forenoon. He said, It was all over in America. We *could* not subdue the colonists; and another gun should not be fired, were it not for decency's sake. He meant, in order to keep up an appearance of power. But I think the lives of our fellow subjects should not be thrown away for such *decency.* He said we may do very well without America and he was for withdrawing our troops altogether, and letting the Canadians fall upon our colonists. I do not think he makes our *right* to tax at all clear. . . .

[239] To the Reverend William Temple, Edinburgh, 12 August 1775.
 . . . I am growing more and more American. I see the unreasonableness of taxing them without the consent of their Assemblies. I think our ministry are mad in undertaking this desperate war.

[II:275] To Edmund Burke, Edinburgh, 8 March 1778.
 . . . Most heartily do I rejoice that our present ministers have at last yielded to conciliation.[1] For amidst all the sanguinary zeal of my countrymen I have professed myself a friend to our fellow-subjects in America, so far as they claim an exemption from being taxed by the representatives of the King's British subjects. I do not perfectly agree with you; for I deny the declaratory act; and I am a warm Tory, in its true constitutional sense. I wish I were a commissioner, or one of the secretaries of the commission, for the grand treaty. I am to be in London this spring, and if his majesty should ask me what I would choose, my answer will be, to assist at the compact between Britain and America. . . .

[II:309] To the Reverend William Temple, Edinburgh, 3 November 1780.
 The state of the nation is indeed wretched; nor do I see any prospect of our being better. It is shocking to think that a new Parliament is returned which will be as subservient to ministry as the last. I agree

---

[1] Parliament had recently authorized the appointment of a commission to negotiate peace with the Americans. An act "for removing all doubts and apprehensions concerning taxation by the Parliament of Great Britain in any of the colonies" was passed 2 March 1778.

with you sincerely, my friend, that it would be better to be a Lord of Session, with an unblemished character, than a peer and Lord Chief Justice, by such means as these promotions have been attained. I would not have been one of those who rejected the petitions from America[2]—no not for half the British Empire. Yet I am a Tory still; for I distinguish between our *limited monarch*, and a *despotick ministry*.

66. Robert Burns, Letters, 1788, 1794

From *The Letters of Robert Burns*, ed. J. DeLancey Ferguson (Oxford: Clarendon Press, 1931). Two volumes. Vol. I, p. 271.

To the Editor of the *Edinburgh Evening Courant*, Nov. 8, 1788
    . . . I dare say, the American Congress, in 1776, will be allowed to have been as able and as enlightened, and, a whole empire will say, as honest, as the English Convention in 1688; and that the fourth of July will be as sacred to their posterity as the fifth of November [Guy Fawkes Day] is to us.

[II:246] To Mrs. Dunlop, June 25, 1794
    . . . I am just going to trouble your critical patience with the first sketch of a stanza I have been framing as I passed along the road. The subject is LIBERTY: you know, my honored friend, how dear the theme is to me. I design it as an irregular Ode for General Washington's birthday. . . . [See document 63.]

67. William Cowper, Letters, 1781–83

From *Private Correspondence of William Cowper*, ed. John Johnson (London: H. Colburn, 1824). Two volumes. Vol. I, p. 174.
    William Cowper (1731–1800) was perhaps the outstanding poet of this period: a conscientious, devout, refined and sensitive Englishman whose works, including his letters, attest even to this day to the vitality of his imagination and the sincerity of his feelings.

---

    [2] Boswell refers to the petitions of the colonists for the redress of grievances, sent to the House of Commons before the outbreak of the Revolution. "Our repeated petitions," reads the Declaration of Independence, "have been answered only by repeated injury."

To the Rev. John Newton, Nov. 27, 1781

First Mr. Wilson, then Mr. Teedon, and lastly Mr. Whitford, each with a cloud of melancholy on his brow, and with a mouth wide open, have just announced to us this unwelcome intelligence from America. We [175] are sorry to hear it, and should be more cast down than we are, if we did not know that this catastrophe was ordained beforehand, and that therefore neither conduct, nor courage, nor any means that can possibly be mentioned, could have prevented it. If the King and his ministry can be contented to close the business here, and, taking poor Dean Tucker's advice, resign the Americans into the hands of their new masters, it may be well for Old England. But if they will still persevere, they will find it, I doubt, an hopeless contest to the last. Domestic murmurs will grow louder, and the hands of faction, being strengthened by this late miscarriage, will find it easy to set fire to the pile of combustibles they have been so long employed in building. These are my politics; and for aught I can see, you and we by our respective fire-sides, though neither connected with men in power, nor professing to possess any share of that sagacity [176] which thinks itself qualified to wield the affairs of kingdoms, can make as probable conjectures, and look forward into futurity with as clear a sight, as the greatest man in the cabinet.

[196] To Rev. William Unwin, Dec. 17, 1781

. . . I see but one feature in the face of our national concerns that pleases me;—the war with America, it seems, is to be conducted on a different plan. This is something; when a long series of measures, of a certain description, has proved unsuccessful, the adoption of others is at least pleasing, as it encourages a hope that they may possibly prove wiser, and more effectual: but, indeed, without discipline, all is lost. Pitt [197] himself could have done nothing with such tools; but he would not have been so betrayed; he would have made the traitors answer with their heads, for their cowardice or supineness, and their punishment would have made survivors active.

[203] To the Rev. John Newton, Jan. 13, 1782

. . . But, alas! what course can Government take? I have heard (for I never made the experiment) that if a man grasp a red-hot iron [204] with his naked hand, it will stick to him, so that he cannot presently disengage himself from it. Such are the colonies in the hands of administration. While they hold them they burn their fingers, and yet they must not quit them. I know not whether your sentiments and mine upon this part of the subject exactly coincide, but you will know, when you understand what mine are. It appears to me that the King is bound, both by the duty he owes to himself and to his people, to consider himself with respect to every inch of his territories, as a trustee deriving his interest in them from God, and invested with them by divine authority for the benefit of his subjects. As he may not sell them or waste them, so he may not resign them to an enemy, or transfer his right to govern them to any, not even to themselves, so long as it is possible for him to keep it. If he does, he betrays at once his own interest, and that of his other dominions. It may be said, suppose Providence has ordained that they [205] shall be wrested from him, how then? I answer, that cannot appear to be the case, till God's purpose is actually accomplished; and in the mean time the most probable prospect of such an event does not release him from his obligation to hold them to the last moment, for as much as adverse appearances are no infallible indication of God's designs, but may give place to more comfortable symptoms, when we least expect it. Viewing the thing in this light, if I sat on his Majesty's throne, I should be as obstinate as he, because if I quitted the contest, while I had any means left of carrying it on, I should never know that I had not relinquished what I might have retained, or be able to render a satisfactory answer to the doubts and enquiries of my own conscience.

[236] To the Rev. John Newton, Jan. 26, 1783
It is reported among persons of the best intelligence at Olney—the barber, the schoolmaster, and the drummer of a corps quartered at this place, that the belligerent powers are at last reconciled, the articles of the treaty adjusted, and that peace is at the door. . . .

[238] . . . the Americans, who, if they had contented themselves with a struggle for lawful liberty, would have deserved applause, seem to me to have incurred the guilt of parricide, by renouncing their parent, by making her ruin their favourite object, and by associating themselves with her worst enemy, for the accomplishment of their purpose. France, and of course, Spain, have acted a treacherous, a thievish part. They have stolen America from England, and whether they are able to possess themselves of that jewel or not hereafter, it was doubtless what they intended. Holland appears to me in a meaner light than any of them. They quarreled with a friend for an enemy's sake. The French led them by the nose, and the English have thrashed them for suffering it. My views of the contest being, and having been always, such, I have conse- [239] quently brighter hopes for England than her situation some time since seemed to justify. She is the only injured party. America, may, perhaps, call her the aggressor; but if she were so, America has not only repelled the injury, but done a greater. . . .

[250] To the Rev. John Newton, Feb. 24, 1783
. . . I am almost sorry to say that I am reconciled to the peace, being reconciled to it not upon principles of approbation, but necessity. The deplorable condition of the country, insisted on by the friends of administration, and not denied by their adversaries, convinces me that our only refuge under Heaven was in the treaty with which I quarreled. The treaty itself I find less objectionable than I did, Lord Shelburne having given a colour to some of the articles that makes them less painful in the contemplation. But my opinion upon the whole affair is, that now is the time (if indeed there is salvation for the country) for Providence to interpose to save it. A peace with the greatest political advantages would not have healed us; a peace with none may procrastinate our ruin for a season, but cannot ultimately

prevent it. The prospect [251] may make all tremble who have no trust in God, and even they that trust may tremble. The peace will probably be of short duration; and, in the ordinary course of things, another war must end us. A great country in ruins will not be beheld with eyes of indifference, even by those who have a better country to look to. But with them all will be well at last.

As to the Americans, perhaps I do not forgive them as I ought; perhaps I shall always think of them with some resentment as the destroyers, intentionally the destroyers, of this country. They have pushed that point farther than the house of Bourbon could have carried it in half a century. I may be prejudiced against them, but I do not think them equal to the task of establishing an empire. Great men are necessary for such a purpose; and their great men, I believe, are yet unborn. They have had passion and obstinacy [252] enough to do us much mischief; but whether the event will be salutary to themselves or not, must wait for proof. I agree with you, that it is possible America may become a land of extraordinary evangelical light; but, at the same time, I cannot discover any thing in their new situation peculiarly favourable to such a supposition. They cannot have more liberty of conscience than they had; at least, if that liberty was under any restraint, it was a restraint of their own making. Perhaps a new settlement in church and state may leave them less.—

From *The Letters of William Cowper*, ed. J. G. Frazer (London: Macmillan, 1912). Two volumes. Vol. I, p. 166.
The following letter is not included in Johnson's edition.

To Joseph Hill, Esq., Dec. 9, 1781

... You know the complexion of my sentiments upon some subjects well enough, and that I do not look upon public events either as fortuitous, or absolutely derivable either from the wisdom or folly of man. These indeed operate as second causes; but we must look for the cause of the decline or the prosperity of an empire elsewhere. I have long since done complaining of men and measures, having learned to consider them merely as the instruments of a higher Power, by which he either bestows wealth, peace, and dignity upon a nation when he favours it; or by which he strips it of all those honours, when public enormities long persisted in provoke him to inflict a public punishment. The counsels of great men become as foolish [167] and preposterous when he is pleased to make them so, as those of the frantic creatures in Bedlam, when they lay their distracted heads together to consider of the state of the nation. But I go still farther. The wisdom, or the want of wisdom, that we observe or think we observe in those that rule us, entirely out of the question, I cannot look upon the circumstances of this country, without being persuaded that I discern in them an entanglement and perplexity that I have never met with in the history of any other, which I think preternatural (if I may use the word on such a subject), prodigious in its kind, and such as human sagacity can never remedy. I have a good opinion of the understanding and integrity of some in power, yet I see plainly that they are unequal to the task. I think as favourably of some that are not in power, yet I am sure they have never yet in any of their speeches recommended the plan that would effect the salutary purpose. If we pursue the war, it is because we are desperate; it is plunging and sinking year after year into still greater depths of calamity. If we relinquish it, the remedy is equally desperate, and would prove I believe in the end no remedy at all. Either way we are undone. Perseverance will only enfeeble us more; we cannot recover the colonies by arms. If we discontinue the attempt, in that case we fling away voluntarily what in the other we strive ineffectually to regain; and whether we adopt the one measure or the other, are equally undone: for I consider the loss of America as the ruin of England. Were we less [168] encumbered than we are at home, we could but ill afford it; but being crushed as we are under an enormous debt that the public credit can at no rate carry much longer, the consequence is sure. Thus it appears to me that we are squeezed to death, between the two sides of that sort of alternative which is commonly called a cleft stick, the most threatening and portentous condition in which the interests of any country can possibly be found. . . .

68. King George III, Letters, 1766–82

From *The Correspondence of King George III*, ed. Sir John W. Fortescue (London: Macmillan, 1927–28). Six volumes. Vol. I, p. 244.
The papers of George III (1738–1820), as they reveal the operations of his mind, demonstrate his sincerity as well as his devotion to the British Empire, of which he considered himself the chief guardian. The portrait that emerges demands that we re-evaluate the stereotype of an inhumane and tyrannical ruler.

The King to Lord Rockingham.
(Jan., 1766)
. . . Talbot is as right as I can desire on the Stamp Act; strong for our declaring our right but willing to repeal, & has handsomely offer'd to attend the House daily & answer the very indecent conduct of those who oppose with so little Manners or Candour.

[268] Memorandum by the King.
(10 February, 1766)
Lord Rockingham this day came & complain'd to Me as if He was accus'd of having wrong stated my opinion on the Stamp Act; I told him I had on *Friday* given him permission to say I prefer'd Repealing to Enforcing the Stamp Act; but [269] that Modification I had ever

thought both more consistent with the honour of this Country, & all the Americans would with any degree of Justice hope for.

Memorandum by the King.
(11 February, 1766)

The late variety of opinions that have been reported to be mine on the Stamp Act, makes it very eligible that I should whilst fresh in my memory put on paper the whole of my conduct during this very arduous transaction.

From the first conversations on the best mode of restoring order & obedience in the American Colonys; I thought the modifying the Stamp Act, the wisest & most efficacious manner of proceeding; 1st. because any part remaining sufficiently ascertain'd the Right of the Mother Country to tax its Colonys & next that it would shew a desire to redress any just grievances; but if the unhappy Factions that divide this Country would not permit this in my opinion equitable plan to be follow'd I thought Repealing infinitely more eligible than Enforcing, which could only tend to widen the breach between this Country & America; my language to all ever continu'd pointing out my wish for Modification; on Friday 6th of February Ld. Rockingham said to Me that now the two partys meant to push for Repeal, or Enforce. I immediately answer'd that in that case I was for the former; He ask'd my permission to say so, which I freely gave. . . .

[275] Lord Rockingham to the King.
(Feb. 22, 1766)

Lord Rockingham humbly presumes to acquaint his Majesty, that upon the Question being proposed for the *Repeal* of the Stamp Act, an Amendment was proposed by Mr. Jenkinson—that instead of the word *Repeal*—the Words—Explain & Amend should be inserted.

After long debate the Question was put upon the *Repeal* & upon division the Numbers were for the *Repeal*. 275—against it—167.

Ld. Rockingham can not nor ought not to disguise from his Majesty the Pleasure he felt upon this Event as he flatters himself—that it is a Confirmation that the Opinion he had humbly submitted to his Majesty was well founded in point of Publick Opinion.

The Joy in the Lobby of the House of Commons which was full of Considerable Merchants both of London & from different Manufacturing Parts of this Country, was extreme.

The Division was about 2 oClock in the Morning, & being so late Ld. Rockingham did not immediately send an account.

[281] Lord Rockingham to the King.
(March 12, 1766)

[In the House of Lords] Lord Mansfield spoke with his Usual Eloquence & Ability but rather anticipating upon the Gloomy Prospect of the Colonies throwing off all Allegiance & turned all his Arguments —as if that Question was immediately before the Lords.

Ld. Camden answered him with Great Force & brought back the Question to the Matter really before us—Exclaimed [282] agt. the Act itself & the total Want of Policy in regard to the Conduct towards America in the Regulations of Trade—Stamp Act &c.

Ld. Rockingham hopes his Majesty will allow him to say that Ld. Camden's Speech was admirable, as indeed It is difficult to restrain from Commendation when one hears ones own Sentiments expressed with real Eloquence.

[435] Memorandum on the American Colonies.
(1766?)

. . . But supposing Forts and Garrisons in the Indian Countries were on the whole useful to Trade; Would not the expence and inconvenience of supporting them greatly exceed any advantages they could produce? And is it proper that this Nation should be at so much charge for that purpose, when the Americans contribute nothing to the maintainence of either. . . .

[436] If we had no Forts, Garrisons, or Settlements in the Indian Country it is probable we should never be in a State of National hostility with those people. Should any of our Colonies by misconduct get themselves into War with the Indians, let them get themselves out of it, as they always us'd to do when they were not so strong: Or else let them beg for Military assistance, acknowledge their want of it, be thankful for it, and pay its expence. . . .

[440] There remains still one more Question, Viz; What should be done with the Troops now dispersed all over that vast Continent when brought together more or less in consequence of a New Arrangement? I will readily give my opinion that in the present disposition of America they should not be brought out of that Country: Where then should they be? . . .

Altho' the conduct of New England, New York & other Provinces, and the temper of their Inhabitants give an equitable pretence to keep Troops among them, & afford strong reason to apprehend they may be wanted there; yet I see Objections to a measure which might unnecessarily provoke: I am persuaded a good Corps of Troops always in readiness within a few days sail of those Colonies would produce the same effect on their [441] minds as if they were actually on the Spot; and probably the insolence of their conduct last year proceeded from a knowledge that it was impossible to assemble such a force as might constrain them to duty & obedience.

[II:36] Lord Hillsborough to the King.
Whitehall July 22d 1768

Sir—The Dispatches I have now the Honour to send to your Majesty and which are just now arrived from Virginia, are still more alarming than those from Massachusetts Bay. . . . As the loss of a few days in Exigencies of the important & dangerous nature that now press, may be of infinite consequence, I humbly submitt to your Majesty whether it may not be proper for me to write to the Lords of the Admiralty to signifie that I have your Majesty's commands to inform their Lordships that it is very probable your Majesty may have occasion for five or six Ships of War and a Body of Marines on very short notice, & that it is your Majesty's pleasure that they do prepare accordingly. But the propriety and expediency of this step I entirely submitt to your Majesty's better Judgement. I have the honour to be Sir Your Most Dutifull Subject.

[III:47] Memoranda by the King.
(1773?)

There is no denying the serious crisis to which the disputes between the Mother Country and its North American Colonies are growing, and that the greatest temper and firmness are necessary to bring matters to a good issue, time is undoubtedly also an ingredient as indispensible on this occasion. Had the Americans in prosecuting their ill grounded claims put on an [III:48] appearance of mildness it might have been very difficult to chalk out the right path to be pursued; but they have boldly thrown off the mask and avowed that nothing less than a total independence of the British Legislature will satisfy them; this indeed decides the proper plan to be followed which is to stop the trade of all those Colonies who obey the mandate of the Congress for non importation, non exportation, and non Consumption, to assist them no further with presents to the Indians and give every kind assistance to those that conduct themselves otherways, which will make them quarrel among themselves their Separate interests must soon effect this and experience will then show them that the interference of the Mother Country is essentially necessary to prevent their becoming rivals.

Perhaps no one period in our History can produce so strange a circumstance, as the Gentlemen who pretend to be Patriots, instead of acting agreeable to such sentiments, avowing the unnatural doctrine of encouraging the American Colonies in their disputes with their Mother Country; this so plainly shews that Men not measures decide their opinions, that it is not necessary to deduce the total want of principle which this motly tribe by their conduct [unfinished]

[III:59] The King to Lord North.

Lord North—Since You left me this day, I have seen Lieutenant General Gage, who came to express his readiness though so lately come from America to return at a day's notice if the conduct of the Colonies should induce the directing coercive measures, his language was very consonant to his Character of an honest determined Man; he says they will be Lyons, whilst we are Lambs but if we take the resolute part they will undoubtedly prove very meek; he thinks the four Regiments intended to Relieve as many Regiments in America if sent to Boston are sufficient to prevent any disturbance; I wish You would see him and hear his ideas as to the mode of compelling Boston to submit to whatever may be thought necessary; indeed all men seem now to feel that the fatal compliance in 1766 has encouraged the Americans annually to encrease in their pretensions that thorough independency which one State has of another, but which is quite subversive of the obedience which a Colony owes to its Mother Country.
Queens House, Feb. 4th 1774

[III:130] The King to Lord North.
Sept. 11, 1774

Lord North,—The letter from the Quakers of Pennsilvania to some of the chiefs of that persuasion in London shews they retain that coolness which is a very strong characteristick of that body of people; but I was in hopes it would have contained some declaration of their submission to the mother-country; whilst by the whole tenour they seem to wish for England giving in [III:131] some degree way to the opinions of North America; the dye is now cast, the Colonies must either submit or triumph. I do not wish to come to severer measures, but we must not retreat; by coolness and an unremitted pursuit of the measures that have been adopted I trust they will come to submit; I have no objection afterwards to their seeing that there is no inclination for the present to lay fresh taxes on them, but I am clear there must always be one tax to keep up the right, and as such I approve of the Tea Duty.

[III:154] The King to Lord North.

Lord North—I return the private letters received from Lieut. General Gage; his idea of Suspending the Acts appears to me the most absurd that can be suggested; the People are ripe for mischief upon which the Mother Country adopts suspending the measures She has thought necessary this must suggest to the Colonies a fear that alone prompts them to their present violence; we must either master them or totally leave them to themselves and treat them as Aliens; I do not by this mean to insinuate that I am for advice [sic] new measures; but I am for Supporting those already undertaken.
Queens House, Nov. 18th 1774

The King to Lord North.
November 18, 1774

Lord North—I am not sorry that the line of conduct seems now chalked out, which the enclosed dispatches thoroughly justify; the New England Governments are in a state of rebellion, blows must decide whether they are to be subject to this country or independent. . . .

[III:156] The King to Lord North.
December 15, 1774

[The King opposed the Commission for Peace, but could not prevent its formation; it was with the greatest difficulty that George III was persuaded to give his consent:]

I am not so fond of the sending Commissioners to examine into the disputes; this looks so like the Mother Country being more afraid of the continuance of the dispute than the Colonies and I cannot think it likely to make them reasonable; I do not want to drive them to despair but to Submission, which nothing but feeling the inconvenience of their situation can bring their pride to submit to.

[III:175] The King to Lord North.
Queens House Feb. 15th 1775

. . . but where violence is with resolution repelled it commonly yields, and I owne though a thorough friend to holding out the Olive Branch I have not the smallest doubt that if it does not succeed that when once vigorous measures appear to be the only means left of bringing the Americans to a due Submission to the Mother Country that the Colonies will Submit. . . .

[III:421] The King to Lord North.
Queens House Feb. 24th 1777

The accounts from America are most comfortable, the Surprize and want of Spirit of the Hessian Officers as well as Soldiers at Trenton is not much to their credit and will undoubtedly rather elate the Rebels who till then were in a state of the greatest despondency; I wish Sir W. Howe had placed None but British Troops in the Out Posts; but I am certain by a letter I have seen from Lord Cornwallis that the Rebells will soon have sufficient reason to fall into the former dejection.

Lord George Germain will tomorrow propose Gen. Clinton for Canada and Burgoyne to join Howe. I thoroughly approve of this. . . .

[IV:350] The King to Lord North.
June 11th, 1779

The object of Sir W. Meredith, pretends to be the desire of Peace with America, that of Mr. Eden is to be employed as a private Negociator with Franklin to effect Peace with America, it is therefore easy to blend my thoughts on both ideas, indeed I rather wish to convey my sentiments to Lord North on so very serious a subject on Paper, as it will enable him at any time to recurr to this when he wants to know my ideas on the Subject.

I should think it the greatest instance among the many I have met with of ingratitude and injustice, if it could be supposed, that any Man in my Dominions more ardently desired the restoration of Peace and solid happiness in every part of this Empire than I do, there is no personal Sacrifice I could not readily yield for so desirable an object, but at the same time no inclination to get out of the present difficulties which certainly keep my mind very far from a state of ease, can incline me to enter into what I look upon as the destruction of the Empire. I have heard Lord North frequently drop that the advantages to be gained by this contest could never repay the expence, I owne that let any War be ever so successful if persons will set down and weigh the Expences they will find as in the last that it has impoverished the State, enriched individuals, and perhaps raised the Name only of the Conquerors, but this is only weighing such events in the Scale of a Tradesman behind his Counter; it is necessary for those in the Station it has pleased Divine Providence to place me to weigh whether expences though very great [IV:351] are not some times necessary to prevent what might be more ruinous to a Country than the loss of money. The present Contest with America I cannot help seeing as the most serious in which any Country was ever engaged it contains such a train of consequences that they must be examined to feel its real weight; whether the laying a Tax was deserving all the Evils that have arisen from it, I should suppose no man could alledge that without being thought more fit for Bedlam than a Seat in the Senate; but step by step the demands of America have risen—independence is their object, that certainly is one which every man not willing to sacrifice every object to a *momentary and* inglorious Peace must concurr with me in thinking that this Country can never submit to; should America succeed in that, the West Indies must follow them, not independence, but must for its own interest be dependent on North America; Ireland would soon follow the same plan and be a separate State, then this Island would be reduced to itself, and soon would be a poor Island indeed, for reduced in Her Trade Merchants would retire with their wealth to Climates more to their Advantage, and Shoals of Manufacturers would leave this country for the New Empire; these self evident consequences, are not worse than what can arise should the Almighty permit every event to turn out to our disadvantage; consequently this Country has but one Sensible, one great line to follow, the being ever ready to make Peace when to be obtained without submitting to terms that in their consequence must annihilate this Empire, and with firmness to make every effort to deserve Success.

[V:297] The King to Lord North.
Windsor, Nov. 3rd, 1781

Lord North will be naturally curious to know what news has been brought this day by Lieut Col. Conway; I have within this half hour seen him and as far as I have been able as yet to collect from him, that having had Sir Henry Clinton's leave to come to England when the campaign in Virginia was supposed to be at an end, and being better able from having later left that Province than anyone at New York to state the situation of Lord Cornwallis, Sir Henry had judged it right still to send him with his Dispatches; his opinion seems to be that Lord Cornwallis will certainly leave the Chesapeak and return to Charles Town after having beat LaFayette, and that both these are likely events, and that before he sailed a report of this had arrived from Philadelphia; on the whole he supposes we shall in very few days hear from Lord Cornwallis, and he trusts Sir Henry Clinton will soon have something decisive to communicate: this I own, gives me satisfaction, with such excellent troops if such an event can be effected I think success must ensue; I feel the justness of our cause; I put the greatest confidence in valour of both Navy and Army and above all in the Assistance of Divine Providence: the moment is certainly anxious; the dye is now cast whether this shall be a Great Empire or the least dignified of the European States; the object is certainly worth struggling for and I trust the Nation is equally determined with myself to meet the conclusion with firmness; if this Country will persist, I think an honourable termination cannot fail, for truth is ever too strong for such a conduct as France has held, and if we have any material success she will become sick of the part she has acted; duplicity can never withstand any disasters. . . . [The King is hoping for a victory by Cornwallis. The news of the disaster at Yorktown reached England on November 25, 1781.]

[V:304] The King to Lord North.
Nov. 28, 1781
I have already directed Lord G. Germain to put on paper the mode that seems most feesible [sic] for conducting the War, that every Member of the Cabinet may have his propositions to weigh by themselves, when I shall expect to hear their sentiments separately, that we may adopt a Plan and abide by it; fluctuating Counsels, and taking up measures with(out) connecting them with the whole of this complicated War must make us weak in every part; with the assistance of Parliament I do not doubt if measures are well concerted a good end may yet be made to this War, but if we despond certain ruin ensues.

The King to Lord North.
Nov. 28, 1781
. . . I have no doubt when Men are a little recovered of the shock felt by the bad news, and feel that if we recede no one can tell to what a degree the consequence of this country will be diminished, that they will then find the necessity of carrying on the War, though the mode of it may require a(l)terations.

[VI:154] The King to Lord Shelburne.
I cannot conclude without mentioning how sensibly I feel the dismemberment of America from this Empire, and that I should be miserable indeed if I did not feel that no blame on that Account can be laid at my door, and did I not also know that knavery seems to be so much the striking feature of its Inhabitants that it may not in the end be an evil that they become Aliens to this Kingdom.
Windsor, Novr. 10th, 1782

[VI:157] The King to Mr. Townshend.
Mr. Townshend may send the Messenger to Paris with the draft of the Preliminary Articles (of peace) and the Dispatches as soon as they are ready, without waiting for my seeing the latter; He cannot be surprised at my not being over anxious for the perusal of them, as Parliament having to my astonishment come into the ideas of granting a Separation to North America, has disabled me from longer defending the just rights of this Kingdom. But I certainly disclaim thinking myself answerable for any evils that may arise from the adoption of this Measure as necessity not conviction had made me subscribe to it.
Windsor, Novr. 19th, 1782

[VI:169] The King to Lord Grantham.
. . . I think Peace so essential, and that the dreadful Resolution

141

of the 27th of February last of the House of Commons has so entirely
removed the real cause of the War to the utter shame of that branch
of the Legislature, that it would be madness not to conclude Peace
on the best possible terms we can obtain.
Windsor, Decr. 3rd, 1782

69. Edward Gibbon, Memoirs

From *The Memoirs of the Life of Edward Gibbon with Various
Observations and Excursions, By Himself*, ed. George Birkbeck
Hill (London: Methuen, 1900). P. 191.
    Edward Gibbon (1737–94) wrote the greatest historical work
in English, *The Decline and Fall of the Roman Empire*, perhaps
the one English history which may be regarded as definitive. Besides being a member of Johnson's famous club, Gibbon was a
member of Parliament from 1774 to 1780, and in 1779 was
appointed as one of the lords commissioners of trade and plantations, a post in which he advised on colonial matters. The
footnotes reprinted here are Birkbeck Hill's.

    I took my seat [in Parliament, 1774] at the beginning of the mem-
orable contest between Great Britain and America, and supported
with many a sincere and silent vote, the rights, though not, perhaps,[1]
the interest, of the mother country. After a fleeting illusive hope, prudence condemned me to acquiesce in the humble station of a mute.

---

  [1] [314] We may well be astonished at the word "perhaps" in the text, when
these "silent and sincere votes" helped to set England at war, not only with
her thirteen colonies, but also with the three chief naval powers of the Continent of Europe—France, Spain, and Holland. . . .
  He might have learnt wisdom from his friend David Hume [the eminent
philosopher], who wrote on October 26, 1775: "Arbitrary power can extend
its oppressive arm to the Antipodes; but a limited government can never long
be upheld at a distance, even where no disgusts have intervened; much less
where such violent animosities have taken place. We must therefore annul all
the charters; abolish every democratical power in every colony; repeal the Ha-
beas Corpus Act with regard to them; invest every governor with full discre-
tionary or arbitrary powers; confiscate the estates of all the chief planters, and
hang three-fourths of their clergy. To execute such acts of destructive violence
twenty thousand men will not be sufficient; nor thirty thousand to maintain
them, in so wide and disjointed a territory. And who are to pay so great an
army? The Colonists cannot at any time, much less after reducing them to
such a state of desolation: we ought not, and indeed cannot, in the overloaded,
or rather overwhelmed and totally ruined state of our finances. Let us therefore
lay aside all anger, shake hands and part friends. Or, if we retain any anger,
let it only be against ourselves for our past folly; and against that wicked mad-
man Pitt, who has reduced us to our present condition." (*Letters of Hume to
Strahan*, p. 289.)

I was not armed by Nature and education with the intrepid energy of mind and voice. . . . Timidity was fortified by pride, and even the success of my [192] pen discouraged the trial of my voice. But I assisted at the debates of a free assembly; I listened to the attack and defence of eloquence and reason; I had a near prospect of the characters, views, and passions of the first men of the age. The cause of government was ably vindicated by Lord North, a statesman of spotless integrity, a consummate master of debate, who could wield, with equal dexterity, the arms of reason and ridicule. He was seated on the Treasury-bench between his Attorney and Solicitor General, the two pillars of the law and state; . . . and the minister might indulge in a short slumber, whilst he was upholden on either hand by the majestic sense of Thurlow, [193] and the skilful eloquence of Wedderburne. From the adverse side of the house an ardent and powerful opposition was supported, by the lively declamation of Barré, the legal acuteness of Dunning, the profuse and philosophic fancy of Burke, and the argumentative vehemence of Fox, who in the conduct of a party approved himself equal to the conduct of an empire. By such men every operation of peace and war, every principle of justice or policy, every question of authority and freedom, was attacked and defended; and the subject of the momentous contest was the union or separation of Great Britain and America. The eight sessions that I sat in parliament were a school of civil prudence, the first and most essential virtue of an historian. . . .

[212] In the first session of the new parliament [1781], administration stood their ground; their final overthrow was reserved for the second. The American war had once been the favourite of the country: the pride of England was irritated by the resistance of her colonies, and the executive power was driven [213] by national clamour into the most vigorous and coercive measures.[2] But the length of a fruitless contest, the loss of armies, the accumulation of debt and taxes, and the hostile confederacy of France, Spain, and Holland, indisposed the public to the American war, and the persons by whom it was conducted; the representatives of the people, followed, at a slow distance, the changes of their opinion, and the ministers who refused to bend, were broken by the tempest. As soon as Lord North had lost, or was about to lose, a majority in the House of Commons, he surrendered his office, and retired to a private station, with the tranquil assurance of a clear conscience and a cheerful temper: the old fabric was dissolved, and the posts of government were occupied by the victorious and veteran troops of opposition.[3]

[2] [317] Gibbon, on October 14, 1775, mentions the Addresses which fill the Gazette—Addresses urging the prosecution of the war (*Corres.*, I, 271). London, Bristol, and the Protestants of Ireland were against the war. The Scotch, "almost to a man, proffered life and fortune in support of the present measures. The same approbation was given, though with somewhat less earnestness and unanimity, by a large number of towns in England. The recruiting service, however, a kind of political barometer with respect to the sentiments of the lowest orders, went on very heavily." (*Annual Register*, 1776.)

[3] [323] The following extracts from Gibbon's Letters show his opinion of the ministry:—

70. Letters from a Soldier in America, 1775–77

From *Letters from America, 1773–1780*, ed. Eric Robson (New York: Barnes & Noble, 1953). P. 16.

These letters were written by Sir James Murray-Pulteney, a young Scottish lord about twenty-five years old, when serving as field officer in the American war. They were sent to his sister back home.

Dublin, Nov. 18th, 1775

Where we are going, how we are going, and what we are going about nobody pretends to conjecture. Our whole force amounts to 2,600 men compleat with which we can make but little impression on the Continent of America. We are perhaps only to be in readiness to receive the [17] proper augmentation of forces and take the field early in the spring, or it is perhaps imagined that a smaller force will be necessary to overawe the southern colonies on account of their Negroes. . . .

Now, my dear Bessy, as you've most probably become somewhat of a politician of late which every country lady ought to be more or less, listen to what I'm going to say. To subdue by force of arms a country of several thousands of miles in extent, almost entirely covered with wood is not an easy operation, if there were no inhabitants at all: but when we consider that there are no less than 3,000,000 exasperated to the last degree and enflamed to the highest pitch of enthusiasm; we have too many instances of what that enthusiasm has been capable of producing not to be very doubtful of the event. During the last war the Americans, those of New England in particular, were most

---

[324] (Jan. 29, 1776) I much fear that our leaders have not a genius which can act at the distance of 3,000 miles.

(August 11, 1777) What a wretched piece of work do we seem to be making of it in America! . . . Upon the whole, I find it much easier to defend the justice than the policy of our measures, but there are certain cases where whatever is repugnant to sound policy ceases to be just.

(December 16, 1777) I shall scarcely give my consent to exhaust still further the finest country in the world in the prosecution of a war from whence no reasonable man entertains any hopes of success.

(December 6, 1781) The present state of public affairs is indeed deplorable, and I fear *hopeless*.

Lord Sheffield, defending his friend, says that "although Mr. Gibbon was not perfectly satisfied with *every* measure, yet he uniformly supported all the principal ones regarding the American war. . . . He liked the brilliant society of a Club, the most distinguished members of which were notorious for their opposition to Government, and might be led, in some degree, to join in their language." (Gibbon's *Misc. Works*, I, 236.)

Unfortunately very few division lists are preserved. I find, however, that on Feb. 2, 1778, he voted for Fox's motion that "no more of the Old Corps be sent out of the Kingdom." Had it been carried, new levies only could have been sent to America. (*Parl. Hist.*, XIX, 684.)

deservedly the contempt [18] of our army, they still continue to act in what we are pleased to call a cowardly manner, witness the efficacy of that manner on Bunkers Hill and in the inaction which our troops have been obliged to preserve since that day. They were entrenched up to the eyes, kept up a constant fire with little or no danger to themselves. . . . The greatest obstacle to an [19] accommodation lies now perhaps on the side of the Americans, who may perhaps be tempted to follow Dr. Jonstone's [Samuel Johnson] advice and encircle with a diadem the brows of Mr. Cushing [a member of the Continental Congress], or at least insist on unreasonable terms. As to the matter of right, if the Americans are convinced that it is more for the good of that country, to be independent of Great Britain and at the same time are able to accomplish it, they are most indisputably in the right to make the attempt. If we can keep them in a dependence beneficial to Great Britain, we have a most undeniable right to preserve that dominion, so that the matter of right cannot well be decided till towards the end of next summer. . . .

We are all in great spirits here, as to myself being appointed to the Light Infantry I have got a double barrel fusee and propose shooting 7 Americans a week exclusive of women and children to teach them to defend their liberties and properties against that Crown and that Parliament from which I receive 10s. a day Irish money. God bless their noble honours. Would it not be hard, now? Would it not be bar- [20] barous? if Government should patch up a peace which can only be considered as an arbitrary Game Act: the most agreeable plan upon the whole considering the tract of country [which] will fall to our share would be that of making them property, which I accordingly hope to submit to the wisdom of the Legislature. . . .

[23]   Long Island Near Charles Town,
                                      S. Carolina, July 7th, 1776
You will, by the time you receive this, hear of our unfortunate attempt upon Charles Town, one of the most singular events that has yet conspired to degrade the name of the British nation. Such another invariable succession of crosses and disappointments, as have hitherto persecuted us in all our attempts, will be sufficient to operate a revolution in my political and religious principles: for I am not even now sufficiently convinced that the Americans are in the right, nor that Providence would so visibly interpose in their favour if they were. . . .

[47]   Head of Elke, Maryland, Sept. 1st, 1777
Mr. Washington is at a place called Wilmington about 23 miles from this. They say that he threatens to fight rather than give up Philadelphia. If he risks an engagement in an accessible situation it will be a sign that he thinks [48] his cause in a very desperate situation, or that he is very little acquainted with the nature of the troops that are to act for and against him. A month or two will enable us to judge with a little more certainty of the event, but I cannot help being still of opinion that the Cause of Liberty is in a very delicate situation: and I sincerely wish that it was over. It is a barbarous business and in

a barbarous country. The novelty is worn off and I see no advantages to be reaped from it. This particular period indeed is so very interesting, and promises to be so active that it makes up for all, and I should interiorly regret it very much if any supernatural accident was to put a stop to the campaign.

[After France entered the war, Murray served on the Leeward Islands, taking part in the operations against the French in St. Lucia, December, 1778; and he was stationed at St. Lucia, Antigua, and Jamaica until 1782.]

71. Horace Walpole, Letters, 1768–83

From *The Letters of Horace Walpole*, ed. Mrs. Paget Toynbee (Oxford: Clarendon Press, 1903). Sixteen volumes. Vol. VII, p. 208.

Horace Walpole (1717–97), the fourth son of the great Prime Minister Sir Robert Walpole, was devoted to the Whig tradition of the Walpole family. A famous antiquarian, art collector, and author, he was also a member of Parliament from 1741 to 1767, representing various districts. His memoirs and letters, considered among the best records of the social scene in England during the second half of the eighteenth century, reveal his wit, charm, and fascination for political intrigue.

To Sir Horace Mann, August 4, 1768

Well! but we have a worse riot, though a little farther off. Boston —not in Lincolnshire, though we have had a riot even there, but in New England, is almost in rebellion, and two regiments are ordered thither. Letters are come in, that say the other provinces disapprove; and even the soberer persons there. In truth, it is believed [209] in the City that this tumult will be easily got the better of. Our navy, too, is in so very formidable plight, that our neighbours will not much care to interfere. It is tremendous the force we have in the river, at Plymouth and Portsmouth. [In this excerpt Walpole is alluding to the Boston riot on June 10, 1768, as a result of the seizure of Hancock's sloop *Liberty* by a British man-of-war.]

[378] To Sir Horace Mann, May 6, 1770

You have seen the accounts from Boston. The tocsin seems to be sounded to America. I have many visions about that country, and fancy I see twenty empires and republics forming upon vast scales over all that continent, which is growing too mighty to be kept in subjection to half a dozen exhausted nations in Europe. . . .

[VIII:418] To Sir Horace Mann, February 2, 1774

. . . there is an ostrich-egg laid in America, where the Bostonians have canted three hundred chests of tea into the ocean [on December 16, 1773], for they will drink tea with our Parliament.

[VIII:423] To the Rev. William Mason, February 14, 1774

The ministers have a much tougher business on their hand, in which even their factotum the Parliament may not be able to ensure success —I mean the rupture with America [as a result of the Boston Tea Party]. If all the black slaves were in rebellion, I should have no doubt in choosing my side, but I scarce wish perfect freedom to merchants who are the bloodiest of all tyrants. I should think the souls of the Africans would sit heavy on the swords of the Americans.

[VIII:436] To Sir Horace Mann, March 28, 1774

. . . The general tone against the Bostonians is threats. It remains to see whether America will be as pliant as we say they must be. I don't pretend to guess, for I seldom guess right; but we could even afford to lose America. Every day gives us more East Indies. Advice has just come that we have taken Tanjore. . . .

[VIII:449] To Sir Horace Mann, May 1, 1774

There is indeed a great business in agitation, and has been for some time; but, without the thorough-bass of opposition, it makes no echo out of Parliament. Its Parliamentary name is *Regulations for Boston* [the Coercive Acts]. Its essence, the question of sovereignty over America. Shall I tell you in one word my opinion? If the Bostonians resist, the dispute will possibly be determined in favour of the crown by force. If they temporize or submit, waiting for a more favourable moment, and preparing for it, the wound, skinned over, will break out hereafter with more violence. . . .

[IX:61] To Sir Horace Mann, October 6, 1774

[News from] America, I doubt, is still more unpromising. There are whispers of their having assembled an armed force, and of earnest supplications arrived for succours of men and ships. A civil war is no trifle; and [IX:62] how we are to suppress or pursue it in such a vast region, with a handful of men, I am not an Alexander to guess. . . .

[IX:86] To Sir Horace Mann, November 14, 1774

There are advices from America that are said to be extremely bad. I don't know the particulars; but I have never augured well of that dispute! I fear we neither know how to proceed or retreat! I believe this is the case with many individuals, as well as with the public.

[IX:106] To the Hon. Henry Seymour Conway, December 1, 1774

The long-expected sloop is arrived at last [from America] and is, indeed, a *man of war*! The General Congress have voted a non-importation, a non-exportation, a non-consumption; that, in case of hostilities committed by the troops at Boston, the several provinces will march to the assistance of their countrymen; that the cargoes of ships at sea shall be sold on their arrival, and the money arising thence given to the poor at Boston; that a letter, in the nature of a petition of rights, shall be sent to the King; another to the House [IX:107] of Commons; a third to the people of England; a demand of repeal of all the Acts of Parliament affecting North America passed during this reign, as also of the Quebec Bill and these resolutions not to be altered till such repeal is obtained. Well, I believe you do not regret being neither in Parliament nor in administration! As you are an idle man, and have nothing else to do, you may sit down and tell one a remedy for all this. . . . We are at our wit's end—which was no great journey. Oh, you conclude Lord Chatham's crutch will be supposed a wand, and be sent for. They might as well send for *my* crutch; and they should not have it; the stile is a little too high to help them over. His Lordship [Chatham] is a little fitter for raising a storm than laying one, and of late seems to have lost both virtues. The Americans at least have acted like men, gone to the bottom at once, and set the whole upon the whole. Our conduct has been that of pert children: we have thrown a pebble at a mastiff, and are surprised it was not frightened. Now we must be worried by it, or must kill the guardian of the house, which will be plundered the moment little master has nothing but the old nurse to defend it. . . .

[IX:150] To the Hon. Henry Seymour Conway, January 22, 1775
Instead of drawing a circle with his [Chatham's] wand round the House of Lords, and ordering them to pacify America, on the terms he prescribed before they ventured to quit the circumference of his commands, he brought a ridiculous, uncommunicated, unconsulted motion for addressing the King immediately to withdraw the troops from Boston, as an earnest of lenient measures. The opposition stared and shrugged; the courtiers stared and laughed. His own two or three adherents left him, except Lord Camden and Lord Shelburne, and except Lord Temple. . . . Himself was not much animated, but very hostile; particularly on Lord Mansfield. . . . He talked of three millions of Whigs in America, and told the ministers they were checkmated and had not a move left to make. Lord Camden was as strong. . . . At eight at night it [the motion] was rejected by 68 to 18. . . . This interlude would be only entertaining, if the scene was not so totally gloomy. The Cabinet have determined on civil war, and regiments are going from Ireland and our West Indian Islands. On Thursday the plan of the war is to be laid before both Houses.

[IX:153] To Sir Horace Mann, January 25, 1775
The times are indeed very serious. Pacification with America is not the measure adopted. More regiments are ordered thither, and to-morrow a plan, I fear equivalent to a declaration of war, is to be laid before both Houses. They are bold ministers, methinks, who do not hesitate on a civil war, in which victory may bring ruin, and disappointment endanger their heads. Lord Chatham has already spoken out: and though his outset (a motion in the Lords last Friday) was

neither wise nor successful, he will certainly be popular again with the clamorous side, which no doubt will become the popular side too, for all wars are costly, and consequently grievous. Acquisition alone can make [IX:154] those burthens palatable; and in a war with our own colonies we must afflict instead of acquiring them, and cannot recover them without having undone them. I am still to learn wisdom and experience, if these things are not so.

[IX:167] To the Rev. William Mason, February 18, 1775
The war with America goes on briskly, that is as far as voting goes. A great majority in both Houses is as brave as a mob ducking a pickpocket. They flatter themselves they shall terrify the colonies into submission in three months, and are amazed to hear that there is no [IX:168] such probability. They might as well have excommunicated them, and left it to the devil to put the sentence into execution.

[IX:171] To Sir Horace Mann, March 20, 1775
The Houses go on fulminating against America; we shall see whether their edicts are regarded, or rather their troops and generals. The province of New York seems to be better disposed than the other colonies; but we must wait for the re-echo of our new Acts, and for the Congress in May. In three months we shall hear whether it will be war or peace. . . .

[IX:191] To Sir Horace Mann, May 7, 1775
There is, indeed, beyond the seas an opposition so big, that most folks call it a rebellion, which if computed by the tract of country it occupies, we, as so diminutive in comparison, ought rather to be called in rebellion to that. All the late letters thence are as hostile as possible; and, unless their heads are as cool as their hearts seem determined, it will not be long before we hear of the overt acts of war. Our three Generals [Burgoyne, Clinton, and Howe] are sailed, and Gage will have a pretty large army. . . . Yet it is that kind of war in which even victory will ruin us.

[IX:203] To Sir Horace Mann, June 5, 1775
You must lower your royal crest a little, for your Majesty's forces have received a check in America; but this is too sad a subject for mirth. [The account of the skirmish at Lexington, April 19, 1775, follows.] [IX:204] So here is this fatal war commenced! "The child that is unborn shall rue The hunting of that day!"

[IX:209] To the Rev. William Mason, June 12, 1775
By the waters of Babylon we sit down and weep, when we think of thee, O America! Tribulation on tribulation! Since Gage's defeat [at Lexington], eighteen, some say twenty-eight thousand men have invested Boston; ten thousand more are on their march from Rhode Island. Two ships laden with provisions for him have been destroyed at New York, and all his Majesty's friends turned out thence. . . . The City [London] says there must be a pacification and a change of

actors [ministers]. Much good may it do those who will read their parts!

[IX:228] To the Rev. William Mason, August 7, 1775
Mrs. Britannia orders her senate to proclaim America a continent of cowards, and vote it should be starved unless it will drink tea with her. She sends her only army to be besieged in one of their towns, and half her fleet to besiege the *terra firma*, but orders her army to do nothing, in hopes that the American senate at Philadelphia will be so frightened at the British army being besieged in Boston, that it will sue for peace. At last she gives her army leave to sally out, but being twice defeated [at Lexington and Bunker Hill], she determines to carry on the war so vigorously till she has not a man left, that all England will be satisfied with the total loss of America; and if everybody is satisfied who can be blamed? Besides is not our dignity maintained? have not we carried our majesty beyond all example? When did you ever read before of a besieged army threatening military execution on the country of the besiegers! . . .

[IX:242] To the Rev. William Mason, September 6, 1775 [from Paris]
You may judge whether they do not stare at all we are doing! They [the French] will not believe me when I tell them that the American war is *fashionable*, for one is forced to use that word to convey to them an idea of the majority. . . . I have not met with a single Frenchman who does not express indignation or sneer contempt at all our late acts of Parliament.

[IX:278] To Sir Horace Mann, October 28, 1775
In both Houses the war [the debate on America] was brisk and warm; the Lords sat till eleven, and the Commons till four, and the court was galled, though it kept the field. . . . In the Commons, Mr. Conway, in a better speech than ever was made, exposed all their [the administration's] outrages and blunders; and Charles Fox told Lord North that nor Alexander nor Caesar had ever conquered so much as he had lost in one campaign. . . . This is a sketch of the present situation: I think it will not mend abroad, and must grow more turbulent at home. France and Spain, by only feeding the war underhand, can baffle all our attempts; and without their declaring themselves, we must exhaust our men, money, navies, and trade. . . .

[IX:316] To Sir Horace Mann, December 26, 1775
I, who am no very good judge, have always thought the American war would be of long duration; and if 200 [Americans] *have* run away, the army besieging Boston and the body under Montgomery (an Irishman) have shown some spirit. . . .

[IX:428] To the Countess of Upper Ossory, October 15, 1776
About the American news, I say what I always have thought and said, that whatever way this war ends, it will be fatal to this country. The liberty of America made it flourish to the prodigious height it did.

If governed by an army, instead of inviting settlers and trade, it will be deserted and be a burthen to us, as Peru and Mexico, with all their mines, have been to Spain. The war has already drained us of men; if the army could be brought back, how many, between climate and other chances, will return? Our ships are entering on their third winter in those seas, and we have flung away in those three years what should have lessened our debt, and prepared against a war with France. . . .
How soon we shall have a French war, I know not; it is much talked of already at Paris; but come when it will, then will be the moment of judging of this war with the colonies. I believe France will then recover Canada, with interest. . . .

[IX:429] To the Hon. Henry Seymour Conway, October 31, 1776
Here is a solution of the Americans declaring themselves independent. [Probably an allusion to the willingness of France to help the Americans. Walpole fears war with France.] Oh! the folly, the madness, the guilt of having plunged us into this abyss! Were we and a few more endued with any uncommon penetration?—No: they who did not see as far [IX:430] *would* not. . . . If the court should receive any more of what they call good news, I think the war with France will be unavoidable. It was the victory at Long Island, and the frantic presumption it occasioned, that has ripened France's measures. . . . I do not enjoy the distress of my country. I think we are undone —I have always thought so; whether we enslaved America, or lost it totally: so we that were against the war could expect no good issue.

[X:32] To Sir Horace Mann, April 3, 1777
It is my opinion that the King's affairs are in a very bad position in America. I do not say that his armies may not gain advantages again; though I believe there has been as much design as cowardice in the behaviour of the provincials, who seem to have been apprised that protraction of the war would be more certainly advantageous to them than heroism. Washington, the dictator, has shown himself both a Fabius and a Camillus. His march through our lines is allowed a prodigy of generalship. In one word, I look upon a great part of America as lost to this country! It is not less deplorable that, between art and contention, such an inveteracy has been sown between the two countries as will probably outlast even the war! Supposing this unnatural enmity should not soon involve us in other wars, which would be extraordinary indeed, what a difference, in a future war with France and Spain, to have the colonies in the opposite scale, instead of being in ours! What politicians are those who have preferred the empty name of *sovereignty* to that of *alliance*, and forced subsidies to the golden ocean of [free] commerce!

[X:182] To the Rev. William Mason, February 4, 1778
The enigma of the day, as he has oft been, is Lord Chatham. He has quarrelled with General Rockingham on the question of independence, and in a manner declared off, yet he is expected today in

the House of Lords to anathematize the new levies [for troops]. There is much talk too of his coming into place, which I doubt; everybody must have discovered that his crutch is no magic wand, and if the lame leads the blind it is not the way of shunning a ditch. . . .

[X:193] To Sir Horace Mann, February 18, 1778

How shall I intimate to you, that you must lower your topsails, waive your imperial dignity, and strike to the colours of the thirteen United Provinces of America? . . . No military *new* event has occasioned this revolution. The sacrifice has been made on the altar of peace. Stop again: peace is not made, it is only implored,—and I fear, only on this side of the Atlantic. In short, yesterday, February 17th, a most memorable era, Lord North opened his conciliatory plan,—no partial, no collusive one. In as few words as I can use, it solicits peace with the States of America: it haggles on no terms; it acknowledges the Congress, or anybody that pleases to treat; it confesses errors, misinformation, ill-success, and impossibility of conquest; it disclaims taxation, desires commerce, hopes for assistance, allows the independence of America, not verbally, yet virtually, and suspends hostilities till June [X:194] 1779. It does a little more: not verbally, but virtually, it confesses that the opposition have been in the right from the beginning to the end. The warmest American cannot deny but these gracious condescensions are ample enough to content that whole continent; and yet, my friend, such accommodating facility had one defect,—it came too late. The treaty between the high and mighty States and France is signed; and instead of peace, we must expect war with the high allies.

[X:214] To the Rev. William Mason, April 8, 1778

Though my daily fellow-labourers [the newspapers] of this morning will give you a minute account of the great event of yesterday, I should be a very negligent gazetteer if I took no notice of it. Lord Chatham fell in the Senate—not by daggers nor by the thunder of Lord Suffolk's eloquence. He had spoken with every symptom of debility, repeated his own phrases, could not recollect his own ideas, and which was no new practice, persisted in our asserting sovereignty over America, [X:215] *though he could not tell by what means.* It was only new to confess his ignorance. The Duke of Richmond answered him with much decency and temper, though Lord Chatham had called *pursuit without means,* timid and pusillanimous conduct. The Earl was rising to reply, but fell down in a second fit of apoplexy, with strong convulsions and slabbering at the mouth. I do not doubt but the *Morning Post* will allow the Duke more rhetoric than it ever acknowledged, in order to ascribe Lord Chatham's fall to his Grace's invectives—but he, who is all tenderness and sensibility, was so affected, that at night the Duchess [of Richmond] desired me not to name it—yet Lord Chatham is not dead and today is better, if existing after two strokes can be called so. To be sure his biographer would have a fairer field, had he died in his vocation [addressing Parliament]. In truth, I see no good he could have done, since he has embraced the idea of still conquering America—but much harm he must have occasioned had the Court adopted him. Now I reckon him politically dead; he will probably neither recover strength or faculties, his family will if possible prevent his reappearance, and the Court will scarce inoculate a half-dead skeleton on their other infirmities. . . .

I can tell you nothing definitive on war or peace. Pacification with France, and even with America, has been much sounded these last days—probably to prop the stocks—but the selection of Governor Johnstone for one of the commissioners [of peace, appointed to treat with the colonies], who even during all the late debates anathematized American independence, implies not only adherence to sovereignty but no thoughts of change—of Johnstone [X:216] it is enough to say that though a Scot in opposition, he never lost sight of the promised land.

[X:272] To the Rev. William Mason, July 4, 1778

. . . What has an army of fifty thousand men fighting for sovereignty achieved in America? retreated from Boston, retreated from Philadelphia, laid down their arms at Saratoga, and lost thirteen provinces! nor is the measure yet full! such are the consequences of our adopting new legislators, new historians, new doctors! Locke and Sidney, for Humes, Johnsons and Dalrymples! When the account is made up and a future historiographer royal casts up debtor and creditor, I hope he will please to state the balance between the last war *for America* [the Seven Years' War] and the present *against* it. The advantages of that we know, Quebec, the [X:273] Havannah, Martinico, Guadeloupe, the East Indies, the French and Spanish fleets destroyed, etc., etc.; all the bills *per contra* are not yet come in! Our writers have been disputing for these hundred and sixty-six years on Whig and Tory principles. Their successors, who I suppose will continue the controversy, will please to allow at least that if the ministers of both parties were equally complaisant when in power, the splendour of the Crown (I say nothing of the happiness of the people which is never taken into the account) has constantly been augmented by Whig administrations, and has faded (and then and now a little more) when Tories have governed! The reason is as plain: Whig principles are founded on sense; a Whig may be a fool, a Tory must be so: the consequence is plain; a Whig when a minister may abandon his principles, but he will retain his sense and will therefore not risk the felicity of his posterity by sacrificing everything to selfish views. A Tory attaining power hurries to establish despotism: the honour, the trade, the wealth, the peace of the nation, all are little to him in comparison with the despotic will of his master [the King]. . . .

[X:283] To the Rev. William Mason, July 18, 1778

As I was going out this evening I stopped in Twickenham, and told that France has declared war. . . . What can be expected from two wars, when one has been so ignominious?—With an army of fifty thousand men against a rabble, and without being beaten, they have lost a continent, and near half that army, and retreated from place to place. Not one general has gained any reputation; our only fleet on this side of the world is to decide whether the two islands [England and Ireland] are not to be fought for on land. Thus have we, the people, been gamed for; and some few of us against our wills! It is very hard, especially on us that remember other days! . . . [X:284] England will one day recollect it had a minister [Sir Robert Walpole, father of Horace], to whom it owed twenty years of prosperity and happiness, and who left it a motto that would have preserved such halcyon days. *Quieta non movere* [not to disturb things at rest] was as wise a saying as any my Lord Bolinbroke bequeathed to my Lord Bute. I do not know whether it is true, what has been said, that my father on being advised to tax America replied, 'It must be a bolder minister than I am.' But that motto of his spoke his opinion.

Well; war proclaimed! and I am near sixty-one; shall I live to see peace again? what a peace! I endeavour to compose my mind, and call in every collateral aid.—I condemn my countrymen. I enjoy the disappointment of the Scots, who had prepared the yoke for the Americans, and for our necks too. I cannot blame the French whom we have tempted to ruin us: yet, to be ruined by France!—There the Englishman in me feels again. . . .

[XI:412] To the Rev. William Mason, March 9, 1781
 . . . for my part, I wish for peace, and I do not care how bad an [XI:413] one; our glory is gone, our constitution gone, our sense gone, but I would save the lives that are left, and then Mr. Gibbon and the University of Oxford may hunt for and find what topics of panegyric they please.

[XI:431] To the Rev. William Mason, April 25, 1781
 . . . As to Lord Chatham, the victories, conquests, extension of our empire within these last five years will annihilate his fame of course, and he may be replaced by Starvation Dundas [Lord Advocate of Scotland] whose pious policy suggested that the devil of *rebellion could be expelled only by fasting* [through closing the port of Boston], though that never drove him out of Scotland. Unfortunately, Dr. Franklin was a truer politician, when he said he would furnish Mr. Gibbon with materials for writing [XI:432] the History of the Decline of the British Empire. . . .

[XII:107] To the Rev. William Mason, November 28, 1781
 You may be unused to horrors, yet if you have read the 10th article of Lord Cornwallis's capitulation, your feelings will bleed afresh. He capitulates for his own person and return, he capitulates for his garrison—but lest the loyal Americans who had followed him should be included in that indemnity, he demands that they should not be punished—is refused—and leaves them to be hanged! now his burning towns, etc., becomes a mere wantonness of war—they were the towns of those whom he calls rebels, though he was one of five who protested against the Stamp Act—but these were his friends, his fellow soldiers! could I fill three pages more with news, I would not—what article could deserve to be coupled with so abominable a deed!

[*XII:110*] To Sir Horace Mann, November 29, 1781

[He laments the defeat of Cornwallis and then remarks:] From the hour that fatal egg, the Stamp Act, was laid, I disliked it and all the vipers hatched from it. I now hear many curse it, who fed the vermin with poisonous weeds. Yet the guilty and the innocent rue it equally! . . . Seven years of miscarriages may sour the sweetest tempers, and the most sweetened. Oh, where is the dove with the olive branch?

[*XII:166*] To the Rev. William Mason, February 14, 1782

I forgot to tell you what perhaps you had not heard. Washington is remarkably silent and serious and when he banqueted his prisoner Lord Cornwallis, spoke little, never smiled, but happening to ask if it was true that Lord Dunmore was returning to resume his government of Virginia, and being answered in the affirmative, the hero burst out into a fit of laughter. This was the philosopher laughing at the ass that has left mumbling *thistles* [Dunmore was a Scot] for clover that is out of his reach.

[*XII:185*] To Sir Horace Mann, March 1, 1782

On Wednesday last, General Conway renewed his motion for an address of pacification with America, and carried the question by a majority of nineteen. His speech was full of wit, spirit, and severity; and after the debate Mr. Fox complimented him publicly on this second triumph, he having been also the mover of the repeal of the Stamp Act.

[*XII:201*] To Sir Horace Mann, March 21, 1782

. . . Lord North rose, and declared the whole administration was dissolved. . . . Not a month is passed since General Conway's successful motion; not that he is entitled to all the glory. Lord Cornwallis's defeat had certainly opened many eyes, which had been obstinately shut to all our other defeats and losses. . . . When some of the ministers had declared the recovery of America impossible, [*XII:202*] others, who had been lulled asleep by that vision, found there was more truth in that revelation than they would believe from opponents. These steps made, Mr. Conway's motion easily found its way.

[*XII:204*] To the Rev. William Mason, March 21, 1782

. . . no change [of ministers] shall ever make me connected with any administration, though I will reverence any that retrieves liberty. I have the comfort of seeing that America may be free if it will. It is the only country that ever had an opportunity of choosing its constitution at once; it may take the best one that ever was, ours, and correct its defects.

[*XII:401*] To the Countess of Upper Ossory, February 8, 1783

The American war is terminated, to my great satisfaction, and there end my politics!

APPENDIX A
Chronology of Events, 1755–83

This chronology is meant to fill out the picture of the period covered in this collection. But it is not meant to be authoritative. Some dates, because authorities (even standard references) differ, must be considered approximate. However, reputable authority supports each of the dates indicated. Should differences in opinion be found, the student will note that they are extremely slight and, for the purposes of this text, inconsequential.

1755

July 9: General Braddock is defeated and killed on the way to Fort Duquesne, occupied by the French; Washington, aide to the General, assumes command of the retreating troops.

August 13: Washington (age twenty-three) is appointed colonel and commander of all Virginia forces defending the frontier against the French and Indians.

Other events: Samuel Johnson, *Dictionary of the English Language*; J. J. Rousseau, *Discourse on Inequality*; John Adams, graduation from Harvard College.

1756

May 17: The Seven Years War with France is formally declared after two years of fighting. The war, called the French and Indian War in America, lasts until 1763.

October 31: William Pitt, the Elder, becomes head of the English Cabinet (to 1761).

1757

June 23: Lord Clive's victory at Plassey makes the English supreme in India.

July 26: Benjamin Franklin arrives in London to become the agent of the Assembly of Pennsylvania (to 1762).

Other events: William Whitehead becomes Poet Laureate (to 1785); the births of Tom Paine and Alexander Hamilton.

1758

July 8: British and colonial troops are defeated at Ticonderoga, N.Y., by the French under General Montcalm. The British lose 2000 killed and wounded.

July 26: Generals Amherst and Wolfe capture Louisbourg, a French fort which then was the key to Canada.

November 25: The British seize Fort Duquesne and rename it Pittsburgh.

Other events: Samuel Johnson's *Idler* (to 1760); admission of John Adams to the Boston bar; election of Washington to Virginia House of Burgesses; birth of James Monroe.

1759

September 18: General Wolfe defeats French General Montcalm and captures Quebec.

Other events: Samuel Johnson, *Rasselas;* Voltaire, *Candide;* Franklin, LL.D. from the University of Edinburgh; birth of Robert Burns.

1760

March 25: Jefferson enters College of William and Mary (graduates 1762).

September 8: The French surrender Montreal, their last stronghold in Canada.

October 25: Upon the death of George II, his grandson George III ascends the throne (reigns to 1820).

1761

February 24: James Otis, of Massachusetts, speaks against the custom collectors' writs of assistance (general search warrants): this is the first strong colonial opposition to British rule.

October 5: William Pitt resigns as Prime Minister.

1762

May 26: Lord Bute becomes Prime Minister.

Other events: Pension grant to Samuel Johnson by British government; J. J. Rousseau, *The Social Contract* and *Emile;* Franklin, D.C.L. (Doctor of Civil Law) from Oxford.

1763

February 10: The Peace of Paris ends the Seven Years War with France. England acquires a new colony, Canada.

April 16: George Grenville becomes Chancellor of the Exchequer and succeeds Lord Bute as Prime Minister (to July, 1765).

May 16: James Boswell meets Samuel Johnson for the first time.

May–October: Pontiac's rising occurs. It is finally suppressed by British soldiers without the assistance of American forces.

October 7: The Proclamation of 1763 forbids the purchase of western territory between the Alleghenies, Florida, Quebec, and the Mississippi and reserves this land for the Indians.

1764

April 5: The Revenue Act (Sugar Act) is passed by Parliament; Massachusetts, Rhode Island, Connecticut, New York, and Virginia protest.

Other events: John Hancock inherits rich uncle's business, at twenty-seven years of age becomes head of Boston's leading mercantile house and the richest man in New England; Franklin, reappointed agent of Pennsylvania, also represents Massachusetts, New Jersey, and Georgia in London.

1765

March 22: The Stamp Act is passed; this internal duty on legal transactions, for the purpose of collecting funds to support imperial troops stationed in America, rouses the opposition of the colonists.

March 24: The Quartering Act permits quartering of British soldiers on the inhabitants of the colonies.

May 30: Patrick Henry's Virginia Resolves on the Stamp Act are passed. The resolves claim that only colonial legislatures can impose taxes on the colonies.

July 13: Because Grenville arouses the King's displeasure upon introducing a Regency Bill that excluded the King's mother from the government, his ministry falls. The Marquis of Rockingham becomes Prime Minister.

August 14, 26–27: Boston Stamp Act riots take place; Lieutenant-Governor Thomas Hutchinson's town house is gutted by a mob.

October 7–24: The Stamp Act Congress meets in New York. Twenty-eight delegates from nine colonies attend to organize united resistance to the act. They resolve to boycott English goods.

November 1: A Stamp Act riot occurs in New York.

Other events: Soame Jenyns, *Objections to the Taxation of Our American Colonies;* Sir William Blackstone, *Commentaries on the Laws of England;* Samuel Johnson, *The Works of Shakespeare;* resolutions of protest against Stamp Act prepared by John Adams for Braintree, Mass.

1766

January 14: George Grenville and William Pitt debate the King's Address in the House of Commons.

January 17: London merchants urge the repeal of the Stamp Act because the American non-importation agreement has injured trade. The Grenville ministry decides to repeal the Stamp Act.

January 21: Franklin is examined before the House of Commons.

February 10: Lord Camden and Lord Northington debate the repeal of the Stamp Act and the accompanying Declaratory Act.

February 24: Lord Camden speaks on American taxation before the House of Lords. A motion to repeal the stamp tax is made in the House of Commons.

March 18: The Stamp Act is repealed by Parliament; but in the Declaratory Act, Parliament confirms its right to tax the colonies and "to bind the colonies . . . in all cases whatsoever."

July 30: The Rockingham ministry falls; Pitt, now the Earl of Chatham, becomes Prime Minister (to 1767).

1767

January–February: In effect, the Duke of Grafton becomes Prime Minister upon Chatham's illness; Townshend takes the lead in the ministry in an attempt to return to Grenville's plans.

May 13: Parliament dissolves the New York Assembly for refusing to comply with all the provisions of the Quartering Act.

June 26, 29, July 2: The Townshend Acts are passed for the purpose of raising revenue to pay salaries of colonial administrators, governors and judges. These duties on colonial imports (glass, lead, paper, paints, and tea) cause furor in America.

November 5: Customs commissioners arrive in Boston to superintend the execution of the Townshend laws.

Other events: Death of Charles Townshend at age forty-one; admission of Jefferson to the bar.

1768

January 20: A separate secretaryship of state for the American colonies is established by the British government. Lord Hillsborough, the first secretary, favors strong action against the colonies.

February 11: The Massachusetts Circular Letter, drafted by Samuel Adams, is sent to the other colonial legislatures. The letter protests against the Townshend Acts. This step towards colonial unity results (July 1) in the dissolution of the General Court (the legislature) of Massachusetts by the British government.

March: Colonial non-importation agreements are initiated in reaction to the Townshend Acts. British goods are boycotted by the colonies in an attempt to coerce the British government.

June 10: A riot over seizure of John Hancock's sloop *Liberty* by the customs commissioners adds to Hancock's local prestige. The commissioners beg Parliament to bring in troops.

June 14: Old South Church, Boston, is the scene of the largest mass meeting ever held in New England. The meeting forwards a petition to the Governor demanding that the British warship which was hindering navigation in the harbor be removed.

August: Boston merchants begin a boycott of English goods in their non-importation agreement. Importations from England are reduced by one-half in 1768 and 1769.

September 22: The Massachusetts Convention meets to protest the presence of British soldiers, who land the next day.

October 4: The Earl of Chatham resigns and the Duke of Grafton becomes Prime Minister.

December 15: Jefferson is elected to the Virginia House of Burgesses.

1769

May 16: Virginia joins the non-importation movement.
Other events: Burke, *Observations on "The Present State of the Nation";* election of Hancock to the General Court of Massachusetts.

1770

January 28: Lord North becomes Prime Minister (to 1782).
March 5: Parliament repeals the Townshend duties, but it excepts the duty on tea in order to make clear its authority in imperial matters.
March 5: Stoned by a mob of men and boys, British troops fire on Boston citizens, killing four ("the Boston Massacre"). Captain Preston, the British officer in command, is tried in a civil court, October 24–30. Defended successfully by John Adams and Josiah Quincy, he is acquitted of the charge of murder.
August: The colonial non-importation agreements break down.
October 24: Franklin is appointed agent for Massachusetts in London.
December 21: Burke is elected colonial agent for New York at a salary of £500. (He at first rejects the invitation to become agent, but accepts it about March 9, 1771.) His duties, like Franklin's, are to represent the interests of the American colony in London before the several political and economic agencies that administer or affect the colonies.
Other events: Burke, *Thoughts on the Present Discontents.*

1772

June 9: Americans burn the British revenue ship *Gaspee*, when it runs aground off Pawtuxet, a few miles south of Providence, R.I.
August 5: Lord Dartmouth, favored by the colonists, succeeds Lord Hillsborough as Secretary of State for the American Colonies.
November 2: Samuel Adams establishes the Boston Committee of Correspondence as an instrument of agitation: "to state the rights of the Colonists and of this Province [Massachusetts] in particular, as men, as Christians, and as Subjects; and to communicate the same to the several towns and to the world."
Other events: Slavery declared illegal in England (slave trade abolished in 1806).

1773

January 6: Governor Hutchinson in a speech to the Massachusetts House of Representatives states, "I know of no line that can be drawn between the supreme authority of Parliament and the total independence of the colonies."
March 12: The Virginia House of Burgesses establishes its Committee of Correspondence and proposes to put committees of correspondence on an intercolonial basis in order to mobilize public opinion more effectively.

April 27: North's Tea Act, passed by Parliament, inflames American opinion again. The act permits the East India Company to export tea directly to the American colonies, free from all duties except the three-penny tax payable in America. The company thus will have a practical monopoly on the tea business in the colonies, cutting out the American merchants as middlemen. By the reduction of the price of tea, smuggling will be made unprofitable.

December 16: In Boston the attempt to land tea leads to the "Tea Party." Tea valued at £18,000 is hurled into the harbor.

1774

January 29: Franklin appears before the Privy Council; denounced by Solicitor-General Wedderburn, Franklin is dismissed from his office as Deputy Postmaster-General for allegedly purloining the private letters of Governor Hutchinson of Massachusetts.

March 31: The first of the Coercive, or Intolerable, Acts is passed in retaliation for the Boston Tea Party. The Boston port is closed to trade and its reopening made conditional upon the payment of damages for losses sustained by the East India Company.

April 19: Burke speaks on American taxation before the House of Commons. In the debate on the tea duty, Burke argues the inexpediency of English government policies. This was his first notable speech on American affairs. He argues for the return to the old position before the Stamp Act, the abandonment of North's Tea Act. Instead the Coercive Acts are passed into law, March–June.

May 17: The first call for an intercolonial congress is issued by Rhode Island and eventually results in the First Continental Congress.

May 20: The British government suspends the Massachusetts charter and again authorizes (June 2) the quartering of soldiers on the inhabitants of the colonies wherever existing quarters are inadequate. Lord Gage carries out the designs of Parliament against Massachusetts.

May 26: Chatham speaks in the House of Lords against all parliamentary taxation of the colonies.

June 17: John Adams and Samuel Adams are chosen as delegates from Massachusetts to the First Continental Congress. (Washington and Jefferson are delegates from Virginia.)

June 22: The Quebec Act is passed by Parliament to secure the loyalty of the Catholic French-Canadians, to whom it grants religious liberty and restitution of their legal and political institutions. The act annexes to the province of Quebec all the territory north of the Ohio River, thus nullifying the western claims of four American colonies and thwarting the expansionist plans of the American land companies. The colonists object to establishing a civil government without a representative assembly and to giving the Catholic Church special privileges.

September 5–October 26: The First Continental Congress convenes in Philadelphia. All thirteen American colonies except Georgia are represented.

October 14: Congress prepares the Declaration of Rights and Grievances, a petition to the King. In this declaration the colonists assert their rights, as loyal English subjects of the King, to "life, liberty, and property," under the principle of the English constitution. They protest such British measures as the Quartering Act, the Townshend Revenue Act, the Coercive Acts of 1774, and the Quebec Act.

October 20: The Continental Merchants Association adopts the colonial non-intercourse agreement; this agreement originates a successful boycott of all British imports. Congress also sends a petition to Parliament reassuring the British by declaring against independence.

November 3: Burke is re-elected to Parliament as the representative of Bristol, a port greatly dependent on American trade.

Other events: Paine emigrates to America; reign of Louis XVI in France begins (to 1792).

1775

January 20: Chatham's motion to withdraw General Gage's troops from Boston is defeated in the House of Lords, 68 to 18.

February 1: Chatham introduces a conciliatory bill for settling the troubles in America, after negotiating with Franklin. This bill limits the supremacy of Parliament with regard to American taxation and the use of troops for coercion and asserts the rights of Parliament in all matters of imperial concern. But Chatham refuses to accept the new claim that troops should be sent to the colonies only with the consent of their legislatures. The bill is rejected 61 to 32.

February 20: Lord North's resolution on conciliation is carried. It provides that any colony can free itself of imperial taxation by making a contribution to imperial defense and due provision for the support of its own civil government.

March 20: Franklin leaves London for good after a final effort at finding a peaceful solution.

March 22: Burke speaks in the House of Commons on conciliation with America.

March 23: At the Second Virginia Convention, Patrick Henry delivers his famous speech against English arbitrary rule and closes with the memorable words, "Give me liberty or give me death."

April 19: American militia engages British soldiers at Lexington Green; a skirmish takes place at Concord. News of these skirmishes reaches London on May 28. Boston, occupied by the British, is besieged by the American Army until March, 1776.

May 10: The Second Continental Congress convenes at Philadelphia. Benedict Arnold and Ethan Allen take Fort Ticonderoga, N.Y.

May 25: British reinforcements arrive at Boston, with Generals Howe, Clinton, and Burgoyne in command.

May 31: The Continental Army is formed.

June 15: Congress appoints Washington Commander-in-Chief of the Continental Army.

June 17: The Battle of Bunker Hill is fought outside Boston. The British lose many officers and troops. News of the battle reaches London on July 25.

July 3: Washington assumes command of the Continental Army at Cambridge, Mass.

July 5: Congress adopts the Olive Branch Petition addressed to King George and Parliament. Congress continues to declare the loyalty of the colonies. But when the petition arrives in London on August 21, Parliament officially refuses to receive it and the King refuses even to read it.

July 6: Congress passes the Declaration of the Causes and Necessity of Taking Up Arms. In the declaration Congress rejects independence but asserts that the colonies will defend their rights.

August 3: General Gage resigns, leaving Sir William Howe in command of the British military forces. Howe takes official command October 10.

August 23: George III issues a proclamation declaring the colonies to be in a state of rebellion.

September 24: Colonial forces under Benedict Arnold march towards Canada.

September 25: Ethan Allen is captured while attacking Montreal; he is kept prisoner in England until the end of the war.

November 10: Lord George Germain, an advocate of strong action, is made Secretary of State for the American Colonies.

November 13: American General Richard Montgomery captures Montreal.

December 6: Congress openly disavows allegiance to the British Parliament though still professing loyalty to the King.

December 22: Parliament passes the Prohibitory Act. This act removes the colonies from the protection of the British Crown, forbids all trade with them, and authorizes seizure and confiscation of American ships at sea. The act, in effect, outlaws the colonies.

December 31: Generals Montgomery and Arnold are repulsed at Quebec; Montgomery is killed.

1776

January 1: Norfolk, Va., is burned by the British.

January 6: Congress again adopts a resolution protesting that it has "no design to set up as an independent nation."

January 9: Thomas Paine publishes his pamphlet *Common Sense*, which is considered the first open and unqualified argument in championship of the doctrine of American independence. In this extremely popular work, Paine attacks the principle of monarchy and issues a republican call to arms for the struggle to separate from the mother country.

February 27: Patriot militia defeats loyalists at Moore's Creek Bridge, near Wilmington, N.C.

March 17: Forced by Washington, who had fortified Dorchester

Heights, the British troops under Howe evacuate Boston. Howe sails for Halifax, Nova Scotia, to await reinforcements. News of the setback reaches London on May 2.

April 6: Congress opens American ports to ships of all nations except Great Britain, inviting other nations to deal with the thirteen united colonies as if they were a separate and independent state.

April 12: The North Carolina Provincial Congress instructs its delegates to the Continental Congress to vote for independence, the first colony to propose independence formally.

May 2: Louis XVI, upon the advice of his Foreign Minister, Vergennes, makes a million livres available to the Americans for the purchase of munitions.

May 8: Admiral Lord Richard Howe is sent to America with instructions to negotiate with the rebellious colonists.

May 15: The Virginia Convention, urged by Patrick Henry, declares in favor of independence, and instructs its delegates in Congress to propose independence.

June 7: Richard Henry Lee of Virginia introduces a resolution in Congress "that these United Colonies are, and of right ought to be, free and independent States." It is seconded by John Adams.

June 28: A British army and navy attack on Charleston, S.C., fails, thus freeing the South from the danger of attack for nearly three years.

July 2: Congress adopts Lee's resolution and votes for independence. The British fleet and army arrive in New York harbor. British forces consist of 30,000 trained troops and over 100 vessels, against 10,000 men under Washington.

July 4: The Second Continental Congress, John Hancock presiding, formally proclaims the Declaration of Independence. This news reaches London on August 11.

July 19: The Howe brothers, Admiral Richard and General William, acting as peace commissioners, attempt reconciliation; but Congress rejects their offer of pardons for the rebels.

August 27: The Battle of Long Island is fought; Howe defeats Washington who retreats to Manhattan.

September 9: Congress resolves that the words "United States" are to replace the words "United Colonies."

September 11: The Howe brothers try for peace again and confer with the American commissioners, among them Franklin and John Adams. They do not offer independence, only clemency to the rebels, excepting John Adams and John Hancock. This peace attempt fails because, as the Americans noted, the colonies had already declared for independence.

September 15: The British occupy New York City.

October 13: British General Carleton defeats American naval forces on Lake Champlain and advances to Crown Point, N.Y., but on the approach of winter withdraws (November 3) his army to Quebec.

October 26: Franklin leaves for France to negotiate a treaty of alliance.

November 6: Rockingham Whigs "secede" and refuse to attend Parliament in protest against British ministerial policy.

November 16–18: The British capture Fort Washington and Fort Lee in New York and seize 2000 prisoners.

December 13: Washington retreats across the Delaware. Congress flees to Baltimore (until March 4, 1777).

December 19: Paine's first *Crisis* pamphlet bolsters American morale: "These are the times that try men's souls."

December 25: Washington recrosses the Delaware and defeats the Hessians at Trenton, capturing 1000 prisoners.

Other events: Gibbon, first volume of the *Decline and Fall of the Roman Empire* (completed 1788); Adam Smith, *The Wealth of Nations;* death of David Hume.

1777

January 3: Washington defeats part of Cornwallis' force at Princeton.

July 6: The Americans lose Fort Ticonderoga to General Burgoyne.

August 1: Lafayette joins Washington.

September 11: Washington is defeated by Howe at Brandywine Creek, Pa.

September 18: Congress flees from Philadelphia to Lancaster and then to York, Pa.

September 27: The British, under Cornwallis, occupy Philadelphia and drive the Continental Army to York.

October 4: At great cost to his forces, Howe defeats Washington at Germantown, Pa.

October 17: Burgoyne, cut off from Canada, surrenders an army of 5000 men at Saratoga, N.Y., to General Horatio Gates.

November 17: Congress presents the Articles of Confederation to the states; the Articles are ratified in 1781.

December 3: John Adams is appointed commissioner (minister) to France to help in the treaty negotiations.

December 17: Washington retires with his troops to Valley Forge, Pa., for the winter.

Other events: American privateers active in English Channel.

1778

February 6: France signs a treaty of alliance with the American government, Franklin being the chief negotiator among the colonial commissioners.

February 17: Lord North's proposals for conciliation are introduced into Parliament. The main acts to which the Americans objected are repealed March 16. Henceforth no taxes will be imposed on the colonies for revenue. Taxes collected for the regulation of trade will be spent in the colonies. A peace commission is to be sent at once to America to negotiate on this basis.

March 17: Britain and France are at war when the Franco-American treaty is officially announced. Soon the French fleet will become a great threat to British security.

March–April: In Paris, Franklin negotiates directly with Hartley, a member of the British Parliament. As the British refuse to grant independence to the colonies as a condition of peace, the overtures come to nothing.

April 7: Chatham makes his last speech in the House of Lords.

May 4: Congress ratifies the treaty of alliance with France.

May 8: Sir Henry Clinton replaces Howe as Commander-in-Chief of the British forces in America.

May 11: Chatham dies at the age of seventy.

June 17: Congress rejects the peace overtures of the British peace commissioners.

June 18: Fearing blockade by the French fleet, the British evacuate Philadelphia and move to New York.

July 8: The French fleet under D'Estaing arrives off the Delaware Capes, threatening Howe's fleet in the Delaware.

September 9: The French forces take the island of Dominica.

December 29: British forces capture Savannah, Ga.

1779

June 1: Jefferson is elected Governor of Virginia, succeeding Patrick Henry.

June 21: Spain declares war upon Great Britain, and a Spanish fleet joins the French. The British expect an invasion of their homeland all through the summer.

July 15: Stony Point is seized by General Anthony Wayne: 600 British are killed or taken prisoner.

September 23: John Paul Jones's *Bonhomme Richard* defeats and captures the British man-of-war *Serapis.*

October 9: The British defeat the combined French and American forces at Savannah.

Other events: William Cowper, *Olney Hymns*; Johnson, *Lives of the Poets* (completed 1781).

1780

March 1: Pennsylvania is the first American state to abolish slavery.

May 12: The British under General Clinton capture a large army of more than 5000 French and American troops at Charleston, S.C.

June 2–9: The savage Gordon riots occur in London, because Parliament passed a mild measure of Roman Catholic relief. These riots may also be considered an expression of the deep discontent of the people in face of the disastrous American policy of the government.

July 10: General Rochambeau's expeditionary force of 6000 men arrives at Newport, R.I., compelling Clinton to return to New York.

August 18: Sumter is defeated by British General Tarleton at Camden, S.C.

September 4: Hancock is elected Governor of Massachusetts.

September 23: Benedict Arnold attempts treason and soon joins the British.

October 2: British Major John André is executed. André was apprehended after he left West Point, which Arnold had agreed to surrender to the British.

December 21: Great Britain declares war on Holland.

1781

March 1: The Articles of Confederation are formally ratified by the American states.

June 4: British General Tarleton raids Monticello and almost captures Governor Jefferson and many legislators.

June 15: Congress agrees on its instructions to American peace commissioners, Franklin, John Adams, and John Jay.

August 30: De Grasse arrives at the Chesapeake. Cornwallis' army at Yorktown, Va., is in grave danger as the French defeat the British fleet and gain control of the sea off Virginia.

October 19: Washington, with the help of a large French fleet and army, defeats Cornwallis, who surrenders his army of 8000 men at Yorktown. This marks the virtual end of the War of Independence.

1782

February 27: A motion to end the American war passes in the House of Commons.

March 20: Lord North resigns. The Rockingham ministry enters negotiations for peace.

July 1: Lord Rockingham dies; the ministry of Lord Shelburne is formed.

November 30: The American commissioners, Franklin, John Adams, and John Jay, sign the Preliminary Articles of Peace between Great Britain and the United States.

1783

January 20: Hostilities between Britain and America cease. Preliminaries of Peace with France and Spain are signed.

September 3: The definitive Treaty of Peace between the United States and Great Britain is signed at Paris, formally ending the Revolutionary War. The boundaries of the United States are defined in this treaty.

November 2: Washington delivers his Farewell Address to the army at Fraunces Tavern, New York.

November 25: The British evacuate New York.

APPENDIX B

Statistics on Population and Trade

From Stella H. Sutherland, *Population Distribution in Colonial America* (New York: Columbia University Press, 1936). Passim.

Estimated population of the colonies in the revolutionary period:

Total—2,504,229 (exclusive of Indians but including about 523,541 Negroes)
Total North—1,298,765 (including about 39,448 Negro slaves)
Total South—1,205,464 (including about 484,093 Negro slaves)
Virginia—504,264 (including 202,913 Negroes)
Massachusetts—290,900 (including 3,761 Negroes)
Pennsylvania—270,518 (Negro population not known)
Maryland—254,633 (including 83,985 Negroes)
North Carolina—246,580 (including 83,195 Negroes)
Connecticut—197,910 (including 6,462 Negroes)
New York—193,167 (including 19,000 Negroes)
South Carolina—169,987 (including 100,000 Negroes)
New Jersey—122,003 (including at least 3,313 Negroes)
New Hampshire—81,050 (including 656 Negroes and "slaves for life")
Rhode Island—58,221 (including 3,768 Negroes)
Maine—47,777 (including 488 Negroes)
Delaware—37,219 (including 2000 Negroes)
Georgia—30,000(?) (including 15,000 Negroes)

In 1790 the first Federal Census indicated a total population of 3,699,525. At this time the population of the four biggest cities was:

New York—22,000
Philadelphia—21,767
Boston—16,000
Charleston—14,000

From *The Gentleman's Magazine*. Vol. XLV (January, 1775), p. 42.

An estimate of the number of souls in the following provinces, made in Congress, September, 1774:

In Massachusetts, 400,000. New Hampshire, 150,000. Rhode Island, 59,678. Connecticut, 192,000. New York, 250,000. New Jersey, 130,000. Pennsylvania, including the lower Counties, 350,000. Maryland, 320,000. Virginia, 650,000. North Carolina, 300,000. South Carolina, 225,000. — Total, 3,026,678.

From William E. H. Lecky, *A History of England in the Eighteenth Century* (New York: D. Appleton, 1877). Vol. I, pp. 213–14; Vol. VI, p. 201.

Estimated population of Great Britain in the 18th century: England and Wales total population in:

> 1700—5,134,561
> 1750—6,039,684
> 1801—9,172,980

The estimated population of the biggest cities was:

> London in 1700—510,000
> London in 1750—610,000
> Bristol in 1700—30,000
> Bristol in 1750—90,000
> Norwich in 1760—57,000
> Manchester in 1760—40,000
> Birmingham in 1760—30,000

From Edward C. K. Gonner, "The Population of England in the 18th Century," *Journal of the Royal Statistical Society*. Vol. LXXVI (1913), p. 286.

In 1775 the population of England and Wales was 7,000,000.

From John Rickman, *Observations on the Results of the Population Act, 41 Geo. III* (1802). As quoted in *English Historical Documents, 1714–1783*, ed. D. B. Horn and Mary Ransome (New York: Oxford University Press, 1957). P. 508.

England and Wales total population in:

> 1760—6,736,000
> 1770—7,428,000
> 1780—7,953,000

From *Harper's Book of Facts* (New York: Harper & Bros., 1898). P. 650.

In 1801, the year of the first official census, the population of Great Britain and Ireland was indicated as 16,237,300; of England and Wales as 8,892,536 (excluding soldiers and sailors).

In 1780, the population of France was estimated as 25,100,000 and that of Spain as 20,200,000.

From Adam Anderson, *An Historical and Chronological Deduction of the Origin of Commerce* (London, 1787–89). Four volumes. Vol. IV. And David Macpherson, *Annals of Commerce* (London, 1805). Four volumes. Vols. III and IV.

Anderson and Macpherson give the figures of the total trade of Great Britain and of the British trade with America, including New England, from 1763 to 1773; but only Macpherson covers the period from 1774 to 1780. Both give figures for the years 1781 to 1784, although their figures for the year 1783 differ. Yet the difference is so slight as to be insignificant. The figures for the British trade with the American colonies scattered through the Anderson and Macpherson works are the sources for the editors' totals. All figures are "official" and in pounds sterling.

	TOTAL BRITISH TRADE (in millions of pounds)		BRITISH TRADE WITH AMERICA (in millions of pounds)		BRITISH TRADE WITH NEW ENGLAND (in thousands of pounds)	
	Imports	Exports	Imports	Exports	Imports	Exports
1763	11.6	16.1	1.1	1.6	74.8	258.8
1764	10.3	16.5	1.1	2.2	88.1	459.7
1765	10.8	14.5	1.1	1.9	145.8	451.2
1766	11.4	14.0	1.4	1.9	141.7	409.6
1767	12.0	13.8	1.4	2.2	128.2	406.0
1768	11.8	15.1	1.7	2.4	148.3	419.7
1769	11.9	13.4	1.5	1.6	129.3	207.9
1770	12.2	14.2	1.0	1.9	148.0	394.4
1771	12.8	17.1	1.3	4.2	150.3	1420.1
1772	14.5	18.7	1.3	3.0	126.2	824.8
1773	12.5	16.6	1.4	2.0	124.6	527.0
1774	14.5	17.6	1.4	2.6	112.2	562.4
1775	14.8	16.9	1.9	.2	116.5	71.6
1776	12.4	15.6	.1	.05	.762	55.0
1777	12.6	14.1	.013	.05	1.879	————
1778	10.9	12.3	.02	.03	.371	————
1779	11.4	13.5	.02	.35	.807	————
1780	11.7	13.6	.02	.8	.032	————
1781	12.7	11.4	.1	.8	2.068	————
1782	10.3	13.2	.03	.3	————	————
1783	13.1	15.4	.3	1.4	26.3	199.5
1784	15.2	14.9	.7	3.7	51.0	526.5

A Selective Bibliography

I. BIBLIOGRAPHIES

Handlin, Oscar, et al. *Harvard Guide to American History*. Cambridge, Mass.: Harvard Univ. Press, 1954. Chapter 10.
Pargellis, Stanley, and D. J. Medley. *Bibliography of British History: The Eighteenth Century, 1714–1789*. Oxford: Clarendon Press, 1951.

II. COLLECTIONS

Beloff, Max. *The Debate on the American Revolution, 1761–1783*. London: Adam & Charles Black, 1960. Second edition.
Commager, Henry S. *Documents of American History*. New York: Appleton-Century-Crofts, 1958. Sixth edition.
Commager, Henry S., and Richard B. Morris. *The Spirit of 'Seventy-Six: The Story of the American Revolution as Told by Participants*. Indianapolis: Bobbs-Merrill, 1958. Two volumes.
Horn, D. B., and Mary Ransome. *English Historical Documents, 1714–1783*. New York: Oxford Univ. Press, 1957.
Jensen, Merrill. *English Historical Documents: American Colonial Documents to 1776*. New York: Oxford Univ. Press, 1955.
Morison, Samuel E. *Sources and Documents Illustrating the American Revolution, 1764–1788*. Oxford: Clarendon Press, 1923. Second edition, 1929.

III. BRITISH HISTORIANS

Acton, John, Lord. *Lectures on Modern History*, "American Revolution." London: Macmillan, 1906.
———. *History of Freedom and Other Essays*. London: Macmillan, 1907.
Butterfield, Herbert. *George III, Lord North, and the People*. London: Bell, 1949.
———. *George III and the Historians*. New York: Macmillan, 1959. Revised edition.
———. *The Whig Interpretation of History*. London: Bell, 1931.
Cambridge Modern History. New York: Macmillan, 1909. Vol. VI.
Churchill, Winston. *A History of the English-Speaking Peoples*. New York: Dodd, Mead, 1956–58. Vol. III.
Egerton, Hugh E. *The Causes and Character of the American Revolution*. Oxford: Clarendon Press, 1923.

Green, John Richard. *History of the English People*. New York: Harper, 1899. Vol. IV.

Guedalla, Philip. *Independence Day*. London: John Murray, 1926.

———. *Fathers of the Revolution*. New York: Putnam's, 1926.

Lecky, William E. H. *History of England in the Eighteenth Century*. London: Longmans, Green, 1878–90. Seven volumes.

———. *The American Revolution, 1763–1783. Being the Chapters and Passages Relating to America from the Author's History of England in the Eighteenth Century*. New York: D. Appleton, 1898.

Macmunn, George F. *The American War of Independence in Perspective*. London: Bell, 1939.

Mumby, Frank A. *George III and the American Revolution*. London: Constable, 1923.

Namier, Lewis B. *England in the Age of the American Revolution*. London: Macmillan, 1930.

———. *Personalities and Powers*. London: Macmillan, 1955. Essay on George III.

Pares, Richard. *King George III and the Politicians*. New York: Oxford Univ. Press, 1953.

Petrie, Charles. *The Four Georges*. Boston: Houghton Mifflin, 1935.

Phillips, W. Alison. "The Declaration of Independence," *Edinburgh Review*, Vol. CCXLIV (July, 1926), pp. 1–17.

Plumb, John H. *Chatham*. New York: Macmillan, 1953.

———. *The First Four Georges*. New York: Macmillan, 1957.

———. *England in the Eighteenth Century*. Baltimore: Penguin Books, 1950.

Rose, J. H., A. P. Newton, and E. A. Benians. *Cambridge History of the British Empire*. Cambridge: University Press, 1929. Vol. I., *The Old Empire*.

Stanhope, Philip Henry, Lord Mahon. *History of England from the Peace of Utrecht to the Peace of Versailles*. London: John Murray, 1858.

Thackeray, William M. *The Four Georges*. In Vol. XXIII of *Works*. Philadelphia: Lippincott, 1901.

Trevelyan, George M. *History of England*. London: Longmans, Green, 1945. Third edition. Vol. I.

Trevelyan, George O. *The American Revolution*. London: Longmans, Green, 1899–1907. Four volumes. [American edition in three volumes.]

———. *George III and Charles Fox*. London: Longmans, Green, 1912–14. Two volumes.

Watson, J. Steven. *The Reign of George III, 1760–1815*. New York: Oxford Univ. Press, 1960.

IV. AMERICAN HISTORIANS

Adams, James T. *The Epic of America*. Boston: Little, Brown, 1931.

Adams, Randolph G. *Political Ideas of the American Revolution*. New York: Barnes & Noble, 1958. First edition, 1922.

Alden, John R. *The American Revolution, 1775–1783.* New York: Harper, 1954.

Andrews, Charles M. *Colonial Background of the American Revolution.* New Haven: Yale Univ. Press, 1943. Last two essays.

———. "The American Revolution: An Interpretation," *American Historical Review,* Vol. XXXI (January, 1926), pp. 219–32.

Beard, Charles A., and Mary R. Beard. *The Rise of American Civilization.* New York: Macmillan, 1934. Chapters 5–6.

Becker, Carl. *The Eve of the Revolution: A Chronicle of the Breach with England.* New Haven: Yale Univ. Press, 1918.

———. *The Declaration of Independence.* New York: Knopf, 1922, 1942.

Brown, Weldon A. *Empire or Independence: A Study in the Failure of Reconciliation, 1774–1783.* Baton Rouge: Louisiana State Univ. Press, 1941.

Clark, Dora M. *British Opinion and the American Revolution.* New Haven: Yale Univ. Press, 1930.

Dickerson, Oliver M. *The Navigation Acts and the American Revolution.* Philadelphia: Univ. of Pennsylvania Press, 1951.

Gipson, Lawrence H. *The Coming of the Revolution, 1763–1775.* New York: Harper, 1954.

Gutteridge, G. H. *English Whiggism and the American Revolution.* Berkeley: Univ. of California Press, 1942.

Hinkhouse, Fred J. *The Preliminaries of the American Revolution as Seen in the English Press, 1763–1775.* New York: Columbia Univ. Press, 1926.

Knollenberg, Bernhard. *Origin of the American Revolution, 1759–1766.* New York: Macmillan, 1960.

McIlwain, Charles H. *The American Revolution: A Constitutional Interpretation.* New York: Macmillan, 1923.

Mahan, Alfred. *The Influence of Sea Power upon History, 1660–1783.* Boston: Little, Brown, 1890, 1898.

Miller, John C. *Origins of the American Revolution.* Boston: Little, Brown, 1943.

———. *Triumph of Freedom, 1775–1783.* Boston: Little, Brown, 1948.

Morgan, Edmund S., and Helen M. Morgan. *The Stamp Act Crisis: Prologue to Revolution.* Chapel Hill: Univ. of North Carolina Press, 1953.

Morison, Samuel E., and Henry S. Commager. *The Growth of the American Republic.* New York: Oxford Univ. Press, 1942. Third edition.

Mullett, Charles F. *Fundamental Law and the American Revolution, 1760–1776.* New York: Columbia Univ. Press, 1933.

Nevins, Allan. *The American States During and After the Revolution, 1775–1789.* New York: Macmillan, 1924.

Ritcheson, Charles R. *British Politics and the American Revolution.* Norman: Univ. of Oklahoma Press, 1954.

Schuyler, R. L. *Parliament and the British Empire.* New York: Columbia Univ. Press, 1929.

Spector, M. M. *The American Department of the British Government, 1768–1782.* New York: Columbia Univ. Press, 1940.

Tyler, Moses C. *The Literary History of the American Revolution.* New York: Putnam's, 1897. Two volumes.

Van Tyne, Claude H. *The American Revolution, 1776–1783.* New York: Harper, 1905.

————. *The Causes of the War of Independence.* Boston: Houghton Mifflin, 1922.

————. *The Loyalists in the American Revolution.* New York: Macmillan, 1902.

————. *The War of Independence: American Phase.* Boston: Houghton Mifflin, 1929.

Wahlke, John C., ed. *The Causes of the American Revolution: Problems in American Civilization Readings.* Boston: Heath, 1950.

Ward, Christopher. *The War of the American Revolution.* New York: Macmillan, 1952. Two volumes.

The Beatles sing "Be Thankful they don't take it all." This attitude was hardly Franklin. When asked —

Suggestions for Papers and Discussion

1. If you were an American living at the time of the conflict between Great Britain and its provinces in America, how would you use Blackstone as a basis for your legalistic argument for American sovereignty (or for American rights) under the British constitution?

2. From your reading of Bernard and Jenyns, state the American side of the argument concerning taxation and representation. Why did the Americans eventually have to give up this argument? What position did the Americans take with regard to the right to tax? (Boswell, among others, comments on this problem.)

3. What is the British constitution? Do you have an idea of the British system of representation in Parliament in the eighteenth century? (Pitt refers to the "rotten" part of the constitution.)

4. Would you in the years 1765 to 1770 have argued for American independence from Britain? (Grenville asserted that Britain protected America and thereby earned her obedience. Do you accept this argument for the years 1765–70?)

5. Analyze Pitt's imperial policy. Distinguish between Pitt's and Grenville's views: which have more merit? Had Pitt's policy been supported by Parliament, would it have averted the American War of Independence? Did Pitt support the idea of American independence from the mother country? (See the Lecky excerpt also.)

6. In Franklin's testimony (1766), can you find evidence of the American wish to separate from the parent country? of the disposition among the Americans to insist upon their rights? of American national feeling? How does Franklin face the problem of taxation? What is Franklin's opinion of the possible relationship between the colonies and the parent country? From the questions asked of Franklin, infer the opinion of the interrogators concerning the colonists—their loyalty, their military ability, their sincerity.

7. What principles are opposed in the debate on the Declaratory Act? Which principle favors the Americans? Show how Blackstone contributes to an understanding of this debate. What underlying attitudes can you detect in the statements of these eminent government officials?

8. What is Burke's attitude toward America? What role in the British Empire does he envisage for America? On what grounds does Burke support the supremacy of the mother country? Distinguish between Burke's views and those of Pitt (and of Camden and others). What is Burke's solution to the American problem? What does he mean by "the ideas of 1766," "the system of 1766"? Do you believe that Burke's views would have satisfied the Americans and averted the Revolutionary War?

9. What is meant by conciliation? Chatham and Whitehead, the poet, see the possibility of mutual conciliation in 1774: show in detail what such conciliation means for Britain and America.

10. Sum up Pitt's (Chatham's) position on America in 1775. (See his speech, January 20, 1775.) Has his opinion altered since 1765–66? Johnson's views in *The Patriot* are diametrically opposed to Chatham's: state them.

11. Summarize the positions taken by those who proposed conciliation and those who advocated punishment for the colonies in 1775. Find the basic principles in the parliamentary debates on America in 1775. Relate these principles to the previous debates on the Stamp Act.

12. American resistance to British taxation is in the tradition of English resistance to arbitrary taxation: can you support this statement? Why is the problem of taxation so important in this phase of American and British history? Were the British taxes on the Americans harsh or excessive? Relate the idea of freedom to that of taxation.

13. Summarize Burke's views on the American character, as described in his 1775 speech on conciliation. What practical policy for Britain does he deduce from his conception of the American character? Do you think that his policy would at this stage of events have kept America within the British Empire? Contrast his views with those of the majority in Parliament.

14. Read the Declaration of Independence and indicate the chief grievances of the Americans against the British government. On the basis of your reading in these collected documents, what do you think of these American grievances? That is to say, do you believe that they are legitimate, from the British point of view? Again, from your reading of the first part of the Declaration, what are the philosophical

reasons for supporting American independence from the mother country? Do the British have good arguments against the American philosophy? Analyze the arguments on "natural and unalienable rights." How are the terms defined in the various expositions of them? What do the Americans mean by these terms?

15. Contrast Johnson's views (*Taxation No Tyranny*) with the American criticisms of the English government made in the Declaration of Independence. What is his principal argument against the Americans? (Account for his emotional hostility to the Americans.) Define the typical Tory view of the colonies as it is illustrated in his essays and in the comments that Boswell makes about him. What are the principal philosophical bases for Johnson's beliefs? What makes his argument so forceful? Is the Tory view much different from the Whig view?

16. What is Adam Smith's view of the relationship between the colonies and the parent country? How does he justify the British government's position with regard to America? According to Smith, are colonies beneficial to the mother country? What is his view of the British Empire? Would Smith have supported Burke, Chatham, or the parliamentary majority?

17. Indicate the attitude of the editor of *The Gentleman's Magazine* towards the American troubles in 1775. What is his solution to the American problem? Whom does he blame for the crisis? Is he hostile to the American point of view? Does he agree with the majority in Parliament that advocated the use of force against the Americans? Evaluate his attitude, and contrast it with the attitude of a writer like Samuel Johnson. Is it unreasonable? How does a reading of the excerpts from *The Gentleman's Magazine* affect your opinions on the Revolution? Since these excerpts appear in a popular English magazine of revolutionary times might it not be expected that they would unequivocally express the pro-British point of view?

18. Chatham, in his speech of November, 1777, supports the Americans as they fight for freedom, but he is against them as they fight for independence: explain this distinction. Is this like Burke's view?

19. Present Boswell's view of the American problem. What is his solution, if any? Explain his disagreement with Burke over the Declaratory Act. Indicate the differences between Johnson and Boswell concerning British policy on America. Do Boswell's views strike you as typically British? Can you explain why Boswell, who calls himself a Tory, supported the Americans?

20. Cowper, a sensitive and intelligent poet, calls himself a Whig, but what is his attitude towards British-American relations? Does he have any solution to the American problem? Compare Cowper's views with Walpole's.

21. Consider the King's character, on the basis of the selections from his letters and personal papers. Is his attitude towards the American problem unreasonable? Does he have support for his views? A recent critic of King George III (John H. Plumb) states that he was stupid in his American policy: do you agree?

22. What is Walpole's policy towards the Americans? Does Walpole provide a solution to the American problem? Is it like Burke's, Chatham's, or Lord North's: does he recommend the use of force, does he believe in appeasement, does he support British sovereignty? Infer Walpole's character from his letters on the American question. Why did Walpole oppose the American war? Whom does he blame for the war? Walpole was a Whig: can you see any resemblance between his views and those of Cowper?

23. Trace the development of English attitudes towards the governing and taxation of the colonies. What factions emerge and where do their interests lie?

24. What role did Boston play in the Revolution? What was British opinion of this role? What were the causes and effects of the Boston Tea Party?

25. After reading the materials in this book, compare and contrast the view of the Revolution which they present with the view of one or two of the major British historians, e.g., Churchill, Lecky, Plumb, G. O. Trevelyan. How have these historians handled these sources? How have they used them in supporting their own particular point of view?

26. Why was 1775 the "crucial year" for British fortunes in America? You will want to define "crucial" very carefully in terms of military fortunes, the legislative-ideological war, trade, or any combination of these facets of British-American relations.

27. What are the problems inherent in the utilization of various types of source materials, such as letters, in the writing of history? What is, in final definition, "history"?

28. Imaginative papers based on these collected materials can also be composed. The following suggestions may appeal to the creative mind:

a) In 1776, Samuel Johnson had dinner with Arthur Lee, whom Boswell, in his *Life of Johnson*, described as "not only a *patriot* but an *American*." Imagine Johnson's reactions to Lee, and reconstruct a conversation between them in which Boswell, who was a good friend of Lee when the latter studied medicine at the University of Edinburgh, also took part. (Lee later became the ambassador from the United States at the court of Madrid.)

b) Imagine a TV documentary like "You Are There," which you will base on an appropriate selection of the materials of this source book. (This approach may produce a paper that is too loosely organized unless there is a sharp focus on some significant idea, motif, or theme.)

c) Imagine you are a member of Parliament writing letters back home to your constituents. Indicate and defend your stand on the American question.

d) Imagine you are a minister delivering a sermon on the troubles with America. Explain the spiritual nature of the struggle.

e) Imagine you are a journalist writing a column for a newspaper or magazine, or an editor explaining the policy of your publication. Explain and defend your position—for or against the Americans.

f) Put yourself in the position of a British soldier (officer or common soldier) fighting in America. What are your attitudes towards the way in which the colonists fight? towards the terrain on which you must live and do battle? towards the prospect of a long war and the issues involved?

SUGGESTED TOPICS

The views of Grenville and Pitt on America.

The grievances of the colonists.

The scope and development of Pitt's arguments.

The attitudes toward America as expressed by the literary men in their poems, letters, and essays.

America and the character of George III.

Changes in British imperial policy as reflected in her post-revolutionary relationships with Canada, India, Nigeria, or Australia.

Causes of the conflict between Britain and America.

Advantages to the colonies of independence from Britain.

Solutions to the American problem.

Patriotism as a cause of the War of American Independence.

Fundamental (or philosophic) causes of the American Revolution.

Attitudes towards America and Americans in the eighteenth century (as a people, as a colony, as a military force, as traders, as slave owners, etc.).

The use of force in solving the American problem (military preparations and activities).

The behavior of the British soldiers in Boston.

The growth of the spirit of colonial independence from Britain.

Parliament and the American problem.

Responsibility for the War of American Independence.

Opinions concerning the American cause (Johnson, the editor of *The Gentleman's Magazine*, Pitt, Boswell, *et al.*). Include the English clergy here.

Reactions to the idea of American independence from Britain.

The opposition in England to the British war against America.

The future of America as an independent nation.

Post-revolutionary relationships between Britain and independent America.

British justification of the war against America (a defensive or an offensive war?).

British attitudes towards Washington, Franklin, and other Americans.

The Stamp Act and American independence.

Index of Topics

Index of Names